Myra L. Fuqua

Fuqua

THE
WORD
BOOK

THE

GLENCOE PRESS
A division of Benziger Bruce and Glencoe, Inc.
Beverly Hills
Collier Macmillan Publishers
London

WORD BOOK

GILBERT KAHN
Late Professor of Business Education
MONTCLAIR STATE COLLEGE
UPPER MONTCLAIR, NEW JERSEY

DONALD J. D. MULKERNE
Professor of Business Education
STATE UNIVERSITY OF NEW YORK AT ALBANY
ALBANY, NEW YORK

Glencoe Press
A division of Benziger Bruce & Glencoe, Inc.
8701 Wilshire Boulevard
Beverly Hills, California 90211
Collier-Macmillan Canada, Ltd.
Library of Congress catalog card number: 74-10137
First printing, 1975

1 2 3 4 5 6 7 8 9 KPt 80 79 78 77 76 75

Contents

Preface

Almost everyone has some difficulty spelling certain words. This desk-sized reference manual provides an instant guide to the correct spelling and word division of nearly 23,000 words. Although it is designed primarily for typists and secretaries, it is equally useful to anyone who has to deal with the written word. Students, teachers, writers, executives—all will find it indispensable; for how often do we wade through page after page of definitions in a dictionary when we are really only seeking the correct spelling of a word?

While *The Wordbook* is basically a word list, alphabetically arranged for quick reference, troublesome homophones are briefly defined and cross-referenced wherever confusion may arise as to which is the proper word. The manual also contains a brief review of punctuation, a gazetteer, and several other quick-reference guides.

The points at which words may be divided are indicated by a tiny hyphen (-) between syllables or, in the case of compounds retaining orthographic hyphens, by a dash (—) between elements of the compound. A short explanation of the accepted rules of word division is also given in the hope that it may shed some light on what otherwise might appear to be a maze of contradictions.

The authority used for the A–Z Word List section of *The Wordbook* is *Webster's New Collegiate Dictionary,* copyright 1973.

The Wordbook is dedicated to the memory of my good friend, long-time associate, and co-author, Dr. Gilbert Kahn.

Donald J. D. Mulkerne

Word Division Guidelines

It would be nice if we could ignore word division; however, because we are accustomed to (and often prefer) seeing relatively even right-hand margins in typewritten and printed materials, we do divide words. The generally accepted guidelines provided below should make word division less bothersome. A brief summary of these rules also appears at the bottom of each left-hand page in the Word List.

1. Whenever possible, avoid word division; however, when it is necessary, try to leave enough of the word on the first line to provide the reader with some hint of what follows.

2. Do not divide a word so that only its first letter appears on the first line.

3. Do not carry over only the last two letters of a word to the second line.

4. Do not divide one-syllable words.

5. Divide words between syllables; however, there are preferred places for word division between syllables:

   a. Divide at prefixes or suffixes which contain at least three letters. (The suffixes *ceous, cion, cious, geous, gious, sial, tion,* and *tious* are not divisible.)

   b. If the final consonant of the root word is doubled before adding a suffix, divide between the two consonants.

   c. If the root word already ends in a double consonant before the suffix is added, divide between the root word and the suffix.

   d. If a word contains a single-letter syllable, divide the word after that letter *except* when the single letter is followed by a two-letter syllable *or,* in the case of *a, i, u,* by *ble, bly, cle,* or *cal.*

   e. Divide compound words which are already hyphenated only at the hyphen.

6. Do not divide the last word on more than two consecutive lines.

Spelling Aids

Spell by syllables. If the spelling of a word looks peculiar or you are in doubt about it, don't take a chance; look it up in the dictionary. Remember, there are exceptions to almost every spelling "rule."

PLURALS

1. Most plurals are formed by adding *s* to the root word, providing the *s* does not result in a new syllable.

   taxis   roofs   bluffs   boats

2. When a noun ends in *s*, *ch*, *sh*, or *x*, its plural is formed by adding *es*.

   kisses   churches   wishes   Joneses   taxes

3. Some nouns ending in *o* add *s* to form plurals; others add *es*.

   magneto–magnetos   embargo–embargoes

4. Words ending in *y* preceded by a consonant are made plural by dropping the *y* and adding *ies*.

   jury–juries   berry–berries

5. Words ending in *y* preceded by a vowel are made plural by adding *s*. Proper names ending in *y* also add *s* for the plural.

   bay–bays   monkey–monkeys   Kennedy–Kennedys

6. If a compound word is hyphenated, *s* is added to the most important part of the word to make it plural.

   mothers-in-law   sisters-in-law

7. If a compound word is *not* hyphenated, add the plural *s* to the end of the word.

   shipyards   housekeepers   hardships

8. The *ie* and *ei* combinations are tricky, and the best help is probably the simple rhyme:

> I before E   (believe, retrieve)
> Except after C   (receive, conceive)
> Or when sounded like A
> As in *neighbor* and *weigh*   (beige, inveigle, eight, weight)

The *ie* order is more common than *ei*.

CONSONANTS, SUFFIXES, AND UNUSUAL WORDS

1. A final single consonant is *not* doubled before a suffix beginning with a vowel *(ed, ing, ish)* if the root word has more than one syllable and is not accented on the last syllable.

    open–opened   meander–meandering

2. A final single consonant *is* doubled before a suffix beginning with a vowel if the word has only one syllable or if it is accented on the last of more than one syllable.

    recur–recurred   clan–clannish

    Exception: the single consonants *h* and *x* are not doubled.

    rush–rushed   box–boxed

3. When a suffix beginning with *e, i,* or *y* is to be added to a word ending with *c,* a *k* is added before the suffix.

    frolic–frolicked   picnic–picnicking   colic–colicky

4. Memorize the spellings of the following:

    super*sede*   ex*ceed*   pro*ceed*   suc*ceed*

    Use *cede* for all other words with this sound.

PREFIXES

1. The prefixes *non*, *semi*, and *pre* are usually added without hyphens unless followed by a root beginning with a capital.

      nonaggression   non-African   prepackage

2. The prefix *self* is usually followed by a hyphen.

      self-defense   self-determined   self-made

3. Most common prefixes are joined to the main word without hyphens.

extraordinary	nonbreakable	preadolescence
reappear	unacquainted	inaccessible
ultraconservative	oversize	

4. If a word ends with a silent *e*, the *e* is usually dropped when the suffix begins with the vowels *e*, *i*, or *u*.

      page–paging   enclose–enclosure

5. If a word ends with a silent *e*, the *e* is retained when the suffix begins with a consonant or the vowels *a* or *o*.

      damage–damageable   courage–courageous

WORD
LIST

WORD
LIST

A

aard-vark
abaci
aba-cus
abaft
aban-don
abase
abash
abate
abater
ab-at-toir
abbé
ab-bess
ab-bey
ab-bre-vi-ate
ab-bre-vi-a-tion
ab-di-ca-ble
ab-di-cate
ab-di-ca-tion
ab-di-ca-tor
ab-do-men
ab-duct
ab-duc-tion
ab-duc-tor
abed
ab-er-rance
ab-er-rancy
ab-er-rant
ab-er-rated
ab-er-ra-tion
abet
abet-ted
abet-ting
abet-tor

or abet-ter
abey-ance
abey-ant
ab-hor
ab-horred
ab-hor-rence
ab-hor-rent
ab-hor-ring
abid-ance
abide
abil-i-ties
abil-ity
ab-ject
ab-jec-tion
ab-jure
ab-jurer
ab-late
ab-la-tion
ab-la-tive
ablaze
able
abler
ablest
able—bodied
ab-luted
ab-lu-tion
ab-ne-gate
ab-ne-ga-tion
ab-nor-mal-i-ties
ab-nor-mal-ity
aboard
abode
abol-ish
abol-isher
ab-o-li-tion
ab-o-li-tion-ism

ab-o-li-tion-ist
A—bomb
abom-i-na-ble
abom-i-na-bly
abom-i-nate
abom-i-na-tion
abom-i-na-tor
ab-orig-i-nal
ab-orig-ine
abort
aborter
abor-tion
abor-tion-ist
abor-tive
abound
about—face *(n.)*
above-board
ab-ra-ca-dabra
abrade
abrader
abra-sion
abra-sive
abreast
abridge
abridg-ment
or abridge-ment
abroad
ab-ro-gate
ab-ro-ga-tion
abrupt
abrup-tion
ab-scess
ab-scise
ab-scis-sa
ab-scond
ab-sence

Plural, past tense, adverbial, and noun derivatives formed by adding
s, d or *ed, ly, ness, ment, ful, less,* or *ing* to an unchanged root word are
not listed, nor are words formed by dropping the final *e* and adding *ing*.

ab-sent
ab-sen-tee
ab-sen-tee-ism
ab-sent-minded
ab-sinthe
or ab-sinth
ab-so-lute
ab-so-lu-tion
ab-so-lut-ism
ab-solve
ab-solver
ab-sorb
ab-sorb-abil-ity
ab-sorb-able
ab-sorber
ab-sor-bance
ab-sor-ben-cies
ab-sor-bency
ab-sor-bent
or ab-sor-bant
ab-sorp-tance
ab-sorp-tion
ab-stain
ab-ste-mi-ous
ab-sten-tion
ab-sten-tious
ab-sti-nence
ab-sti-nent
ab-stract
ab-strac-tion
ab-strac-tion-ism
ab-strac-tor
or ab-stracter
ab-strac-tive
ab-surd
ab-surd-ism

ab-surd-i-ties
ab-surd-ity
abun-dance
abun-dant
abus-able
abuse
abu-sive
abut
abut-ted
abut-ting
abys-mal
abyss
abys-sal
ac-a-de-mia
ac-a-demic
or ac-a-dem-i-cal
acad-e-mi-cian
acad-e-mies
acad-emy
ac-cede (give consent)
 cf. ex-ceed (go beyond)
ac-cel-er-ate
ac-cel-er-a-tion
ac-cel-er-a-tive
ac-cel-er-a-tor
ac-cent
ac-cen-tual
ac-cen-tu-ate
ac-cen-tu-a-tion
ac-cept (receive)
 cf. ex-cept (other than)
ac-cept-abil-ity
ac-cept-able
ac-cep-tance
ac-cess (entry)
 cf. ex-cess (too much)

ac-ces-si-bil-ity
ac-ces-si-ble
ac-ces-si-bly
ac-ces-sion
ac-ces-sory
or ac-ces-sary
ac-ces-so-ries
or ac-ces-sa-ries
ac-ci-dent
ac-ci-den-tal
ac-claim
ac-cla-ma-tion
ac-cli-mate
ac-cli-ma-tion
ac-cli-ma-ti-za-tion
ac-cli-ma-tize
ac-cliv-ity
ac-co-lade
ac-com-mo-date
ac-com-mo-da-tion
ac-com-mo-da-tive
ac-com-pa-ni-ment
ac-com-pa-nist
ac-com-pany
ac-com-plice
ac-com-plish
ac-com-plish-able
ac-cord
ac-cor-dance
ac-count
ac-count-abil-ity
ac-coun-tancy
ac-coun-tant
ac-credit
ac-crete
ac-crual

2

Do not divide one-syllable words. Divide words by syllables, but leave at least two letters of the word on the first line and three letters on the following line. For additional guidelines, see page ix.

ac-crue
ac-cul-tur-ate
ac-cul-tu-ra-tion
ac-cu-mu-late
ac-cu-mu-la-tion
ac-cu-mu-la-tive
ac-cu-mu-la-tor
ac-cu-ra-cies
ac-cu-ra-cy
ac-cu-rate
ac-cursed
or ac-curst
ac-cu-sal
ac-cu-sa-tion
ac-cu-sa-tive
ac-cu-sa-tory
ac-cuse
ac-cus-tom
ac-cus-tom-ation
ace
ac-er-ate
ac-er-bate
acer-bic
acer-vate
ace-tate
acet-y-lene
ache
achiev-able
achieve
achiever
acid
acid-i-fi-ca-tion
acid-ify
acid-ity
ack-ack
ac-knowl-edge-able

ac-knowl-edg-ment
or ac-knowl-edge-ment
acme
ac-o-lyte
acne
acous-tic
acous-ti-cal
ac-ous-ti-cian
ac-quaint
ac-quain-tance
ac-quain-tance-ship
ac-qui-esce
ac-qui-es-cence
ac-qui-es-cent
ac-quir-able
ac-quire
ac-qui-si-tion
ac-qui-si-tional
ac-quis-i-tive
ac-quit
ac-quit-tal
ac-quit-ted
ac-quit-ting
acre
acre-age
acre—foot *(n.)*
ac-rid
ac-ri-mo-ni-ous
ac-ri-mo-nies
ac-ri-mony
ac-ro-bat
ac-ro-batic
ac-ro-nym
ac-ro-pho-bia
acrop-o-lis
across

across—the—board *(adj.)*
acrylic
act
ac-tion
ac-ti-vate
ac-ti-va-tion
ac-ti-va-tor
ac-tive
ac-tiv-ism
ac-tiv-is-tic
ac-tiv-i-ties
ac-tiv-i-ty
ac-tor
ac-tress
ac-tual
ac-tu-al-i-ties
ac-tu-al-ity
ac-tu-al-iza-tion
ac-tu-al-ize
ac-tu-ar-ial
ac-tu-ar-ies
ac-tu-ary
ac-tu-ate
ac-tu-a-tion
ac-tu-a-tor
acu-ities
acu-ity
acu-men
acu-punc-ture
acute
acuter
acut-est
ad-age
ada-gio
ad-a-mant
adapt (make suitable)

Plural, past tense, adverbial, and noun derivatives formed by adding
s, d or *ed, ly, ness, ment, ful, less,* or *ing* to an unchanged root word are
not listed, nor are words formed by dropping the final *e* and adding *ing*.

3

cf. **adept** (skilled)	**ad hoc**	**ad-mi-ra-tion**
cf. **adopt** (take over)	**adi-a-batic**	**ad-mire**
adapt-abil-ity	**adieu**	**ad-mirer**
adapt-able	**adieus**	**ad-mis-si-bil-ity**
ad-ap-ta-tion	*or* **adieux** *(n. pl.)*	**ad-mis-si-ble**
adapter	**ad in-fi-ni-tum**	**ad-mis-sion**
or **adap-tor**	**adios**	**ad-mis-sive**
adap-tive	**ad-ja-cent**	**ad-mit**
ad-denda *(n. pl.)*	**ad-jec-tive**	**ad-mit-tance**
ad-den-dum	**ad-join**	**ad-mit-ted**
ad-dict	**ad-journ**	**ad-mit-ting**
ad-dic-tion	**ad-judge**	**ad-mon-ish**
ad-dic-tive	**ad-ju-di-cate**	**ad-mon-isher**
ad-di-tion	**ad-ju-di-ca-tive**	**ad-mo-ni-tion**
ad-di-tive	**ad-ju-di-ca-tor**	**ad nau-seam**
ad-dress	**ad-junct**	**adobe**
ad-dress-able	**ad-ju-ra-tion**	**ad-o-les-cence**
ad-dressed	**ad-jure**	**ad-o-les-cent**
ad-dressee	**ad-just**	**Ado-nis**
ad-dresser	**ad-just-able**	**adopt** (take over)
ad-duce	**ad-juster**	*cf.* **adapt**
ad-duct	*or* **ad-jus-tor**	(make suitable)
ad-e-noid	**ad-ju-tant**	*cf.* **adept** (skilled)
adept (skilled)	**ad—lib**	**adopt-abil-ity**
cf. **adapt**	**ad—libbed**	**adopt-able**
(make suitable)	**ad—libbing**	**adopter**
cf. **adopt** (take over)	**ad-min-is-ter**	**adop-tion**
ad-e-qua-cies	**ad-min-is-tra-ble**	**adop-tive**
ae-e-quacy	**ad-min-is-trate**	**ador-able**
ad-e-quate	**ad-min-is-tra-tion**	**ad-o-ra-tion**
ad-here	**ad-min-is-tra-tive**	**adore**
cf. **ad-her-ents** (sup-	**ad-min-is-tra-tor**	**adorer**
porters)	**ad-min-is-tra-tri-ces**	**adorn**
ad-her-ent	*(n. pl.)*	**ad-re-nal**
ad-he-sion	**ad-min-is-tra-trix**	**adroit**
ad-he-sive	**ad-mi-ra-ble**	**ad-sorb**
	ad-mi-ra-bly	**ad-sorb-able**

Do not divide one-syllable words. Divide words by syllables, but leave
at least two letters of the word on the first line and three letters on the
following line. For additional guidelines, see page ix.

4

ad-sorp-tion
ad-sorp-tive
ad-u-late
ad-u-la-tion
adult
adul-ter-ate
adul-ter-a-tion
adul-terer
adul-ter-ess
adul-ter-ous
adul-tery
adult-hood
ad-vance
ad-van-tage
ad-van-ta-geous
ad-vec-tion
Ad-vent
ad-ven-ture
ad-ven-turer
ad-ven-ture-some
ad-ven-tur-ess
ad-ven-tur-ous
ad-verb
ad-ver-bial
ad-ver-sar-ies
ad-ver-sary
ad-verse
ad-ver-si-ties
ad-ver-sity
ad-vert (refer to)
  cf. **avert** (avoid)
ad-ver-tise
ad-ver-tiser
ad-vice *(n.)*
  (counsel)
  cf. **ad-vise** *(v.)* (give
  advice)

ad-vis-abil-ity
ad-vis-able
ad-vise (*v.* give advice)
  cf. **ad-vice**
  (*n.* counsel)
ad-viser
  or ad-vi-sor
ad-vi-sory
ad-vo-cacy
ad-vo-cate
ad-vo-ca-tor
adz
  or adze
aer-ate
aer-a-tion
aer-a-tor
ae-rial
ae-ri-al-ist
aer-o-bat-ics
aero-naut
aero-nau-tics
aero-plane
aero-sol
aero-space
aero-sphere
aes-thetic
aes-thet-i-cal
af-fa-bil-ity
af-fa-ble
af-fa-bly
af-fect (influence)
  cf. **ef-fect** (result)
af-fect-abil-ity
af-fect-able
af-fec-ta-tion
af-fec-tion
af-fec-tion-ate

af-fec-tive
af-fi-da-vit
af-fil-i-ate
af-fil-i-a-tion
af-fin-i-ties
af-fin-ity
af-firm
af-fir-ma-tion
af-fir-ma-tive
af-fix
af-fix-a-tion
af-flict
af-flic-tion
af-flic-tive
af-flu-ence
af-flu-en-cies
af-flu-ency
af-flu-ent (wealthy)
  cf. **ef-flu-ent**
  (flowing forth)
af-ford
af-ford-able
af-for-est
af-for-es-ta-tion
af-fray
af-front
aflame
afore-men-tioned
afore-said
afore-thought
afraid
A—frame
Afro—American
aft
after
after—hours *(adj.)*
af-ter-noon

Plural, past tense, adverbial, and noun derivatives formed by adding
s, d or *ed, ly, ness, ment, ful, less,* or *ing* to an unchanged root word are
not listed, nor are words formed by dropping the final *e* and adding *ing*.

after—shave *(n.)*
af-ter-ward
again
against
agate
age
age-ing
or ag-ing
agen-cies
agency
agenda
agen-dum
or agen-dums
  (n. pl.)
agent
ag-glom-er-ate
ag-glom-er-a-tion
ag-glu-ti-nate
ag-glu-ti-na-tion
ag-gran-dize
ag-gra-vate
ag-gra-va-tion
ag-gre-gate
ag-gre-ga-tion
ag-gre-ga-tive
ag-gres-sion
ag-gres-sive
ag-gres-sor
ag-grieve
aghast
ag-ile
agil-i-ties
agil-ity
ag-i-tate
ag-i-ta-tion
ag-i-ta-tor
ag-i-ta-tive

aglow
ag-nos-tic
ag-nos-ti-cism
ago
agog
a—go—go
ag-o-nies
ag-o-nist
ag-o-nis-tic
ag-o-nize
ag-ony
agrar-ian
agrar-i-an-ism
agree
agree-able
ag-ri-cul-ture
ag-ri-cul-tur-al-ist
agron-omy
ague
ahead
aid (help)
  cf. aide (assistant)
aide—de—camp
aides—de—camp
  (n. pl.)
ail
aim
air (atmosphere)
  cf. heir (inheritor)
air base
air-borne
air—condition *(v.)*
air con-di-tioner *(n.)*
air-plane
aisle (pathway)
  cf. isle (island)
ajar

akimbo
akin
al-a-bas-ter
a la carte
a la mode
alac-rity
alarm
alarm-ist
al-beit
al-bum
al-che-mist
al-chemy
al-co-hol
al-co-holic
al-co-hol-ism
al-cove
al-der-man
alert
al-falfa
alga
algae
or algas *(n. pl.)*
al-ge-bra
al-ge-braic
al-ge-bra-ically
ALGOL
or Al-gol
al-go-rithm
alias
al-ibi
alien
alien-ate
alien-ation
align
or aline
al-i-men-tary
  (nourishing)

Do not divide one-syllable words. Divide words by syllables, but leave at least two letters of the word on the first line and three letters on the following line. For additional guidelines, see page ix.

cf. **el-e-men-tary** (simple)
al-i-mony
alive
al-kali
al-ka-line
al-ka-lin-ity
all (whole)
cf. **awl** (tool)
all—American *(n.)* *(adj.)*
all—around *(adj.)*
al-lay
al-lege
al-le-giance
al-le-gor-i-cal
al-le-gory
al-le-luia
or **hal-le-lu-jah**
al-ler-gic
al-lergy
al-le-vi-ate
al-ley (street)
cf. **ally** (friend)
al-li-ance
al-lied
al-lo-cate
al-lo-ca-tion
all—or—nothing *(adj.)*
al-lot
al-lot-ted
al-lot-ting
al-low
al-low-able
al-low-ance
al-loy

all right *(adj.)* (satisfactory)
cf. **al-right** *(adv.)* *(adj.)* (okay)
all—star *(n.)*
al-lude
al-lure
al-lu-sion (indirect reference)
cf. **il-lu-sion** (false impression)
al-lu-sive (hint)
cf. **elu-sive** (evade)
ally (friend)
cf. **al-ley** (street)
alma ma-ter
al-ma-nac
al-mighty
al-most
alms
alone
along
aloof
aloud
al-paca
al-pha-bet
al-pha-bet-i-cal
al-pha-bet-ize
al-pha-meric
al-pha-mer-i-cal
al-pha-nu-meric
al-pha-nu-mer-i-cal
al-ready (before this time)
cf. **all ready** (completely ready)
al-right *(adv.)* *(adj.)* (okay)
cf. **all right** *(adj.)* (satisfactory)

al-tar (table in church)
cf. **al-ter** (make different)
al-ter-able
al-ter-ation
al-ter-ca-tion
al-ter ego
al-ter-nate
al-ter-na-tion
al-ter-na-tive
al-ter-na-tor
al-tim-e-ter
al-ti-tude
al-ti-tu-di-nal
al-to-gether (wholly)
cf. **all to-gether** (everyone in a group)
al-tru-ism
al-tru-ist
al-tru-is-tic
alu-mi-nate (metallic oxide)
cf. **il-lu-mi-nate** (light up)
alu-mi-num
alu-mi-nize
alumna
alum-nae *(n. pl)*
alum-nus
al-ways
amal-gam-ate
amal-gam-ation
am-a-teur
am-a-teur-ish
am-a-teur-ism
am-a-tive
am-a-tory
amaze
am-a-zon

Plural, past tense, adverbial, and noun derivatives formed by adding *s, d* or *ed, ly, ness, ment, ful, less,* or *ing* to an unchanged root word are not listed, nor are words formed by dropping the final *e* and adding *ing*.

am-bas-sa-dor
am-bas-sa-do-rial
am-bas-sa-dor-ship
am-ber
am-bi-dex-ter-ity
am-bi-dex-trous
am-bi-gu-ities
am-bi-gu-ity
am-big-u-ous
am-bi-tion
am-bi-tious
am-biv-a-lence
am-biv-a-lent
am-ble
am-bu-lance
am-bu-lant
am-bu-late
am-bu-la-tory
am-bus-cade
am-bush
ame-lio-rate
ame-lio-ra-tion
ame-lio-ra-tive
ame-lio-ra-tory
ame-na-ble
ame-na-bly
amend
amend-able
ame-ni-ties
ame-nity
ami-able
ami-a-bly
am-i-ca-ble
am-i-bly
amid
or amidst

am-mo-nia
am-mu-ni-tion
am-ne-sia
am-nes-ties
am-nesty
amoeba
amoe-bas
or amoe-bae *(n. pl)*
among
amoral
am-o-rous
amor-phous
am-or-tiz-able
am-or-tize
amount
amour
am-per-age
am-pere
am-per-sand
am-phib-ian
am-phib-i-ous
am-phi-the-ater
am-ple
am-ply
am-pli-fi-ca-tion
am-pli-fied
am-pli-fier
am-plify
am-pli-tude
am-pu-tate
am-pu-tee
am-u-let
amuse
anach-ro-nism
anach-ro-nis-tic
or ana-chronic

or anach-ro-nous
an-aes-the-sia
an-aes-thetic
ana-gram
an-al-ge-sia
an-al-ge-sic
an-a-log
or an-a-logue
anal-o-gist
anal-o-gize
anal-o-gous
anal-o-gies
an-a-logue
or an-a-log
anal-ogy
anal-y-ses
anal-y-sis
an-a-lytic
an-a-lyst
an-a-lyze
an-ar-chism
an-ar-chist
an-ar-chy
anath-ema
anath-e-ma-tize
anat-omy
an-ces-tor
an-ces-tral
an-ces-tress
an-ces-try
an-chor
an-chor-age
an-cho-vies
an-chovy
an-cient
an-cil-lary

Do not divide one-syllable words. Divide words by syllables, but leave at least two letters of the word on the first line and three letters on the following line. For additional guidelines, see page ix.

8

and
and-iron
and/or *(conj.)*
an-droid
an-ec-dot-age
an-ec-dotal
an-ec-dote
ane-mia
ane-mic
anem-one
an-es-the-sia
an-es-the-si-ol-o-gist
an-es-the-si-ol-ogy
an-es-thetic
anes-the-tist
anes-the-tize
an-eu-rysm
anew
an-gel
an-ger
an-gina
angle
an-gler
an-gli-cize
Anglo—Saxon
an-grier
an-gri-est
an-grily
an-gry
an-guish
an-gu-lar
an-i-mal
an-i-mal-ism
an-i-mal-is-tic
an-i-mate
an-i-ma-tion

an-i-mos-i-ties
an-i-mos-ity
an-kle
an-kle-bone
an-nal-ist
an-nex
an-nex-a-tion
an-ni-hi-late
an-ni-hi-la-tion
an-ni-ver-sa-ries
an-ni-ver-sary
anno Do-mini
an-no-tate
an-no-ta-tion
an-no-ta-tor
an-nounce
an-nouncer
an-noy
an-noyer
an-nual
an-nu-ities
an-nu-ity
an-nul
an-nulled
an-nul-ling
an-nun-ci-ate (announce)
  cf. enun-ci-ate (pronounce)
an-nun-ci-a-tion
an-ode
anoint
anom-a-lous
anom-a-lies
anom-aly
anon
an-o-nym-ity
anon-y-mous

an-other
an-swer
an-swer-able
ant
ant-acid
an-tag-o-nism
an-tag-o-nist
an-tag-o-nis-tic
an-tag-o-nize
ant-arc-tic
an-te-bel-lum
an-te-cede
an-te-ced-ence (priority)
  cf. an-te-ced-ents (ancesto
an-te-ced-ent
an-te-date
an-te-lope
an-tenna
an-ten-nae
or an-ten-nas
an-te-ri-or (toward the front
  cf. in-te-ri-or (inside)
an-them
an-thol-o-gies
an-thol-ogist
an-thol-ogy
an-thra-cite
an-thro-poid
an-thro-pol-o-gist
an-thro-pol-ogy
an-thro-po-log-i-cal
an-ti-air-craft
an-ti-bi-otic
an-tic
An-ti-christ
an-tic-i-pate

Plural, past tense, adverbial, and noun derivatives formed by adding
s, d or *ed, ly, ness, ment, ful, less,* or *ing* to an unchanged root word are
not listed, nor are words formed by dropping the final *e* and adding *ing*.

an-tic-i-pa-tion
an-tic-i-pa-tive
an-tic-i-pa-tory
an-ti-cli-mac-tic
an-ti-cli-max
an-ti-clock-wise
an-ti-dotal
an-ti-dote
an-ti-freeze
an-ti-his-ta-mine
an-ti-pasto
an-tip-a-thies
an-tip-a-thy
an-ti-quar-ian
an-ti-quate
an-tique
an-tiq-u-ties
an-tiq-uity
an-ti—Sem-i-tism *(n.)*
an-ti-sep-tic
an-ti-so-cial
an-tith-e-ses *(n. pl.)*
an-tith-e-sis
an-ti-toxin
ant-ler
ant-onym
anx-i-eties
anx-i-ety
anx-ious
any
any-body
A—OK
A 1
apart
apart-heid
ap-a-thetic

ap-a-thy
ape
ape—man *(n.)*
aper-i-tif
ap-er-ture
apex
apexes
or api-ces *(n. pl.)*
aphid
aph-o-rism
aph-ro-dis-iac
api-ary
apiece
aplenty
aplumb
apoc-a-lypse
apo-gee
Apollo
apol-o-getic
apol-o-gies
apol-o-gize
apol-ogy
ap-o-plexy
apos-tle
ap-os-tolic
apos-tro-phe
apoth-e-car-ies
apoth-e-cary
ap-pall
or ap-pal
ap-pa-ra-tus
ap-pa-ra-tuses
or ap-pa-ra-tus *(n.pl)*
ap-parel
ap-par-ent
ap-pa-ri-tion

ap-peal
ap-pear
ap-pear-ance
ap-pease
ap-pel-late
ap-pel-la-tion
ap-pend
ap-pend-age
ap-pen-dec-to-mies
ap-pen-dec-tomy
ap-pen-di-ci-tis
ap-pen-dix
ap-pen-dixes
or ap-pen-di-ces *(n. pl.)*
ap-per-ceive
ap-per-cep-tion
ap-pe-tite
ap-pe-tizer
ap-plaud
ap-plause
ap-ple
ap-pli-ance
ap-pli-ca-ble
ap-pli-ca-bil-ity
ap-pli-cant
ap-pli-ca-tion
ap-point
ap-poin-tee
ap-por-tion
ap-po-site
ap-po-si-tion
ap-praise
ap-pre-cia-ble
ap-pre-cia-bly
ap-pre-ci-ate
ap-pre-ci-a-tion

Do not divide one-syllable words. Divide words by syllables, but leave at least two letters of the word on the first line and three letters on the following line. For additional guidelines, see page ix.

ap-pre-cia-tive
ap-pre-hend
ap-pre-hen-si-ble
ap-pre-hen-si-bly
ap-pre-hen-sion
ap-pre-hen-sive
ap-pren-tice
ap-prise (to inform)
cf. **ap-prize** (to value)
ap-proach
ap-proach-able
ap-pro-bate
ap-pro-ba-tion
ap-propri-ate
ap-pro-pri-a-tion
ap-proval
ap-prove
ap-prox-i-mate
ap-prox-i-ma-tion
apron
ap-ro-pos
apt
ap-ti-tude
aqua-cade
aqua-naut
aquar-ium
Aquar-ius
aquatic
aq-ue-duct
ar-a-ble
ar-bi-ter
ar-bi-tra-ble
ar-bi-trarily
ar-bi-trary
ar-bi-trate
ar-bi-tra-tion

ar-bi-tra-tive
ar-bi-tra-tor
ar-bor
ar-bo-re-tum
arc
ar-cade
arch
ar-chae-ol-o-gist
or ar-che-ol-o-gist
ar-chae-ol-o-gy
or ar-che-ol-o-gy
ar-chaic
arch-di-o-cese
arch-duch-ess
arch-duchy
arch-duke
arch-en-e-mies
arch-en-emy
ar-cher
ar-chery
ar-chi-pel-ago
ar-chi-tect
ar-chi-tec-tural
ar-chi-tec-ture
ar-chive
arc-tic
ar-dent
ar-dor
ar-du-ous
area (surface)
cf. **aria** (melody)
area code *(n.)*
arena
ar-gu-able
argue
ar-guer

ar-gu-ment
ar-gu-men-ta-tion
ar-gu-men-ta-tive
aria (melody)
cf. **area** (surface)
arid
arid-ity
arise
ar-is-toc-ra-cies
ar-is-toc-racy
aris-to-crat
aris-to-cratic
arith-me-tic
ar-ith-met-i-cal
ark
arm
ar-mada
ar-ma-ment
ar-ma-ture
arm-chair
ar-mi-stice
ar-mor
ar-mo-ries
ar-mies
ar-mory
army
aroma
around
around—the—clock *(adj.)*
arouse
ar-raign
ar-range
ar-ray
ar-rear
ar-rest
ar-rival

Plural, past tense, adverbial, and noun derivatives formed by adding
s, d or *ed, ly, ness, ment, ful, less,* or *ing* to an unchanged root word are
not listed, nor are words formed by dropping the final *e* and adding *ing*.

11

ar-rive
ar-ro-gance
ar-ro-gant
ar-row
ar-se-nal
ar-se-nate
ar-se-nic
ar-son
ar-te-rio-scle-ro-sis
ar-ter-ies
ar-tery
ar-te-sian well (n.)
ar-thritic
ar-thri-tis
ar-ti-choke
ar-ti-cle
ar-tic-u-late
ar-tic-u-la-tion
ar-ti-fact
ar-ti-fi-cial
ar-ti-fi-cial-i-ties
ar-ti-fi-ci-al-ity
ar-til-lery
ar-ti-san
art-ist
ar-tis-tic
art-istry
art-work
Aryan
as-bes-tos
or as-bes-tus
as-cend
as-cend-able
or as-cend-ible
as-cen-dance
or as-cen-dence

as-cen-dancy
or as-cen-dency
as-cent (rising)
cf. as-sent (agree)
as-cer-tain
as-cetic
ascor-bic acid
as-cot
as-cribe
asex-ual
ash
ashamed
ashen
Asian
Asi-atic
aside
as-i-nine
as-i-nin-ity
ask
askance
or askant
askew
asleep
asp
as-pect
as-perse
as-per-sion
as-phalt
as-phyx-i-ate
as-pic
as-pi-rant
as-pi-ra-tion
as-pire
as-pi-rin
as-sail
as-sail-ant

as-sas-sin
as-sas-si-nate
as-sas-si-na-tion
as-sas-si-na-tor
as-sault
as-saulter
as-say (analyze ore)
cf. es-say (theme)
as-sem-blage
as-sem-ble
as-sem-bly
as-sent (agree)
cf. as-cent (rising)
as-sert
as-ser-tion
as-ser-tive
as-sess
as-sess-able
as-ses-sor
as-set
as-sev-er-ate
as-sev-er-a-tion
as-sev-er-a-tive
as-si-du-ity
as-sid-u-ous
as-sign
as-sig-na-tion
as-signee
as-signer
as-sim-i-late
as-sim-i-la-tion
as-sim-i-la-tor
as-sist
as-sis-tance (help)
cf. as-sis-tants (helpers)
as-so-ci-ate

Do not divide one-syllable words. Divide words by syllables, but leave at least two letters of the word on the first line and three letters on the following line. For additional guidelines, see page ix.

12

as-so-ci-a-tion	asym-me-try	at-ten-u-ate
as-so-cia-tive	at all (in any way)	at-ten-u-a-tion
as-sort	*cf.* atoll (coral island)	at-test
as-suage	athe-ism	at-tes-ta-tion
as-sua-sive	athe-ist	at-tic
as-sume	athe-is-tic	at-tire
as-sum-abil-ity	athe-is-ti-cal	at-ti-tude
as-sum-able	ath-lete	at-ti-tu-di-nal
as-sump-tion	ath-letic	at-ti-tu-di-nize
as-sump-tive	at-las	at-tor-nies
as-sur-ance	at-mos-phere	at-tor-ney
as-surer	at-mos-pheric	attorney—at—law
or as-suror	atoll (coral island)	attorneys-at-law *(n. pl.)*
as-ter-isk	*cf.* at all (in any way)	at-tract
astern	atom	at-trac-tion
as-ter-oid	atom bomb	at-trac-tive
asthma	atomic	at-trib-ute
as-tig-matic	at-om-ize	at-trib-ut-able
astig-ma-tism	atone	at-trib-u-tion
as-ton-ish	atop	at-trib-u-tive
as-tound	atro-cious	at-tri-tion
astrad-dle	atroc-i-ties	at-tune
as-tral	atroc-ity	atyp-i-cal
astride	at-ro-phy	au-burn
as-tro-dome	at-tach	auc-tion
as-trol-ogy	at-ta-ché	auc-tion-eer
as-tro-naut	at-tack	au-da-cious
as-tro-nav-i-ga-tion	at-tain	au-dac-ity
as-tron-o-mer	at-tar	au-di-ble
as-tron-om-i-cal	at-tempt	au-di-ence
as-tron-omy	at-tend	au-dio
as-tute	at-ten-dance (act of	au-di-ol-ogy
asun-der	attending)	au-dio-vi-sual
asy-lum	*cf.* at-ten-dants (helpers)	au-dit
asym-met-ric	at-ten-tion	au-di-tion
asym-met-ri-cal	at-ten-tive	au-di-tor

Plural, past tense, adverbial, and noun derivatives formed by adding
s, d or *ed, ly, ness, ment, ful, less,* or *ing* to an unchanged root word are
not listed, nor are words formed by dropping the final *e* and adding *ing*.

13

au-di-to-rium
au-di-tory
au-ger
aught (zero)
  cf. ought (should)
aug-ment
au gra-tin
au-gust
au jus
auld lang syne
aunt
au-ral (hearing)
  cf. oral (spoken)
au re-voir
au-ri-cle (heart)
  cf. or-a-cle (person)
aus-pice
aus-pi-cious
aus-tere
aus-ter-i-ties
aus-ter-ity
au-then-tic
au-then-ti-ca-tion
au-then-tic-ity
au-thor
au-thor-i-tar-ian
au-thor-i-tar-i-an-ism
au-thor-i-ta-tive
au-thor-i-ties
au-thor-ity
au-thor-i-za-tion
au-thor-ize
au-thor-ship
au-to-bio-graph-i-cal
au-to-bi-og-ra-phy
au-to-bi-og-ra-pher

au-to-cade
au-toc-racy
au-to-crat
au-to-cratic
au-to-crat-i-cal
au-to-graph
au-to-mate
au-to-matic
au-to-ma-tion
au-tom-a-tism
au-tom-a-ti-za-tion
au-tom-a-ton
au-to-mo-bile
au-to-mo-tive
au-ton-o-mous
au-ton-o-mies
au-ton-omy
au-topsy
au-tumn
aux-il-ia-ries
aux-il-iary
avail
avail-abil-ity
avail-able
av-a-lanche
av-a-rice
av-a-ri-cious
avast
avenge
avenger
av-e-nue
aver
av-er-age
averse
aver-sion
averred

aver-ring
avert (avoid)
  cf. ad-vert (refer to)
avi-ary
avi-a-tion
avi-a-tor
avid
av-o-cado
av-o-ca-tion
avoid
avoid-able
avoid-ance
av-oir-du-pois
avouch
avow
avowal
await
awake
awaken
aware
away (from a place)
  cf. aweigh (to lift anchor)
awe
aweigh (to lift anchor)
  cf. away (from a place)
aw-ful
awk-ward
awl (tool)
  cf. all (whole)
awry
ax
or axe
axes (pl. of ax and axis)
  cf. axis (imaginary line
  through an object)
ax-iom

Do not divide one-syllable words. Divide words by syllables, but leave at least two letters of the word on the first line and three letters on the following line. For additional guidelines, see page ix.

ax-i-om-atic
axis
axle
aye *(yes)*
  cf. **eye** (organ of sight)
az-i-muth
azure

B

bab-ble
babies *(n. pl.)*
baby
baby—sitter *(n.)*
bac-ca-lau-re-ate
bach-e-lor
bach-e-lor-hood
ba-cil-lus
back
back-fire
back-ground
back-lash
back-stage
back-track
ba-con
bac-te-ria *(n. pl.)*
bac-te-rial
bac-te-ri-ol-o-gist
bac-te-ri-ol-ogy
bac-te-rium *(n. sing.)*
bad
bade

badger
bad-min-ton
bad—mouth *(v.)*
baf-fle
ba-gel
bag-gage
bag-ging
baggy
bag-pipe
bail (bond or dip)
  cf. **bale** (large bundle)
bai-liff
bai-li-wick
bait
bake
baker
bak-er-ies
bak-ery
bal-ance
bal-co-nies
bal-cony
bald
bale (large bundle)
  cf. **bail** (bond or dip)
balk
balky
ball (sphere)
  cf. **bawl** (cry)
bal-lad
ball—and—socket joint *(n.)*
bal-last
ball bear-ing *(n.)*
bal-let
bal-lis-tic
bal-loon
bal-lot

ball—point (pen)
bal-ly-hoo
balm
balm-ier
balm-i-est
balsa
bal-sam
bal-us-trade
bam-boo
ban
ba-nana
band
band-age
ban-danna
or ban-dana
ban-do-lier
or ban-do-leer
band saw *(n.)*
bang
ban-gle
ban-ish
ban-is-ter
or ban-nis-ter
banjo
banjos
or ban-joes *(n. pl.)*
bank
bank note
bank-roll
bank-rupt
bank-rupt-cies
bank-ruptcy
ban-ner
ban-quet
ban-tam
ban-zai

Plural, past tense, adverbial, and noun derivatives formed by adding
s, d or *ed, ly, ness, ment, ful, less,* or *ing* to an unchanged root word are
not listed, nor are words formed by dropping the final *e* and adding *ing*.

bap-tism
bap-tize
bar
barb
bar-bar-ian
bar-bar-i-an-ism
bar-baric
bar-ba-rism
bar-bar-ity
bar-ba-rous
bar-be-que
bar-ber
bar-ber-shop
bar-bi-tu-rate
bare (without covering)
 cf. bear (animal; endure)
bare-leg-ged
bar-gain
barge
bark
bar-i-tone
bar mitz-vah (ceremony
 for male)
barn
bar-na-cle
barn dance (n.)
barn-storm
ba-rom-e-ter
baro-met-ric
baron (nobleman)
 cf. barren (fruitless)
bar-on-ess
bar-onet
bar-rage
bar-rel
bar-ren (fruitless)

cf. baron (nobleman)
bar-ri-cade
bar-rier
bar-ris-ter
bar-ter
basal
base
base-ball
based (resting on)
 cf. baste (stitch)
base hit (n.)
bash
ba-sic
ba-sin
bas-ket
bas mitz-vah (ceremony
 for female)
bass
bas-si-net
baste (stitch)
 cf. based (resting on)
bas-tion
bat
batch
bate
bath (n.)
bathe (v.)
bathy-sphere
ba-ton
bat-ted
bat-ter
bat-ter-ies
bat-tery
bat-ting
bat-tle
bawl (cry)

cf. ball (sphere)
Bayes-ian
bay-o-net
ba-zaar (market)
 cf. bi-zarre (grotesque)
be (v.) (to be)
 cf. bee (n.) (bug)
beach (sandy shore)
 cf. beech (tree)
bea-con
beam
bear (animal; endure)
 cf. bare (without covering)
bear-able
beard
bearer
beast
beat (strike)
 cf. beet (vegetable)
beaten
beat-nik
beau (suitor)
 cf. bow (bend; weapon)
beaus
 or beaux
beau-te-ous
beau-ti-ful
beau-tify
be-came
be-cause
bed
bed-ded
bed-ding
be-devil
bed-lam
be-drag-gle

Do not divide one-syllable words. Divide words by syllables, but leave
at least two letters of the word on the first line and three letters on the
16   following line. For additional guidelines, see page ix.

bed-rid-den	**be-hest**	**be-med-aled**
bee (n.) (bug)	**be-hind**	_or_ **be-med-alled**
_cf._ **be** (v.) (to be)	**behind–the–scenes** (adj.)	**be-moan**
beech (tree)	**be-hold**	**be-muse**
_cf._ **beach** (sandy shore)	**be-holden**	**bench**
beefy	**be-holder**	**bench mark** (n.)
bee-hive	**beige**	**bench war-rant** (n.)
beer (beverage)	**be-labor**	**bend**
_cf._ **bier** (coffin rest)	**be-lated**	**be-neath**
beet (vegetable)	**be-lay**	**bene-dic-tion**
_cf._ **beat** (strike)	**belch**	**bene-dic-tory**
bee-tle	**bel-fries**	**bene-fac-tor**
be-fit-ting	**bel-fry**	**be-nefic**
be-fore	**be-lie**	**be-nef-i-cence**
be-fore-hand	**be-lief**	**be-nef-i-cent**
be-friend	**be-liev-able**	**ben-e-fi-cial**
be-fud-dle	**be-liev-ably**	**ben-e-fi-cia-ries**
beg	**be-lieve**	**ben-e-fi-ciary**
be-gan	**be-liever**	**ben-e-fi-ci-ate**
beg-gat	**be-lit-tle**	**ben-e-fit**
begged	**be-lit-tler**	**ben-e-fited**
beg-ging	**bell** (hollow metal cup)	_or_ **ben-e-fit-ted**
be-gin	_cf._ **belle** (girl)	**be-nev-o-lence**
be-gin-ner	**bell—bottoms** (n.)	**be-nev-o-lent**
be-gin-ning	**bell-boy**	**be-nign**
be-gone	**belle** (girl)	**be-nig-nancy**
be-gun	_cf._ **bell** (hollow metal cup)	**be-nig-nant**
be-grudge	**bell-hop**	**ben-zene**
be-guile	**bel-lig-er-ence**	**ben-zi-dine**
be-guiler	**bel-lig-er-ency**	**ben-zine**
be-half	**bel-lig-er-ent**	**be-queathal**
be-have	**bel-low**	**be-quest**
be-hav-ior	**bell-wether**	**be-rate**
be-hav-ioral	**be-long**	**be-reave**
be-hav-ior-ism	**be-loved**	**be-reaved**
be-held	**below**	_or_ **be-reft**

Plural, past tense, adverbial, and noun derivatives formed by adding
s, d or ed, ly, ness, ment, ful, less, or ing to an unchanged root word are
not listed, nor are words formed by dropping the final e and adding ing.   17

be-ret
ber-ries
berry
ber-serk
berth (place)
 cf. birth (coming to life)
be-seech
be-set
be-set-ting
be-side (prep.) (near)
be-sides (adv.) (also)
be-siege
be-smear
be-smirch
be-spec-ta-cled
best
bes-tial
bes-ti-al-i-ties
bes-ti-al-ity
best man (n.)
be-stow
best—seller (n.)
bet
beta
be-to-ken
be-tray
be-trayal
be-trayer
be-troth
be-trothal
bet-ter (superior)
bet-tor (one who bets)
be-tween
be-twixt
bevel
bev-er-age

be-ware
be-wil-der
be-witch
be-yond
bias
bib
bi-ble
bib-li-cal
bib-lio-graphic
bib-li-o-graph-i-cal
bib-li-og-ra-phies
bib-li-og-ra-phy
bi-cen-te-nary
bi-cen-ten-nial
bi-ceps
bicker
bi-cy-cle
bid
bid-den
bid-ding
bide
bi-en-nial
bier (coffin rest)
 cf. beer (beverage)
bi-fo-cal
bi-fur-cate
bi-fur-ca-tion
big-a-mous
big-a-mist
big-amy
big-ger
big-gest
bigot
big-otry
bi-kini
bi-lat-eral

bi-lat-er-al-ism
bile
bilge
bi-lin-gual
bi-lin-gual-ism
bil-ious
bilk
bill
bill-board
bil-let
billet—doux
billets—doux (n. pl.)
bil-lion
bil-lion-aire
bil-low
bi-modal
bi-monthly
bin
bi-nary
bind
binder
bind-er-ies
bind-ery
binge
bin-oc-u-lar
bi-no-mial
bio-de-grad-able
bio-graph-i-cal
bio-graphic
bi-og-ra-phies
bi-og-ra-phy
bi-o-logic
bi-o-log-i-cal
bi-ol-o-gist
bi-op-sies
bi-opsy

Do not divide one-syllable words. Divide words by syllables, but leave
at least two letters of the word on the first line and three letters on the
following line. For additional guidelines, see page ix.

bi-par-ti-san	blank	bliss-fully
bi-par-ti-san-ism	blan-ket	blis-ter
bi-par-ti-san-ship	blare	blis-tery
birch	blasé	blithe
birch-bark	blas-pheme	blithe-some
bird	blas-phemer	blitz
birth (coming to life)	blas-phe-mous	blitz-krieg
cf. **berth** (place)	blas-phe-mies	bliz-zard
birth-day	blas-phemy	bloat
birth-rate	blast	blob
bis-cuit	**blast-off** *(n.)*	**bloc** (group)
bi-sect	bla-tant	*cf.* **block** (solid substance)
bi-sec-tor	blaze	block-ade
bi-sex-ual	bleach	block-age
bishop	bleach-able	**blond** (male)
bish-op-ric	bleak	**blonde** (female)
bi-son	blear-ily	blood
bit	blear-i-ness	blood-ier
bite	bleary	blood-i-est
bit-ter	bled	blood-hound
bi-tu-men	bleed	blood-stain
bi-tu-mi-nous	bleeder	bloody
bi-var-i-ate	blem-ish	bloom
biv-ouac	blend	blos-som
bi-weekly	blender	blot
bi-zarre (grotesque)	bless	blotch
cf. **ba-zaar** (market)	blessed	blotchy
black	*or* **blest**	blot-ted
black-mail	*blew* (past tense of blow)	blot-ter
black-mar-ket	*cf.* **blue** (color)	blot-ting
black-out	blight	blouse
black-top	blimp	blow
blade	blind	blown
blame	blind-fold	blud-geon
blanch	blink	**blue** (color)
bland	bliss	*cf.* **blew** (past tense of blow)

Plural, past tense, adverbial, and noun derivatives formed by adding *s, d* or *ed, ly, ness, ment, ful, less,* or *ing* to an unchanged root word are not listed, nor are words formed by dropping the final *e* and adding *ing.*   19

blue book	bo-he-mian	boom
blue chip	boil	boo-mer-ang
blue—collar (adj.)	boiler	boon
blue-ing	bois-ter-ous	boon-docks
or blu-ing	bold	booster
bluer	bo-lo-gna	boot
bluff	bol-she-vism	boo-tee (baby shoe)
blu-ish	bol-ster	or bootie
blun-der	bolt	cf. booty (plunder)
blun-derer	bomb	bo-rax
blunt	bom-bard	bor-der
blur	bom-bar-dier	bore (uninteresting)
blurb	bomber	cf. boar (animal)
blurred	bona fide	bored (disinterested)
blur-ring	bo-nanza	cf. board (plank of wood)
blurry	bond	bore-dom
blush	bond-able	born (brought to life)
boar (animal)	bond-age	cf. borne (carried)
cf. bore (uninteresting)	bone	bor-ough (town)
board (plank of wood)	bon-fire	cf. burro (animal)
cf. bored (disinterested)	bon-ier	cf. bur-row (hole)
boarder	bon-i-est	bor-row
board-walk	bon-net	bo-som
boast	bo-nus	boss
bob	bon vi-vant	boss-ier
bob-bin	bon voy-age	boss-i-est
bode	bony	boss-ism
bod-ice	or boney	bossy
bod-ies	boogie—woogie	bo-tan-i-cal
bod-ily	book	bot-a-nist
body	book-end	bot-any
bog	book-keeper	both
bogged	book-keep-ing	bother
bog-ging	book-let	both-er-some
boggy	book-mo-bile	bot-tle
bo-gus	Bool-ean	bot-tle-neck

Do not divide one-syllable words. Divide words by syllables, but leave at least two letters of the word on the first line and three letters on the following line. For additional guidelines, see page ix.

20

bot-tom
bot-tom-most
bot-u-lism
bou-doir
bough (branch)
  cf. **bow** (bending of head)
bought
bouil-lon (soup)
  cf. **bul-lion** (gold)
boul-der
bou-le-vard
bounce
bounc-ier
bounc-i-est
bouncy
bound
bound-aries
bound-ary
bounder
boun-te-ous
boun-ti-ful
boun-ties
bounty
bou-quet
bour-geois
bour-geoi-sie
bout
bou-tique
bou-ton-niere
bow (bend; weapon)
  cf. **beau** (suitor)
bow-ery
bowl
box
boxes
box-car

boy (young male)
  cf. **buoy** (marker in water)
boy-cott
boy-friend
boy scout
boy-sen-ber-ry
brace
brace-let
bracket
brack-ish
brad
brag
brag-ga-do-cio
brag-gart
bragged
brag-ger
braid
braille
brain
brain—picking *(n.)*
brain-storm
brain-wash
brake (stop movement)
  cf. **break** (take apart)
bram-ble
bran
branch
brand
bran-dish
brandy
brash
brass
bras-sard
bras-siere
bra-vado
bra-va-does

or bra-va-dos
brave
brav-ery
bravo
brawl
brawn
bra-zen
bra-zier
breach
breaches (breaks)
  cf. **breeches** (trousers)
bread (food)
  cf. **bred** (raised)
breadth
break (take apart)
  cf. **brake** (stop movement)
break-able
break-age
break-down
breaker
break-wa-ter
breast
breath
breathe
breath-tak-ing
bred (raised)
  cf. **bread** (food)
breed
breeder
breeze
breez-ier
breez-i-est
breez-ily
breez-i-ness
breezy
breth-ren

Plural, past tense, adverbial, and noun derivatives formed by adding
s, d or *ed, ly, ness, ment, ful, less,* or *ing* to an unchanged root word are
not listed, nor are words formed by dropping the final *e* and adding *ing*.

21

brev-ity
brew
brew-er-ies
brew-ery
bribe
brib-ery
bric—a—brac
brick
brick-layer
bridal (wedding)
 cf. bridle (restrain)
bride-groom
brides-maid
bridge
bridge-head
bridge-work
bridle (restrain)
 cf. bridal (wedding)
brief
brief-case
brier
brig
bri-gade
brig-and
brig-a-dier
bright
brighten
bril-liance
bril-liancy
bril-liant
brim
brimmed
brim-ming
brine
bring
brin-ier

brin-i-est
brink
brink-man-ship
briny
brisk
bris-tle
brit-tle
brit-tler
brit-tlest
broach
broad
broad-cast
broad-caster
broaden
broader
broad—minded (adj.)
bro-cade
bro-chure
broi-der
broi-dery
broil
broiler
broke
bro-ken
broken—down (adj.)
bro-ken-hearted
bro-ker
bro-ker-age
bron-chial
bron-chi-tis
bron-cho-pneu-mo-nia
bron-cho-scope
bron-chi (n. pl)
bron-chus
bronco
bronze

brooch
brood
brook
broom
broom-stick
broth
brother
brother—in—law
brothers—in—law (n. pl.)
brought
brow
brow-beat
brown
browse
browser
bru-cel-lo-sis
bruise
bruit (spread rumor)
 cf. brute (beast)
brunch
bru-net
 or bru-nette
brunt
brush
brush-fire
brusque
 or brusk
bru-tal
bru-tal-i-ties
bru-tal-ity
bru-tal-iza-tion
bru-tal-ize
brute (beast)
 cf. bruit (spread rumor)
brut-ish
bub-ble

Do not divide one-syllable words. Divide words by syllables, but leave at least two letters of the word on the first line and three letters on the following line. For additional guidelines, see page ix.

22

bub-ble gum
bub-blier
bub-bli-est
bub-bly
buc-ca-neer
buck
bucket
buckle
buck-shot
buck-skin
buck-tooth
buck-wheat
bu-colic
bud
bud-ded
Bud-dha
Bud-dhism
Bud-dhist
bud-dies
bud-ding
buddy
budge
bud-get
buff
buf-falo
buf-fa-loes *(n. pl.)*
or buf-falo
or buf-fa-los
buffer
buf-fet
buf-foon
buf-foon-er-ies
buf-foon-ery
bug
bug-a-boo
buggy

bu-gle
bu-gler
build
builder
built
built—up *(adj.)*
bulb
bul-bous
bulge
bulk
bulk-ier
bulk-i-est
bulk-i-ness
bulky
bull
bull-dog
bull-doze
bull-dozer
bull-fight
bul-le-tin
bul-lion (gold)
cf. bouil-lon (soup)
bul-lied
bul-lies
bull-ish
bull-pen
bull's—eye
bully
bul-wark
bum-ble
bum-bler
bump
bumper
bump-ier
bump-i-est
bump-kin

bump-tious
bumpy
bunch
bunco
or bunko
bun-dle
bun-ga-low
bun-gle
bun-gler
bun-ion
bunk
bunker
bunt
buoy (marker in water)
cf. boy (young male)
buoy-ance
buoy-ancy
buoy-ant
bur-den
bur-den-some
bu-reau
bu-reau-cra-cies
bu-reau-cracy
bu-reau-cratic
bu-reau-cra-ti-za-tion
bu-reau-cra-tize
bur-glar
bur-glar-ies
bur-glar-ize
bur-glary
bur-go-mas-ter
burial
bur-ied
bur-lap
bur-lesque
burn

Plural, past tense, adverbial, and noun derivatives formed by adding
s, d or *ed, ly, ness, ment, ful, less,* or *ing* to an unchanged root word are
not listed, nor are words formed by dropping the final *e* and adding *ing*.

burner	bu-tane	cab-a-ret
bur-nish	butcher	cabin
burr (sound; tool)	butch-er-ies	cab-i-net
burred	butch-ery	ca-ble
burrer	but-ler	ca-ble-gram
burro (animal)	butt (target; hit)	ca-ble TV
cf. bor-ough (town)	*cf.* but (on the other hand)	ca-cao
cf. bur-row (hole)	butte	cache (hiding place)
bursa	but-ter	*cf.* cash (money)
bur-sar	but-ter-fly	cac-tus
bur-si-tis	but-tock	ca-daver
burst	but-ton	cad-die
bury	but-ton-hole	*or* caddy
bus (vehicle)	but-tress	ca-dence
cf. buss (kiss)	buxom	ca-denza
buses *(n. pl.)*	buy (purchase)	ca-det
or bus-ses	*cf.* by (near to)	cadre
bush	buyer	ca-du-ceus
bushel	buzz	café
bush-ier	buzzer	caf-e-te-ria
bush-i-est	by (near to)	caf-feine
bushy	*cf.* buy *(purchase)*	cage
bus-ied	by—line *(n.)*	cagy
bus-ier	by-pass	*or* cagey
bus-ily	by-stander	ca-jole
busi-ness		ca-lam-i-ties
busi-ness-like		ca-lam-ity
busi-ness-man		cal-cif-er-ous
busi-ness-woman		cal-ci-fi-ca-tion
buss (kiss)		cal-ci-fied
cf. bus (vehicle)	**C**	cal-cify
bust		cal-cium
bus-tle	cab	cal-cu-la-ble
busy	cab-bage	cal-cu-late
but (on the other hand)	ca-bal-lero	cal-cu-la-tion
cf. butt (target; hit)	ca-bana	cal-cu-la-tor

Do not divide one-syllable words. Divide words by syllables, but leave
at least two letters of the word on the first line and three letters on the
following line. For additional guidelines, see page ix.

24

cal-en-dar
calf
cal-i-ber
or cal-i-bre
cal-i-brate
cal-i-per
or cal-li-per
cal-is-then-ics
or cal-lis-then-ics
calk
cal-lous *(adj.)*
cal-lus *(n.)*
calm
ca-loric
cal-o-rie
or cal-ory
ca-lypso
cameo
cam-era
cam-ou-flage
cam-paign
cam-paigner
cam-phor
camp-site
camp-stool
cam-pus
can
ca-nal
can-apé (appetizer)
 cf. can-opy (awning)
can-cel
can-cel-la-tion
or can-cel-ation
can-cer
can-de-la-bra
can-did

can-di-dacy
can-di-date
can-dle
can-dor
can-dies
can-died
cane
ca-nine
can-ing
can-is-ter
or can-nis-ter
can-ker
can-na-bis
canned
can-ni-bal
can-ni-bal-ism
can-ni-bal-is-tic
can-ning
can-non (gun)
 cf. canon (church law)
can-nily
can-ni-ness
canny
ca-noe
canon (church law)
 cf. can-non (gun)
can-o-pied
can-opy (awning)
 cf. can-apé (appetizer)
can-ta-loupe
can-tan-ker-ous
can-teen
can-ter (pace)
 cf. can-tor (liturgical
 singer)
can-tina

can-vas (cloth)
or can-vass
 cf. can-vass (examine)
 or can-vas
can-yon
cap
ca-pa-bil-i-ties
ca-pa-bil-ity
ca-pa-ble
ca-pac-ity
ca-per
cap-il-lary
cap-i-tal (city; resources)
 cf. cap-i-tol (building)
cap-i-tal-ism
cap-i-tal-ist
cap-i-tal-is-tic
cap-i-tal-iza-tion
cap-i-tal-ize
ca-pit-u-late
ca-pit-u-la-tion
capped
cap-ping
ca-price
ca-pri-cious
cap-size
cap-stan
cap-sule
cap-tain
cap-tion
cap-ti-vate
cap-ti-va-tion
cap-ti-va-tor
cap-tiv-ity
cap-ture
ca-rafe

Plural, past tense, adverbial, and noun derivatives formed by adding
s, d or *ed, ly, ness, ment, ful, less,* or *ing* to an unchanged root word are
not listed, nor are words formed by dropping the final *e* and adding *ing*.

car-a-mel
carat (weight)
or karat
 cf. car-rot (vegetable)
 cf. caret (printer's
 mark)
car-bine
car-bo-hy-drate
car-bon
car-bu-re-tor
car-cass
car-diac
car-di-nal
ca-reen
ca-reer
ca-ress
caret (printer's mark)
 cf. carat (weight)
or karat
 cf. car-rot
 (vegetable)
cargo
car-goes
or car-gos
car-hop
car-i-ca-ture
car-nal
car-na-tion
car-ni-val
car-niv-o-rous
ca-rouse
car-pen-ter
car-pen-try
car-pet
car-port
car-riage
car-ried

car-rier
car-ries
car-rot (vegetable
 cf. carat (weight)
or karat
 cf. caret
 (printer's mark)
carry
carte blanche
car-ti-lage
car-tog-ra-phy
car-ton
car-toon
car-toon-ist
car-tridge
carve
carver
cas-cade
cash (money)
 cf. cache (hiding place)
cash-ier
cash-mere
cas-ket
cas-sette
or ca-sette
cast (throw; list)
 cf. caste (social class)
cas-ti-gate
cas-tle
cas-trate
ca-sual
ca-su-al-ties
ca-su-alty
cat-a-comb
cat-a-log
or cat-a-logue
cat-a-loger

or cat-a-loguer
cat-a-lyst
cat-a-pult
cat-a-ract
ca-tas-tro-phe
cat-a-strophic
catch
catcher
catchup
or cat-sup
or ketchup
catchy
cat-e-chism
cat-e-go-ries
cat-e-gory
cater
ca-the-dral
cath-e-ter-ize
cath-ode
cath-o-lic (universal)
 cf. **Cath-o-lic**
 (Roman Catholic)
Ca-thol-i-cism
cat—o'—nine—tails *(n.)*
cat-sup
or catchup
or ketchup
cat-tle
cau-cus
causal
cau-sal-ity
cau-sa-tion
cause-way
caus-tic
cau-ter-ize
cau-tion
cau-tious

Do not divide one-syllable words. Divide words by syllables, but leave
at least two letters of the word on the first line and three letters on the
following line. For additional guidelines, see page ix.

cav-al-cade
cav-a-lier
cav-alry
cave
cave—in
cave-man
cav-ern
cav-ern-ous
cav-iar
or **cav-i-are**
cav-i-ties
cav-ity
ca-vort
cease
ce-dar
cede (yield)
  cf. **seed** (germ)
ceil-ing
cel-e-brate
cel-e-bra-tion
ce-leb-ri-ty
cel-ery
ce-les-tial
cel-i-bate
cell (small room)
  cf. **sell** (exchange for money)
cel-lar (basement)
  cf. **seller** (one who sells)
cel-lo-phane
cel-lu-lose
ce-ment
cem-e-ter-ies
cem-e-tery
cen-ser
  (incense container)
  cf. **cen-sor** (judge)

cen-sor-ship
cen-sure
cen-sus
cent (one penny)
  cf. **scent** (odor)
  cf. **sent**
    (did send)
cent-are
cen-ten-nial
cen-ter
cen-ter-piece
cen-ti-grade
cen-ti-me-ter
cen-tral
cen-tral-iza-tion
cen-tral-ize
cen-trif-u-gal
cen-tu-ries
cen-tury
ce-ramic
ce-real (food)
  cf. **se-rial**
    (story in installments)
ce-re-bral
cer-e-mo-nial
cer-e-mo-nies
cer-e-mo-ni-ous
cer-e-mony
cer-tain
cer-tainty
cer-tif-i-cate
cer-ti-fi-ca-tion
cer-ti-fied
cer-tify
ce-sar-ean
or **ce-sar-ian**
ces-sa-tion

ces-sion (surrender)
  cf. **ses-sion**
    (meeting)
chafe
chaff
cha-grin
chain
chain—reaction *(n.)*
chain—smoke *(v.)*
chair
chair lift
chair-man
chair-woman
chaise lounge
chal-ice (cup)
  cf. **chal-lis** (fabric)
chalk
chal-lenge
chal-lenger
chal-lis (fabric)
  cf. **chal-ice** (cup)
cha-me-leon
cham-ber
cham-ber-maid
cham-bray
cham-ois
or **chammy**
cham-pagne
cham-pion
chan-cel-lery
or **chan-cel-lory**
chan-cel-lor
chan-de-lier
change
change-able
change-over *(n.)*
chan-nel

Plural, past tense, adverbial, and noun derivatives formed by adding *s, d* or *ed, ly, ness, ment, ful, less,* or *ing* to an unchanged root word are not listed, nor are words formed by dropping the final *e* and adding *ing*.

Cha-nu-kah	chasm	cheer-leader
or Ha-nuk-kah	chas-sis	cheese
chaos	chaste *(pure)*	chees-ier
cha-otic	*cf.* chased *(pursued)*	chees-i-ness
chap	chas-ten	cheesy
chap-ar-ral	chas-tise	chef
chapel	chas-tity	chem-i-cal
chap-eron	chat	chem-is-try
or chap-er-one	châ-teau	che-nille
chap-lain	châ-teaus *(pl.)*	cher-ish
chapped	*or* châ-teaux	cher-ries
chap-ping	chatted	cherry
char	chat-tel	cherub
char-ac-ter-is-tic	chat-ter	che-ru-bic
char-ac-ter-iza-tion	chat-ting	cher-ubs *(pl.)*
char-ac-ter-ize	chatty	*or* cher-u-bim
cha-rade	chauf-feur	chess
char-coal	chau-vin-ism	chest
charge	chau-vin-ist	chest-ier
charge-able	cheap *(inexpensive)*	chesty
charge—a—plate *(n.)*	*cf.* cheep *(bird sound)*	chev-ron
or charge plate	cheat	chew
charger	cheater *(swindler)*	chew-able
char-iot	*cf.* chee-tah *(animal)*	chewy
cha-ris-ma	check	chi-can-ery
or char-ism	check-book	Chi-cano
cha-ris-mata *(pl.)*	check-er-board	chick
or char-isms	check-mate	chicken
charmer	check-out *(n.)*	chicken pox
char-ter	check out *(v.)*	chick-pea *(n.)*
char-treuse	cheep *(bird sound)*	chide
chase	*cf.* cheap *(inexpensive)*	chief
chased *(pursued)*	cheer	chief-tain
cf. chaste *(pure)*	cheer-ier	chif-fon
chaser	cheer-i-ness	child
chas-ing	cheerio	child-birth

Do not divide one-syllable words. Divide words by syllables, but leave
at least two letters of the word on the first line and three letters on the
28   following line. For additional guidelines, see page ix.

child-hood
child-ish
chil-dren
chili (hot-tasting food)
or chile
or chilli
  cf. chilly (cold)
chill
chill-ier
chilly (cold)
  cf. chili (hot
  tasting food)
or chile
or chilli
chime
chim-ney
chim-pan-zee
china
chin-chil-la
chip
chipped
chip-per
chip-ping
chi-ro-prac-tic
chi-ro-prac-tor
chisel
chis-eled
or chis-elled
chit-chat
chiv-al-rous
chiv-alry
chlo-ride
chlo-ri-nate
chlo-ri-na-tion
chlo-rine
chlo-ro-form

chlo-ro-phyll
chock
chock—full *(adj.)*
choc-o-late
choice
choir (singers)
  cf. quire (measure)
chol-era
cho-les-terol
choose
chop
chop—chop *(adv.)*
chopped
chop-ping
choppy
chop-stick
chop suey
cho-ral (musical)
  cf. cho-rale (hymn tune)
or cho-ral
chord (tone)
  cf. cord (wood measure)
chordal
chore
cho-re-og-ra-pher
cho-re-og-ra-phy
cho-ris-ter
chorus
chose
cho-sen
chow-der
chrome
chronic
chron-i-cle
chro-no-log-i-cal
chro-nol-o-gies

chro-nol-ogy
chub-bier
chub-i-ness
chubby
chuckle
chunk
chunk-ier
church
church-goer
chute (inclined trough)
  cf. shoot (fire at)
ci-ca-trix
ci-ca-tri-ces *(pl.)*
ci-der
ci-gar
cig-a-rette
or cig-a-ret
cin-der
cin-ema
cin-na-mon
ci-pher
circa
cir-cle
cir-cuit
cir-cu-itous
cir-cu-lar
cir-cu-lar-ize
cir-cu-late
cir-cu-la-tion
cir-cu-la-tory
cir-cum-fer-ence
cir-cum-lo-cu-tion
cir-cum-nav-i-gate
cir-cum-scribe
cir-cum-spect
cir-cum-stance

Plural, past tense, adverbial, and noun derivatives formed by adding
s, d or *ed, ly, ness, ment, ful, less,* or *ing* to an unchanged root word are
not listed, nor are words formed by dropping the final *e* and adding *ing.*

cir-cum-stan-tial
cir-cum-stan-ti-ate
cir-cum-vent
cir-cum-ven-tion
cir-cus
cir-rho-sis
cis-tern
cit-a-del
ci-ta-tion
cite (quote)
 cf. **sight** (vision)
 cf. **site** (place)
cit-i-zen
cit-i-zenry
cit-ron
cit-rus
ci-ties
city
city-scape
civic
civic—minded *(adj.)*
civil
ci-vil-ian
ci-vil-ity
civ-i-li-za-tion
civ-i-lize
civil rights *(pl. only)*
claim
claim-able
claim-ant
claimer
clair-voy-ance
clair-voy-ant
clam-mier
clammy
clamor

clam-or-ous
clan
clan-des-tine
clans-man
claret
clar-i-fi-ca-tion
clar-i-fied
clar-ify
clar-i-net
clar-ity
clasp
class
clas-sic
clas-si-cal
clas-si-cism
clas-si-cist
clas-si-fi-ca-tion
clas-si-fied
clas-si-fier
clas-sify
class-room
clause (words)
 cf. **claws** (talons)
claus-tro-pho-bia
claws (talons)
 cf. **clause** (words)
clean
clean—cut *(adj.)*
cleaner
clean-li-ness
cleanse
cleanser
clear
clear—cut *(adj.)*
clear-headed
cleav-age

cleave
cleaver
clem-ency
clench
cleric
cler-i-cal
clerk
clew
 or **clue**
cli-ché
click (noise)
 cf. **clique** (exclusive group)
cli-en-tele
cliff—hanger *(n.)*
cli-mate
cli-matic
cli-max
climb
climb-able
clinch
clincher
cling
clingy
clinic
clin-i-cal
clip
clipped
clip-per
clip-ping
clique (exclusive group)
 cf. **click** (noise)
cloak
clois-ter
close (shut)
 cf. **clothes** (apparel)
closer

Do not divide one-syllable words. Divide words by syllables, but leave at least two letters of the word on the first line and three letters on the following line. For additional guidelines, see page ix.

closet
clo-sure
cloth
clothe
clothed
or clad
clothes (apparel)
  cf. close (shut)
cloth-ing
cloud
cloudy
clown
club
clubbed
club-bing
clum-sier
clum-si-ness
clumsy
clus-ter
clutch
clut-ter
coach
co-ag-u-late
co-ag-u-la-tion
co-ali-tion
coarse (rough)
  cf. course (direction)
coarsen
coarser
coast
coaster
coax
co-ax-ial
co-balt
CO-BOL
or Co-bol

co-caine
cock-ier
cock-i-ness
cocky
co-co-nut
co-coon
co-deine
cod-i-cil
cod-i-fi-ca-tion
cod-i-fied
cod-ify
coed
co-ed-u-ca-tion
co-ef-fi-cient
co-er-cion
co-ex-ist
co-ex-is-tence
co-ex-is-tent
cof-fee
cof-fer
cof-fin
cog-i-tate
cog-nac
cog-ni-tive
cog-ni-zant
co-habit
co-hab-i-tant
co-hab-i-ta-tion
co-her-ence
co-her-ent
co-he-sion
co-he-sive
co-hort
coif-fure
coin-age
co-in-cide

co-in-ci-dence
co-in-ci-den-tal
co-itus
col-an-der
cold—blooded *(adj.)*
cold-hearted
cole-slaw
colic
col-i-seum
col-lab-o-rate
col-lab-o-ra-tion
col-lab-o-ra-tor
col-lapse
col-laps-ible
col-lar
col-lat-eral
col-league
col-lect
col-lect-ible
col-lec-tion
col-lec-tive
col-lec-tiv-ism
col-lege
col-le-gian
col-le-giate
col-lide
col-li-sion (crash)
  cf. col-lu-sion (agreement)
col-lo-quial
col-lo-qui-al-ism
col-lo-quies
col-lo-quy
col-lu-sion (agreement)
  cf. col-li-sion (crash)
col-lu-sive
co-logne

Plural, past tense, adverbial, and noun derivatives formed by adding
s, d or ed, ly, ness, ment, ful, less, or *ing* to an unchanged root word are
not listed, nor are words formed by dropping the final *e* and adding *ing.*

co-lon	com-i-cal	com-mit-ted
col-o-nel (officer)	comma (punctuation)	com-mit-tee
cf. ker-nel (nut)	*cf.* coma (stupor)	com-mit-tee-man
co-lo-nial	com-mand	com-mit-tee-woman
col-o-nies	com-man-dant	com-mit-ting
col-o-nist	com-man-deer	com-mode
col-o-ni-za-tion	com-mander	com-mod-i-ties
col-o-nize	com-mander in chief	com-mod-i-ty
col-ony	com-mem-o-rate	common—law *(adj.)*
co-los-sal	com-mem-o-ra-tion	com-mon law *(n.)*
col-os-seum	com-mem-o-ra-tive	com-mon-wealth
col-umn	com-mence	com-mu-nal
col-um-nist	com-mend	com-mune
coma (stupor)	com-mend-able	com-mu-ni-ca-ble
cf. comma (punctuation)	com-men-da-tion	com-mu-ni-cate
co-ma-tose	com-men-da-tory	com-mu-ni-ca-tion
com-bat	com-men-su-ra-ble	com-mu-ni-ca-tive
com-bat-ant	com-men-su-ra-bly	com-mu-nion
com-bat-ive	com-men-su-rate	com-mu-nism
com-bi-na-tion	com-ment	com-mu-nist
com-bine	com-men-tar-ies	com-mu-nis-tic
com-bus-ti-ble	com-men-tary	com-mu-ni-ties
com-bus-tion	com-men-ta-tor	com-mu-ni-ty
co-me-dian (male)	com-merce	com-mu-ta-tion
co-me-di-enne (female)	com-mer-cial	com-mute
com-e-dies	com-mer-cial-ism	com-muter
com-edy	com-mer-cial-iza-tion	com-pact
come-lier	com-mer-cial-ize	com-pan-ion
comely	com-mis-er-ate	com-pan-ion-able
come—on *(n.)*	com-mis-er-a-tion	com-pa-nies
come on *(v.)*	com-mis-sar	com-pany
comet	com-mis-sary	com-pa-ra-ble
com-fort	com-mis-sion	com-par-a-tive
com-fort-able	com-mis-sioner	com-pare
com-forter	com-mit	com-par-i-son
comic	com-mit-tal	com-part-ment

Do not divide one-syllable words. Divide words by syllables, but leave at least two letters of the word on the first line and three letters on the following line. For additional guidelines, see page ix.

com-pass
com-pas-sion
com-pas-sion-ate
com-pat-i-bil-ity
com-pat-i-ble
com-pel
com-pelled
com-pel-ling
com-pen-sate
com-pen-sa-tion
com-pen-sa-tor
com-pen-sa-tory
com-pete
com-pe-tence
com-pe-ten-cies
com-pe-tency
com-pe-tent
com-pe-ti-tion
com-pet-i-tive
com-pet-i-tor
com-pi-la-tion
com-pile
com-pla-cence (self-satisfaction)
  cf. **com-plai-sance** (courteousness)
com-pla-cency
com-pla-cent
com-plain
com-plain-ant
com-plainer
com-plai-sance (courteousness)
  cf. **com-pla-cence** (self-satisfaction)
com-plai-sant

com-plected
com-ple-ment (that which completes)
  cf. **com-pli-ment** (favorable remark)
com-ple-men-tary
com-plete
com-ple-tion
com-plex
com-plex-ion
com-plex-ity
com-pli-ance
com-pli-cate
com-pli-ca-tion
com-plic-ity
com-pli-ment (favorable remark)
  cf. **com-ple-ment** (that which completes)
com-pli-men-tary
com-plied
com-ply
com-po-nent
com-pose
com-poser
com-pos-ite
com-po-si-tion
com-po-sure
com-pound
com-pre-hend
com-pre-hen-si-ble
com-pre-hen-sion
com-pre-hen-sive
com-press
com-pres-sion
com-pres-sor

com-prise
com-pro-mise
com-pro-miser
comp-trol-ler
  or con-trol-ler
com-pul-sion
com-pul-sive
com-pul-sory
com-punc-tion
com-pu-ta-tion
com-pute
com-puter
com-put-er-ize
com-rade
com-rad-ery
con-cave
con-ceal
con-ceal-able
con-cede
con-ceit
con-ceiv-able
con-ceive
con-cen-trate
con-cen-tra-tion
con-cen-tric
con-cept
con-cep-tual
con-cern
con-cert
con-certo
con-ces-sion
con-ces-sion-aire
con-cil-i-ate
con-cil-i-a-tion
con-cil-i-a-tor
con-cil-ia-tory

Plural, past tense, adverbial, and noun derivatives formed by adding
s, d or *ed, ly, ness, ment, ful, less,* or *ing* to an unchanged root word are
not listed, nor are words formed by dropping the final *e* and adding *ing*.

con-cise
con-clave
con-clude
con-clu-sion
con-clu-sive
con-coct
con-coc-tion
con-com-i-tant
con-crete
con-cur
con-curred
con-cur-rence
con-cur-ring
con-cus-sion
con-demn
con-dem-na-tion
con-dens-able
or con-dens-ible
con-den-sa-tion
con-dense
con-denser
con-de-scend
con-de-scen-sion
con-di-ment
con-di-tion
con-di-tional
con-dole
con-do-lence
con-done
con-du-cive
con-duct
con-duc-tive
con-duc-tor
con-duit
cone
con-fec-tion

con-fec-tion-ary
con-fec-tion-ery
con-fed-er-acy
con-fed-er-ate
con-fed-er-a-tion
con-fer
con-feree
con-fer-ence
con-ferred
con-fer-ring
con-fess
con-fes-sion
con-fes-sional
con-fes-sor
con-fetti
con-fi-dant (trusted person)
  cf. con-fi-dent (sure)
con-fi-dante (female
  trusted person)
con-fide
con-fi-dence
con-fi-dent (sure)
  cf. con-fi-dant
  (trusted person)
con-fi-den-tial
con-fine
con-firm
con-fir-ma-tion
con-fis-cate
con-fis-ca-tion
con-fla-gra-tion
con-flict
con-flu-ent
con-form
con-form-ance
con-for-ma-tion

con-form-ist
con-form-ity
con-found
con-front
con-fron-ta-tion
con-fuse
con-fu-sion
con-geal
con-ge-nial
con-ge-ni-al-ity
con-gen-i-tal
con-gest
con-ges-tion
con-ges-tive
con-glom-er-ate
con-gom-er-a-tion
con-grat-u-late
con-grat-u-la-tion
con-grat-u-la-tory
con-gre-gate
con-gre-ga-tion
con-gre-ga-tional
con-gress
con-gres-sio-nal
con-gress-man
con-gress-woman
con-gru-ence
con-gru-ent
con-gru-ity
con-gru-ous
co-ni-fer
co-nif-er-ous
con-jec-tural
con-jec-turer
con-ju-gal
con-ju-gate

Do not divide one-syllable words. Divide words by syllables, but leave
at least two letters of the word on the first line and three letters on the
following line. For additional guidelines, see page ix.

con-ju-ga-tion
con-junc-tion
con-junc-tive
con-jure
con-jurer
or con-juror
con-nect
con-necter
or con-nec-tor
con-nec-tion
con-nec-tive
con-niv-ance
con-nive
con-niver
con-nois-seur
con-no-ta-tion
con-note
con-nu-bial
con-quer
con-que-ror
con-quest
con-quis-ta-dor
con-quis-ta-do-res
con-science
con-sci-en-tious
con-scio-na-ble
con-scious
con-script
con-se-crate
con-se-cra-tion
con-se-cra-tor
con-sec-u-tive
con-sen-sus
con-sent
con-senter
con-se-quence

con-se-quent
con-se-quen-tial
con-ser-va-tion
con-ser-va-tion-ist
con-ser-va-tism
con-ser-va-tive
con-serve
con-sider
con-sid-er-able
con-sid-er-ate
con-sid-er-ation
con-sign
con-sign-able
con-signee
con-signor
con-sist
con-sis-tence
con-sis-tency
con-sis-tent
con-so-la-tion
con-sole
con-sol-i-date
con-sol-i-da-tion
con-sommé
con-so-nance
con-so-nant
con-spic-u-ous
con-spir-a-cies
con-spir-acy
con-spire
con-sta-ble
con-stab-u-lary
con-stant
con-stancy
con-stel-la-tion
con-ster-na-tion

con-stit-u-en-cies
con-stit-u-ency
con-stit-u-ent
con-sti-tute
con-sti-tu-tion
con-sti-tu-tional
con-sti-tu-tion-al-ity
con-strain
con-straint
con-strict
con-stric-tion
con-stric-tive
con-stric-tor
con-struct
con-struct-ible
con-struc-tion
con-struc-tive
con-struc-tor
con-stru-able
con-strue
con-sul
con-sul-ate
con-sular
con-sult
con-sul-tant
con-sul-ta-tion
con-sume
con-sumer
con-sum-mate
con-sum-ma-tion
con-sump-tion
con-sump-tive
con-tact
con-ta-gion
con-ta-gious
con-tain

Plural, past tense, adverbial, and noun derivatives formed by adding *s, d* or *ed, ly, ness, ment, ful, less,* or *ing* to an unchanged root word are not listed, nor are words formed by dropping the final *e* and adding *ing*.

con-tainer
con-tam-i-nate
con-tam-i-na-tion
con-tam-i-na-tor
con-tem-plate
con-tem-pla-tion
con-tem-po-ra-ne-ous
con-tem-po-rary
con-tempt
con-tempt-ible
con-temp-tu-ous
con-tend
con-tender
con-tent
con-ten-tion
con-test
con-test-able
con-test-ant
con-text
con-tex-tual
con-ti-gu-ity
con-tig-u-ous
con-ti-nence
(self restraint)
cf. con-ti-nents
(land)
con-ti-nen-tal
con-tin-gency
con-tin-ent
con-tin-ual
con-tin-u-ance
con-tin-u-a-tion
con-ti-nu-ity
con-tin-u-ous
con-tort
con-tor-tion
con-tor-tion-ist

con-tour
con-tra-band
con-tra-cep-tion
con-tra-cep-tive
con-tract
con-tract-ible
con-trac-tion
con-trac-tor
con-tra-dict
con-tra-dict-able
con-tra-dic-tion
con-tra-dictor
con-tra-dic-tory
con-trail
con-trari-ness
con-trary
con-trast
con-trast-able
con-tra-vene
con-trib-ute
con-tri-bu-tion
con-trib-u-tor
con-trib-u-tory
con-trite
con-tri-tion
con-triv-ance
con-trive
con-triver
con-trol
con-trol-la-ble
con-trolled
con-trol-ler
or comp-trol-ler
con-trol-ling
con-tro-ver-sial
con-tro-versy
con-tu-sion

con-va-lesce
con-va-les-cence
con-va-les-cent
con-vec-tion
con-vene
con-ve-nience
con-ve-nient
con-vent
con-ven-tion
con-ven-tional
con-verge
con-ver-gence
con-ver-gent
con-ver-sant
con-ver-sa-tion
con-ver-sa-tional
con-verse
con-ver-sion
con-vert
con-verter
or con-ver-tor
con-vert-ibil-ity
con-vex
con-vey
con-vey-ance
con-veyer
or con-veyor
con-vict
con-vic-tion
con-vince
con-vincer
con-viv-ial
con-viv-ial-ity
con-vo-ca-tion
con-voy
con-vulse
con-vul-sion

Do not divide one-syllable words. Divide words by syllables, but leave at least two letters of the word on the first line and three letters on the following line. For additional guidelines, see page ix.

con-vul-sive
cool
coolly
or cooly
coop (pen)
  cf. coupe (*small car*)
co-op-er-ate
co-op-er-a-tion
co-op-er-a-tive
co-or-di-nate
co-or-di-nat-ing
co-or-di-na-tor
cope
co-pi-lot
co-pi-ous
cop—out (*n.*)
cop-per
cop-u-late
cop-ies
copy
copy-holder
co-quet
or co-quette
co-quet-tish
coral
  (stony substance)
  cf. choral (musical)
  cf. chor-ale
  (hymn tune)
coral snake
cord
  (wood measure)
  cf. chord (tone)
cord-age
cor-dial
cor-dial-ity
cor-don

core (central part)
  cf. corps.
  (military branch)
co-re-late
co-re-la-tion
co-re-spon-dent (legal term)
  cf. cor-re-spon-dent (one
  who exchanges letters)
cor-nea
cor-nu-co-pia
cor-o-nary
cor-o-na-tion
cor-o-ner
cor-po-ral
cor-po-rate
cor-po-ra-tion
corps (military branch)
  cf. core (central part)
cor-pu-lence
cor-pu-lent
cor-pus-cle
cor-ral (animal pen)
cor-ralled
cor-ral-ling
cor-rect
cor-rect-able
cor-rec-tion
cor-rec-tive
cor-rec-tor
cor-re-late
cor-re-la-tion
cor-re-spond
cor-re-spon-dence
cor-re-spon-dent (one who
  exchanges letters)
  cf. co-re-spon-dent
  (legal term)

cor-ri-dor
cor-rob-o-rate
cor-rob-o-ra-tion
cor-rob-o-ra-tive
cor-rob-o-ra-tor
cor-rode
cor-ro-sion
cor-ro-sive
cor-ru-gate
cor-rupt
cor-rupter
or cor-rup-tor
cor-rupt-ible
cor-rupt-ibil-ity
cor-rup-tion
cor-sage
cor-tege
  (or) cor-tège
cor-ti-sone
co-sine (angle)
  cf. co-sign (jointly sign)
cos-metic
cos-me-tol-o-gist
cos-me-tol-ogy
cos-mic
cos-mo-naut
cos-mo-pol-i-tan
co—star
cost—of—living index (*n.*
couch
cou-gar
cough
coun-cil (group of people)
  cf. coun-sel
  (exchanging ideas)
coun-cil-lor
or coun-cilor

Plural, past tense, adverbial, and noun derivatives formed by adding
s, d or *ed, ly, ness, ment, ful, less,* or *ing* to an unchanged root word are
not listed, nor are words formed by dropping the final *e* and adding *ing*.

coun-selor
or coun-sel-lor
coun-selor—at—law
(attorney)
coun-selors—at—law
(attorneys)
count-able
count-down
coun-te-nance
counter
coun-ter-ac-tion
coun-ter-clock-wise
coun-ter-es-pi-o-nage
coun-ter-feit
coun-tri-fied
or coun-try-fied
coun-try
coup
coup de grace
coup d'état
coupe (small car)
cf. coop (pen)
coups de grace *(pl.)*
coups d'état *(pl.)*
cou-ple
cou-pon
cour-age
cou-ra-geous
cou-rier
course (direction)
cf. coarse (rough)
court
court-house
cour-te-ous
cour-te-san
cour-tesy
court—martial

courts—martial
(pl.)
cousin
cove
co-ven
cov-e-nant
cover
cov-er-all *(n.)*
cover—all *(adj.)*
co-vert
cover—up *(n.)*
cov-et-ous
cow-ard
cow-ard-ice
cow-ard-li-ness
cow-boy
cow-hand
cow-hide
coy
co-zier
cozy
crab
crabbed
crab-bing
crack
crack-down *(n.)*
crack down *(v.)*
cracker—barrel
crack—up *(n.)*
crack up *(v.)*
cra-dle
craft
craft-ier
crafts-man
crafts-man-ship
crafty
cram

crammed
cram-ming
crane
cra-nium
crank
crank-ier
cranky
crash dive *(n.)*
crash hel-met *(n.)*
crash—land *(v.)*
crate
crater
crave
cra-ven
crawl
crayon
craze
cra-zier
cra-zi-ness
crazy
creak (noise)
cf. creek
(stream)
creak-ier
creak-ily
cream
cream-ery
crease
cre-ate
cre-ation
cre-ative
cre-ator
crea-ture
cre-dence
cre-den-tial
cred-i-ble
cred-i-bil-ity

Do not divide one-syllable words. Divide words by syllables, but leave
at least two letters of the word on the first line and three letters on the
following line. For additional guidelines, see page ix.

credit
cred-it-abil-ity
cred-it-ably
credit card (n.)
cred-i-tor
credo
cred-u-lous
creed
creek (stream)
  cf. creak
  (noise)
cre-scendo
cres-cent
crest
cre-vasse
crev-ice
crew
crew cut (n.)
crib
crib-bage
cribbed
cribber
crib-bing
crick
cricket
crime
crim-i-nal
crim-i-nol-o-gist
crim-i-nol-ogy
crim-son
cringe
crin-kle
crip-ple
cri-ses (pl.)
cri-sis (sing.)
crisp
crisp-ier

crispy
criss-cross
cri-te-ria (pl.)
  or cri-te-rions
cri-te-rion (sing.)
critic
crit-i-cal
crit-i-cism
crit-i-cize
crit-i-cizer
cri-tique
croak
cro-chet
crock-ery
croc-o-dile
cro-nies
crony
crop
cropped
crop-ping
cro-quet (game)
  cf. cro-quette
  (food)
cross
cross—country (n.)
cross—examination (n.)
cross—examine
cross—reference
cross-road
crou-pier
cru-cial
cru-ci-ble
cru-ci-fied
cru-ci-fix
cru-ci-fix-ion
cru-cify
crude

cruder
cru-dity
cruel
cru-el-ties
cru-elty
cruise
cruiser
crumb
crum-ble (make crumbs o
  cf. crum-ple (wrinkle)
crummy
  or crumby
crunch
cru-sade
cru-sader
crus-ta-cean
crutch
crux
cried
cries
cry
cryp-tic
cryp-to-gram
crys-tal
crys-tal-line
crys-tal-li-za-tion
crys-tal-lize
  or crys-tal-ize
cub-by-hole
cube
cubic
cu-bi-cal (shaped like a
  cube) cf. cu-bi-cle
  (very small room)
cub-ism
cub-ist
cuck-old

Plural, past tense, adverbial, and noun derivatives formed by adding
s, d or ed, ly, ness, ment, ful, less, or ing to an unchanged root word are
not listed, nor are words formed by dropping the final e and adding ing.

cud-dle
cud-dly
cue (hint)
cf. queue
(braid; line)
cui-sine
cuff link
cul—de—sac
cu-li-nary
cull
cul-mi-nate
cul-mi-na-tion
cul-pa-ble
cul-prit
cult
cul-ti-va-ble
or cul-ti-vat-able
cul-ti-vate
cul-ti-va-tion
cul-ti-va-tor
cul-tural
cul-ture
cul-vert
cum-ber-some
cum laude
cum-mer-bund
cu-mu-late
cu-mu-la-tion
cu-ne-ate
cun-ning
Cu-pid
cur-able
cure
cure—all *(n.)*
cur-dle
cur-few
cu-rio

cu-ri-os-ity
cu-ri-ous
curl
curler
curl-i-que
or curly-cue
curl-ier
cur-rant
(berry)
cf. cur-rent (topical;
movement)
cur-ren-cies
cur-rency
cur-ric-ula *(pl.)*
or cur-ric-u-lums
cur-ric-u-lar
cur-ric-u-lum
curry
curse
cur-sive
cur-sory
curt
cur-tail
curt-sied
or curt-seyed
curt-sies
or curt-seys
curtsy
or curt-sey
cur-va-ceous
or cur-va-cious
cur-va-ture
cush-ion
cus-tard
cus-to-dial
cus-to-dian
cus-tody

cus-tom
cus-tom-arily
cus-tom-ary
custom—built *(adj.)*
cus-tomer
custom—made
custom—tailor
cut
cut—and—dried *(adj.)*
or cut—and—dry
cut-lery
cut-off *(n.) (adj.)*
cu-ti-cle
cut-lass
cut-ter
cut-ting
cy-an-a-mide
cy-a-nide
cy-ber-netic
cy-cle
cy-clic
cy-cli-cal
cy-clist
cyl-in-der
cy-clone
cy-clonic
cy-lin-dri-cal
cym-bal
(percussion instrument)
cf. sym-bol (image)
cynic
cyn-i-cal
cyn-i-cism
cyst
czar
cza-rina
czar-ism

Do not divide one-syllable words. Divide words by syllables, but leave
at least two letters of the word on the first line and three letters on the
following line. For additional guidelines, see page ix.

D

dab-ble
dab-bler
dachs-hund
Da-cron
dag-ger
da-guerre-o-type
dahlia
daily
dain-tier
dain-tily
dain-ti-ness
dainty
dair-ies
dairy
dais
dai-sies
daisy
dal-li-ance
dal-lied
dal-lier
dally
dam
  (holds water)
  cf. **damn** (curse)
dam-age
damned
dam-ming
dam-na-ble
dam-na-tion
damp
dampen
damper
dam-sel
dance

dancer
dan-de-lion
dan-ger
dan-ger-ous
dan-gle
dare
dare-devil
darer
dark
Dark Ages
darken
darn
dart
Dar-win
Dar-win-ian
Dar-win-ism
data *(pl.)*
  or da-tums
da-ta-ma-tion
date
datum *(sing.)*
date
daub
daugh-ter
daunt-less
daw-dle
daw-dler
dawn
day—care *(adj.)*
daze
  (confusion)
  cf. **days** (time)
daz-zle
daz-zler
D day
dea-con
dea-con-ess

dead
deaden
dead-line
dead-li-ness
dead-lock
deaf
deafen
deaf—mute *(n.)*
deal
dealer
dealt
dean
dear
  (much loved)
  cf. **deer** (animal)
dearth
death
death-bed
de-ba-cle
de-bark
de-bar-ka-tion
de-base
de-baser
de-bat-able
de-bate
de-bater
de-bauch
de-baucher
de-bauch-er-ies
de-bauch-ery
de-ben-ture
de-bil-i-tate
debit
deb-o-nair
de-bris *(sing. pl.)*
debt
debtor

Plural, past tense, adverbial, and noun derivatives formed by adding
s, d or *ed, ly, ness, ment, ful, less,* or *ing* to an unchanged root word are
not listed, nor are words formed by dropping the final *e* and adding *ing.*

41

de-bug
de-but
deb-u-tante
de-cade
dec-a-dence
dec-a-dent
de-cal
de-canter
de-cap-i-tate
de-cap-i-ta-tion
de-cay
de-cease
de-ce-dent
de-ceit
de-ceive
de-ceiver
de-cel-er-ate
de-cel-er-a-tion
de-cency
de-cent
de-cen-tral-iza-tion
de-cen-tral-ize
de-cep-tion
de-cep-tive
deci-bel
de-cide
de-cid-u-ous
dec-i-mal
dec-i-mal point
dec-i-mate
dec-i-ma-tion
de-ci-pher
de-ci-pher-able
de-ci-sion
de-ci-sive
deck

de-claim
de-clam-a-tory
dec-la-ra-tion
de-clar-a-tive
de-clare
de-clas-si-fied
de-clas-sify
de-clin-able
de-cline
de-code
dé-col-le-tage *(n.)*
dé-col-le-té *(adj.)*
de-com-pos-able
de-com-pose
de-com-po-si-tion
de-con-ges-tant
de-con-tam-i-nate
de-cor
or dé-cor
dec-o-rate
dec-o-ra-tion
dec-o-ra-tive
dec-o-ra-tor
de-co-rum
de-coy
de-crease
de-cree
de-crepit
de-cry
ded-i-cate
ded-i-ca-tion
de-duce
de-duc-ible
de-duct
de-duct-ible
de-duc-tion

de-duc-tive
deem
deep
deepen
deep—freeze *(v.)*
deep—six *(v.)*
deep six *(n.)*
deer (animal)
   cf. **dear** (much loved)
de-face
de facto
def-a-ma-tion
de-fam-a-tory
de-fame
de-famer
de-fault
de-faulter
de-feat
de-feat-ism
de-feat-ist
def-e-cate
de-fect
de-fec-tion
de-fec-tor
de-fec-tive
de-fend
de-fend-able
de-fen-dant
de-fense
or de-fence
de-fen-si-bil-ity
de-fen-si-ble
de-fen-sive
de-fer
def-er-ence
def-er-en-tial

Do not divide one-syllable words. Divide words by syllables, but leave at least two letters of the word on the first line and three letters on the following line. For additional guidelines, see page ix.

de-ferred
de-fer-ring
de-fi-ance
de-fi-ant
de-fi-cien-cies
de-fi-cient
def-i-cit
de-fied
de-fier
de-file
de-filer
de-fin-able
de-fine
def-i-nite
def-i-ni-tion
de-fin-i-tive
de-flate
de-fla-tion
de-fla-tor
de-flect
de-flec-tor
de-flo-ra-tion
de-flower
de-fo-li-ant
de-fo-li-ate
de-for-est
de-for-es-ta-tion
de-form
de-for-ma-tion
de-form-i-ties
de-form-ity
de-fraud
de-fray
de-fray-able
de-funct
defy

de-gen-er-acy
de-gen-er-ate
de-gen-er-a-tion
de-grad-able
deg-ra-da-tion
de-grade
de-gree
de-hu-man-ize
de-hu-mid-ify
de-hy-drate
de-hy-dra-tion
de-icer
de-i-fi-ca-tion
de-i-fied
de-ify
de-ism
de-ist
de-is-tic
de-i-ties
de-ity
de-jected
de-jec-tion
de-lec-ta-ble
del-e-gate
del-e-ga-tion
de-lete
de-le-tion
del-e-te-ri-ous
de-lib-er-ate
de-lib-er-a-tion
del-i-ca-cies
del-i-cacy
del-i-cate
del-i-ca-tes-sen
de-li-cious
de-lin-eate

de-lin-ea-tion
de-lin-ea-tor
de-lin-quency
de-lin-quent
de-lir-i-ous
de-lir-ium
de-liver
de-liv-er-able
de-liv-er-ance
de-liv-erer
de-liv-er-ies
de-liv-ery
de-lude
de-lu-sion
de-lu-sive
del-uge
de-luxe
delve
dem-a-gogue
or dem-a-gog
de-mand
de-mar-ca-tion
or de-mar-ka-tion
de-mean
de-mented
de-men-tia
de-men-tia prae-cox
de-merit
de-mil-i-ta-ri-za-tion
de-mil-i-ta-rize
de-mise
dem-i-tasse
de-mo-bi-li-za-tion
de-mo-bi-lize
de-moc-racy
dem-o-crat

Plural, past tense, adverbial, and noun derivatives formed by adding
s, d or *ed, ly, ness, ment, ful, less,* or *ing* to an unchanged root word are
not listed, nor are words formed by dropping the final *e* and adding *ing*.   43

dem-o-cratic
de-moc-ra-ti-za-tion
de-moc-ra-tize
de-mol-ish
dem-o-li-tion
de-mon
 or dae-mon
de-monic
 or de-mon-i-cal
de-mon-stra-ble
dem-on-strate
dem-on-stra-tion
dem-on-stra-tor
de-mor-al-iza-tion
de-mor-al-ize
de-mor-al-izer
de-mote
de-mo-tion
de-mur (object)
 cf. de-mure (coy)
de-murred
de-murer
de-nial
denim
de-nom-i-na-tion
de-nom-i-na-tional
de-nom-i-na-tor
de-note
de-nounce
dense
den-si-ties
den-sity
den-tal
den-ti-frice
den-tist
den-ture

de-nun-ci-a-tion
de-nied
deny
de-odor-ant
de-odor-ize
de-odor-izer
de-part
de-part-men-tal
de-par-ture
de-pend
de-pend-abil-ity
de-pend-able
de-pen-dence
 or de-pen-dance
de-pen-den-cies
de-pen-dency
de-pen-dent
 or de-pen-dant
de-pict
de-plete
de-ple-tion
de-plor-able
de-plore
de-ploy
de-port
de-por-ta-tion
de-pose
de-posit
de-pos-i-tary (person or
 company)
 cf. de-pos-i-tory (place)
de-pos-i-tor
dep-o-si-tion
de-pot
de-prave
de-prav-ity

dep-re-cate
dep-re-ca-tion
dep-re-ca-tory
de-pre-cia-ble
de-pre-ci-ate
de-pre-ci-a-tion
de-press
de-pres-sant
de-pres-sion
dep-ri-va-tion
de-prive
depth
dep-u-ties
dep-u-tize
dep-uty
de-rail
de-range
der-e-lect
der-e-lic-tion
de-ride
de-riv-able
der-i-va-tion
de-riv-a-tive
de-rive
de-rog-a-tory
der-rick
der-ri-ere
 or der-ri-ère
der-rin-ger
de-scend
de-scend-ible
de-scent
de-scen-dant
 or de-scen-dent
de-scrib-able
de-scribe

Do not divide one-syllable words. Divide words by syllables, but leave
at least two letters of the word on the first line and three letters on the
following line. For additional guidelines, see page ix.

44

de-scrib-er
de-scrip-tion
de-scrip-tive
des-e-crate
des-e-crater
or des-e-cra-tor
de-seg-re-gate
de-seg-re-ga-tion
de-sen-si-tize
de-sert (abandon)
 cf. des-ert (wasteland)
 cf. des-sert (pie, etc.)
de-serter
de-ser-tion
de-serve
de-sign
de-signer
des-ig-nate
des-ig-na-tion
de-sir-abil-ity
de-sir-able
de-sire
de-sir-ous
de-sist
des-o-late
des-o-la-tion
de-spair
des-per-ado
des-per-ate
des-per-a-tion
de-spi-ca-ble
de-spise
de-spite
de-spoil
de-spoiler
de-spond

de-spon-dence
de-spon-dency
des-pot
des-potic
des-po-tism
des-sert (pie, etc.)
 cf. de-sert (abandon)
 cf. des-ert (wasteland)
des-sert-spoon
des-ti-na-tion
des-ti-nies
des-tiny
des-ti-tute
des-ti-tu-tion
de-stroy
de-stroyer
de-struc-ti-bil-ity
de-struc-ti-ble
de-struc-tion
de-struc-tive
des-ul-tory
de-tach
de-tach-able
de-tail
de-tain
de-tect
de-tect-able
de-tec-tion
de-tec-tor
de-ten-tion
de-ter
de-ter-gent
de-te-ri-o-rate
de-te-ri-o-ra-tion
de-ter-min-able
de-ter-mi-nant

de-ter-mi-nate
de-ter-mi-na-tion
de-ter-mine
de-ter-rence
de-ter-rent
de-test
de-test-able
de-throne
det-o-na-ble
det-o-nate
de-tour
de-tox-i-fi-ca-tion
de-tox-i-fied
de-tox-ify
de-tract
de-trac-tion
de-trac-tive
de-trac-tor
de-train
det-ri-ment
det-ri-men-tal
de-val-u-ate
de-val-u-a-tion
de-value
dev-as-tate
dev-as-ta-tion
de-velop
de-vel-op-able
de-vel-oper
de-vi-ance
de-vi-ate
de-vi-a-tion
de-vi-a-tor
de-vice
devil
dev-il-ish

dev-ilry
or dev-il-try
de-vi-ous
de-vis-able
de-vise
de-viser
de-vi-sor
de-void
de-volve
de-vote
dev-o-tee
de-vo-tion
de-vour
de-vourer
de-vout
dew (moisture)
cf. do (act)
cf. due (owed)
dew point
dex-ter-ity
dex-ter-ous
dex-trose
di-a-be-tes
di-a-betic
di-a-bolic
di-a-bol-i-cal
di-ag-nose
di-ag-no-ses
di-ag-no-sis
di-ag-o-nal
di-a-gram
di-a-gram-matic
dial
di-a-lect
di-a-lec-tic
di-a-lec-ti-cal

di-a-logue
or di-a-log
di-al-y-sis
di-am-e-ter
di-a-met-ric
di-a-mond
di-a-per
di-a-phragm
di-ar-rhea
or di-ar-rhoea
di-a-ries
di-ary
di-a-stolic
diced
di-chot-omy
dic-ing
dic-tate
dic-ta-tion
dic-ta-tor
dic-ta-tor-ship
dic-tion
dic-tio-nar-ies
dic-tio-nary
die (expire; tool)
cf. dye (coloring)
die—hard *(adj.)*
die-hard *(n.)*
die—off *(n.)*
die out *(v.)*
die-sel
diet
di-eti-tian
or di-eti-cian
di-etary
dif-fer
dif-fer-ence

dif-fer-ent
dif-fer-en-tial
dif-fer-en-ti-ate
dif-fer-en-ti-a-tion
dif-fi-cult
dif-fi-cul-ties
dif-fi-dence
dif-fi-dent
dif-fuse
dif-fu-sion
dig
di-gest
di-gest-ible
di-ges-tion
di-ges-tive
digged
dig-ging
dig-i-tal
dig-ni-fied
dig-nify
dig-ni-tar-ies
dig-ni-tary
dig-nity
di-gress
di-gres-sion
di-gres-sive
dike
di-lap-i-date
di-lap-i-da-tion
di-late
di-lemma
dil-et-tante
dil-et-tantes
or dil-et-tanti
dil-i-gence
dil-i-gent

Do not divide one-syllable words. Divide words by syllables, but leave at least two letters of the word on the first line and three letters on the following line. For additional guidelines, see page ix.

dil-ly-dally
di-lute
di-lu-tion
di-men-sion
di-men-sion-al
di-min-ish
di-min-ish-able
dim-i-nu-tion
di-min-u-tive
dim-ple
dim-wit *(n.)*
dim—witted *(adj.)*
diner (person; place)
 cf. din-ner (meal)
ding-a-ling *(n.)*
dinghies
din-ghy
din-gier
dingy
din-ner-ware
di-no-saur
di-oc-e-san
di-o-cese
di-orama
diph-the-ria
diph-thong
di-ploma
di-plo-macy
dip-lo-mat
dip-lo-matic
dip-lo-mat-i-cally
dire
di-rect
di-rec-tion
di-rec-tional
di-rec-tive

di-rec-tor
di-rec-to-ries
di-réc-tory
dirge
di-ri-gi-ble
dirt
dirt farmer
dirt-ier
dirty
dis-a-bil-i-ties
dis-a-bil-ity
dis-able
dis-ad-van-tage
dis-ad-van-ta-geous
dis-agree
dis-agree-able
dis-al-low
dis-ap-pear
dis-ap-pear-ance
dis-ap-point
dis-ap-prove
dis-arm
dis-ar-ma-ment
dis-ar-range
dis-ar-ray
dis-as-ter
dis-as-trous
dis-avow
dis-avowal
dis-band
dis-bar
dis-barred
dis-bar-ring
dis-be-lief
dis-be-lieve
dis-burse (pay out)

cf. **dis-perse** (scatter)
disc
disc brake
dis-cern
dis-cern-ible
or dis-cern-able
dis-charge
dis-charge-able
dis-ci-ple
disc jockey *(n.)*
dis-claim
dis-claimer
dis-close
dis-clo-sure
dis-color
dis-col-or-ation
dis-com-bob-u-late
dis-com-fort
dis-con-nect
dis-con-so-late
dis-con-tent
dis-con-tinue
dis-con-tinu-ance
dis-cord
dis-cord-ance
dis-cord-ant
dis-co-theque
dis-count
dis-counter
dis-cour-age
dis-course
dis-cour-te-ous
dis-cour-tesy
dis-cover
dis-cov-er-able
dis-cov-erer

Plural, past tense, adverbial, and noun derivatives formed by adding
s, d or *ed, ly, ness, ment, ful, less,* or *ing* to an unchanged root word are
not listed, nor are words formed by dropping the final *e* and adding *ing*.   47

dis-cov-er-ies
dis-cov-ery
dis-credit
dis-cred-it-able
dis-creet (cautious)
 cf. dis-crete (separate)
dis-crep-an-cies
dis-crep-ancy
dis-cre-tion
dis-cre-tion-ary
dis-crim-i-nate
dis-crim-i-na-tion
dis-crim-i-na-tive
dis-crim-i-na-tor
dis-cur-sive
dis-cus
dis-cuss
dis-cuss-able
 or dis-cuss-ible
dis-cus-sant
dis-cus-sion
dis-dain
dis-ease
dis-em-bark
dis-em-bar-ka-tion
dis-em-body
dis-en-gage
dis-favor
dis-fran-chise
dis-grace
dis-grun-tle
dis-guise
dis-gust
dish-cloth
dis-hearten
dis-hon-est

dis-hon-esty
dis-honor
dis-hon-or-able
dish-washer
dis-il-lu-sion
dis-in-cli-na-tion
dis-in-cline
dis-in-fect-ant
dis-in-herit
dis-in-te-grate
dis-in-te-gra-tion
dis-in-te-gra-tor
dis-in-ter
dis-in-ter-est
disk
 or disc
dis-lik-able
dis-like
dis-lo-cate
dis-lo-ca-tion
dis-lodge
dis-loyal
dis-loy-alty
dis-mal
dis-man-tle
dis-may
dis-mem-ber
dis-miss
dis-missal
dis-mount
dis-obe-di-ence
dis-obe-di-ent
dis-o-bey
dis-or-der
dis-or-der-li-ness
dis-or-ga-nize

dis-ori-ent
dis-ori-en-tate
dis-ori-en-ta-tion
dis-own
dis-par-age
dis-par-i-ties
dis-par-ity
dis-pas-sion-ate
dis-patch
dis-patcher
dis-pel
dis-pelled
dis-pel-ling
dis-pens-able
dis-pens-abil-ity
dis-pen-sa-ries
dis-pen-sary
dis-pen-sa-tion
dis-pense
dis-penser
dis-perse (scatter)
 cf. dis-burse (pay out)
dis-persal
dis-perser
dis-pers-ible
dis-per-sion
dis-place
dis-play
dis-please
dis-pos-able
dis-posal
dis-pose
dis-po-si-tion
dis-pos-sess
dis-pos-ses-sion
dis-pos-ses-sor

Do not divide one-syllable words. Divide words by syllables, but leave at least two letters of the word on the first line and three letters on the following line. For additional guidelines, see page ix.

dis-pro-por-tion
dis-pro-por-tional
dis-pro-por-tion-ate
dis-prove
dis-pu-ta-ble
dis-pute
dis-qual-i-fi-ca-tion
dis-qual-i-fied
dis-qual-ify
dis-re-gard
dis-rep-u-ta-ble
dis-re-pute
dis-re-spect
dis-robe
dis-rupt
dis-rupter
dis-rup-tion
dis-rup-tive
dis-sat-is-fac-tion
dis-sat-is-fac-tory
dis-sat-is-fied
dis-sat-isfy
dis-sect
dis-sec-tion
dis-sem-i-nate
dis-sem-i-na-tion
dis-sem-i-na-tor
dis-sen-sion
dis-sent
dis-senter
dis-sen-sient
dis-ser-ta-tion
dis-ser-vice
dis-si-dence
dis-si-dent
dis-si-pate

dis-si-pater
dis-si-pa-tion
dis-sol-u-ble
dis-solve
dis-solv-able
dis-taff
dis-tance
dis-tant
dis-taste
dis-tem-per
dis-tend
dis-till
dis-til-late
dis-til-la-tion
dis-tiller
dis-till-ery
dis-tinct
dis-tinc-tion
dis-tinc-tive
dis-tin-guish
dis-tin-guish-able
dis-tort
dis-tor-tion
dis-traught
dis-tress
dis-trib-ute
dis-tri-bu-tion
dis-trib-u-tor
dis-trict
dis-trust
dis-turb
dis-turb-ance
dis-unity
ditch-dig-ger
ditto
di-ur-nal

dive
dive—bomb (v.)
dive—bomber (n.)
diver
di-verge
di-ver-gence
di-ver-gent
di-verse
di-ver-si-fi-ca-tion
di-ver-si-fied
di-ver-sion
di-ver-sion-ary
di-ver-sity
di-vert
di-verter
di-vest
di-vid-able
di-vide
div-i-dend
di-vider
di-vine
diving bell (n.)
divining rod (n.)
di-vis-i-ble
di-vi-sion
di-vi-sive
di-vi-sor
di-vorce
di-vorcé (male)
di-vor-cée (female)
di-vot
di-vulge
diz-zier
diz-zily
diz-zi-ness
dizzy

Plural, past tense, adverbial, and noun derivatives formed by adding
s, d or *ed, ly, ness, ment, ful, less,* or *ing* to an unchanged root word are
not listed, nor are words formed by dropping the final *e* and adding *ing.*

do (act)	**dog-ma-tizer**	**dor-mant**
cf. **dew** (moisture)	**do—gooder** *(n.)*	**dor-mer**
cf. **due** (owed)	**dog-tag**	**dor-mi-to-ries**
doc-ile	**dol-drums**	**dor-mi-tory**
do-cil-ity	**dole**	**dor-sal**
dock	**dol-lar**	**dos-age**
docket	**dol-phin**	**dose**
dock-yard	**do-main**	**do—si—do**
doc-tor	**do-mes-tic**	**dot-age**
doc-trine	**do-mes-ti-cally**	**dou-ble**
doc-trinal	**do-mes-ti-cate**	**double—breasted** *(adj.)*
doc-u-ment	**do-mes-ti-ca-tion**	**double—cross** *(v.)*
doc-u-men-tary	**do-mi-cile**	**double—dealing** *(n.)*
doc-u-men-ta-tion	**dom-i-nance**	**double—header** *(n.)*
dod-der	**dom-i-nant**	**double—talk** *(n.)*
dodge	**dom-i-nate**	**dou-bloon**
dodger	**dom-i-na-tion**	**dou-bly**
dodo	**dom-i-na-tor**	**doubt**
dodoes	**dom-i-neer**	**dough** (flour)
or **dodos**	**do-min-ion**	*cf.* **doe** (animal)
doe (animal)	**dom-ino**	**dough-nut**
cf. **dough** (flour)	**dom-i-noes**	**douse**
dog	*or* **dom-i-nos**	**dove-tail**
dog-cart	**do-nate**	**dow-ager**
dog—ear *(n.)*	**do-na-tion**	**dowd-ier**
dog—eared *(adj.)*	**don-ny-brook**	**dowd-i-ness**
dog—eat—dog *(adj.)*	**doo-dle**	**dowdy**
dog-face	**dooms-day**	**dowel**
dog-gie bag	**door**	**down**
dog-house	**door-bell**	**down—and—out** *(adj.)*
dogma	**door-knob**	**down-fall**
dog-matic	**door-step**	**down-grade**
dog-ma-tism	**door—to—door** *(adj.)*	**down-hearted**
dig-ma-tist	**door-way**	**dow-ries**
dog-ma-ti-za-tion	**dopey**	**dowry**
dog-ma-tize	*or* **dopy**	**dowse**

Do not divide one-syllable words. Divide words by syllables, but leave at least two letters of the word on the first line and three letters on the following line. For additional guidelines, see page ix.

drab
draft
draftee (military
 conscript)
cf. **drafty** (windy)
draft-ier
drafty (windy)
cf. **draftee** (military
 conscript)
drag-net
dragon
drain
drain-age
drama
dra-matic
dra-ma-tist
dra-ma-ti-za-tion
dra-ma-tize
drape
dra-per-ies
dra-pery
dras-tic
dras-ti-cally
draw
draw-back
drawl
drawn
dread
dream
dreamed
or **dreamt**
dreamer
dream-ier
dreamy
drea-rier
dreary

dredge
drench
dresser
dress-maker
dressy
drib-ble
drier
or **dryer**
drift
drill
driller
drink
drink-able
drinker
drip
dripped
drip-ping
drive—in *(n.)*
drivel
driz-zle
droll
drone
drool
droop
drop-let
drought
or **drouth**
drown
drowse
drows-ier
drows-ily
drows-ing
drudge
drudg-ery
drug
drugged

drug-ging
drug-gist
drug-store
drum
drum-beat
drum major
drummed
drum-mer
drum-ming
drunk
drunk-ard
drunken
dry
dried
drier
or **dryer**
dry cell
dry—clean *(v.)*
dual (two)
cf. **duel** (fight)
du-al-ity
du-bi-ous
duct
dud
dude
due(owed)
cf. **dew** (moisture)
cf. **do** (act)
duel (fight)
cf. **dual** (two)
du-eler
du-el-ist
duet
dumb
dumb-found
or **dum-found**

Plural, past tense, adverbial, and noun derivatives formed by adding
s, d or *ed, ly, ness, ment, ful, less,* or *ing* to an unchanged root word are
not listed, nor are words formed by dropping the final *e* and adding *ing*. 51

E

dum-mies
dummy
dump
dunce
dun-geon
dun-nage
dupe
du-plex
du-pli-cate
du-pli-ca-tion
du-plic-ity
du-ra-ble
du-ra-bil-ity
du-ress
dusk-ier
dusk-i-ness
dusky
du-ties
du-ti-ful
duty
dwarf
dwarf-ish
dwell
dweller
dwelt
or dwelled
dwin-dle
dye (coloring)
cf. die (expire; tool)
dyed—in—the—wool *(adj.)*
dy-namic
dy-na-mite
dy-namo
dy-nas-ties
dy-nasty
dys-tro-phy

ea-ger
eager beaver
ea-gle
ear
ear-ache
ear-drum
ear-mark
ear-muffs
ear-phone
ear-ring
ear-shot
ear-lier
early
earn (be paid)
cf. urn (vase)
ear-nest
earth
earthen
earth-en-ware
earth-quake
earth-ward
earth-worm
earthy
ease
ea-sel
ease-ment
eas-ier
easy
eas-y-going
eat
eat-able
eaves-drop
ebb

ebb tide *(n.)*
ebony
ec-cen-tric
ec-cen-tric-i-ties
ec-cen-tric-ity
ec-cle-si-as-ti-cal
ech-e-lon
echo
eclec-tic
eclipse
eclip-tic
eco-log-ical
ecol-o-gist
ecol-ogy
eco-nomic
eco-nom-i-cal
econ-o-mist
econ-o-mize
econ-o-mizer
econ-omy
ec-sta-sies
ec-stasy
ec-static
ec-to-morph
ec-to-mor-phic
ec-to-plasm
ec-zema
edge
edgeways
or edge-wise
eddy
edema
edgy
ed-i-ble
edict
ed-i-fi-ca-tion

Do not divide one-syllable words. Divide words by syllables, but leave
at least two letters of the word on the first line and three letters on the
following line. For additional guidelines, see page ix.

ed-i-fice
ed-i-fied
ed-ify
edit
edi-tion
ed-i-tor
ed-i-to-rial
ed-i-to-ri-al-ize
ed-u-ca-ble
ed-u-cate
ed-u-ca-tion
ed-u-ca-tive
ee-rie
or eery
ee-rily
ef-face
ef-face-able
ef-facer
ef-fect (result)
 cf. af-fect (influence)
ef-fec-tive
ef-fec-tual
ef-fec-tu-ate
ef-fer-vesce
ef-fer-ves-cence
ef-fer-ves-cent
ef-fi-ca-cious
ef-fi-cacy
ef-fi-ciency
ef-fi-cient
ef-fi-gies
ef-figy
ef-flu-ent (flowing forth)
 cf. af-flu-ent (wealthy)
ef-fort
ef-fron-tery

egal-i-tar-ian
egg
egg-beater
egg-nog
egg-plant
egg-shell
ego
ego-cen-tric
ego-ism
ego-ist
ego-tism
ego-tist
ego-tis-tic
ego—trip *(n.)*
egress
eight
eight ball
eight-een
ei-der
ei-der-down
eighth
eight-i-eth
eighty
ei-ther
ejec-tion
ejec-tor
eke
eke out *(v.)*
elab-o-rate
elab-o-ra-tion
elab-o-ra-tive
elapse
elas-tic
elas-tic-ity
elate
ela-tion

el-bow
el-bow grease
el-bow-room
elder
elect
elect-able
elec-tion
elec-tive
elec-tor
elec-toral
elec-tor-ate
elec-tric
elec-tri-cal
elec-tric eye
elec-tri-cian
elec-tric-ity
elec-tri-fi-ca-tion
elec-tri-fied
elec-trify
elec-trode
elec-tron
elec-tronic
el-e-gance
el-e-ment
el-e-men-tal
el-e-men-tary (simple)
 cf. al-i-men-tary (nourishing
el-e-phant
el-e-phan-tine
el-e-vate
el-e-va-tion
el-e-va-tor
eleven
elf
elfin
elf-ish

elicit (draw forth)	eman-ci-pa-tion	em-cee
cf. il-licit (forbidden)	eman-ci-pa-tor	em-er-ald
el-i-gi-ble	emas-cu-late	emerge
el-i-gi-bil-ity	emas-cu-la-tion	emer-gence
Eli-jah	em-balm	emer-gen-cies
elim-i-nate	em-balmer	emer-gency
elim-i-na-tion	em-bank-ment	emer-gent
Eli-sha	em-bargo	emer-ita (female)
elite	em-bar-goes	emer-iti (pl.)
elixir	em-bark	emer-i-tus (male)
el-lipse	em-bar-ka-tion	emer-sion
el-lip-ses	em-bar-rass	em-i-grant (leaving a
el-lip-sis	em-bas-sies	country) cf. im-mi-grant
el-lip-ti-cal	em-bassy	(one entering a country)
el-o-cu-tion	em-bat-tle	em-i-grate
el-o-cu-tion-ist	em-bed	ém-i-gré
elon-gate	em-bed-ded	or emi-gré
elon-ga-tion	em-bed-ding	em-i-nent (distinguished)
elope	em-bel-lish	cf. im-mi-nent (impending)
eloper	em-bez-zle	em-i-nent do-main
el-o-quence	em-bez-zler	em-is-sar-ies
el-o-quent	em-bit-ter	em-is-sary
else-where	em-blem	emis-sion
elu-ci-date	em-bod-ied	emis-sive
elu-ci-da-tion	em-bod-i-ment	emit
elude	em-body	emit-ted
elu-sion (escape)	em-bo-lism	emit-ter
cf. al-lu-sion (indirect	em-brace	emit-ting
reference)	em-brace-able	e-mol-lient (softener)
cf. il-lu-sion (false	em-bra-sure	cf. e-mol-u-ment (profit)
impression)	em-broi-der	emote
elu-sive (evade)	em-broi-derer	emo-tion
cf. al-lu-sive (hint)	em-broi-dery	emo-tion-al-ism
elves	em-broil	em-pathic
ema-ci-ate	em-bryo	em-pa-thy
ema-ci-a-tion	em-bry-onic	em-pa-thize

Do not divide one-syllable words. Divide words by syllables, but leave at least two letters of the word on the first line and three letters on the following line. For additional guidelines, see page ix.

54

em-peror	en-code	en-force-able
em-pha-ses *(pl.)*	en-core	en-forcer
em-pha-sis	en-coun-ter	en-fran-chise
em-pha-sized	en-cour-age	en-gage
em-phatic	en-croach	en-gen-der
em-pire	en-cum-ber	en-gine
em-pir-i-cal	en-cum-brance	en-gi-neer
em-pir-i-cism	en-cyc-li-cal	En-glish
em-pir-i-cist	en-cy-clo-pe-dia	en-gorge
em-ploy	*or* en-cy-clo-pae-dia	en-grave
em-ploy-able	en-cy-clo-pe-dic	en-graver
em-ployee	*or* en-cy-clo-pae-dic	en-gross
or em-ploye	en-dan-ger	en-gulf
em-ployer	en-dear	en-hance
em-power	en-deavor	enigma
em-press	en-dorse	en-join
emp-tied	en-dors-able	en-joy
emp-ties	en-dorsee	en-joy-able
emp-ti-ness	en-dorser	en-large
empty	en-dow	en-larger
empty—handed *(adj.)*	en-dur-ance	en-lighten
em-u-late (try to equal)	en-dur-able	en-list
cf. im-mo-late (kill as	en-dure	en-liven
a sacrifice)	end zone	en masse
em-u-la-tion	en-ema	en-mi-ties
emul-si-fied	en-e-mies	en-mity
emul-sify	en-emy	en-no-ble
emul-sion	en-er-getic	enor-mity
en-able	en-er-get-i-cally	enor-mous
en-act	en-er-gies	enough
enamel	en-er-gize	en-quire
en-chant	en-er-gizer	en-quiry
en-chan-tress	en-ergy	en-rage
en-cir-cle	en-fee-ble	en-rapt
en-close	en-fold	en-rap-ture
en-clo-sure	en-force	en-rich

Plural, past tense, adverbial, and noun derivatives formed by adding
s, d or *ed, ly, ness, ment, ful, less,* or *ing* to an unchanged root word are
not listed, nor are words formed by dropping the final *e* and adding *ing*.

55

en-roll
or en-rol
en-rollee
en route
en-sconce
en-sconced
en-sem-ble
en-shrine
en-sign
en-slave
en-snare
en-sue
en-tail
en-tan-gle
en-ter
en-ter-prise
en-ter-tain
en-thrall
or en-thral
en-throne
en-thuse
en-thu-si-asm
en-thu-si-ast
en-thu-si-as-tic
en-tice
en-tire
en-tirety
en-ti-tle
en-ti-ties
en-tity
en-tomb
en-to-mol-ogy
en-tou-rage
en-train
en-trance (entry)
 cf. en-trants (people)

en-trap
en-treat
en-treat-ies
en-treaty
en-treé
or en-tree
en-trench
en-tre-pre-neur
en-tries
en-trust
en-twine
enu-mer-a-ble
enu-mer-ate
enu-mer-a-tion
enu-mer-a-tive
enu-mer-a-tor
enun-ci-ate (pronounce)
 cf. an-nun-ci-ate
 (announce)
enun-ci-a-tion
en-velop (surround)
 cf. en-ve-lope (cover
 for letter)
en-vi-able
en-vi-ous
en-vi-ron
en-vi-ron-men-tal
en-vi-ron-men-tal-ist
en-vi-rons
en-vis-age
en-vi-sion
en-voy
en-vied
en-vies
envy
en-zyme

épée
ephem-eral
epic
ep-i-cure
ep-i-demic
ep-i-lepsy
ep-i-lep-tic
ep-i-logue
epis-co-pal
Epis-co-pa-lian
ep-i-sode
epis-tle
ep-i-taph
ep-i-thet
epit-ome
epit-o-mize
ep-och
ep-ochal
equal
equal-ity
equal-iza-tion
equal-ize
equal-izer
equa-nim-ity
equate
equa-tion
equa-tor
equa-to-rial
eques-trian (male)
eques-tri-enne (female)
equi-lat-eral
equi-lib-rium
equine
equi-nox
equip
equipped

Do not divide one-syllable words. Divide words by syllables, but leave
at least two letters of the word on the first line and three letters on the
following line. For additional guidelines, see page ix.

56

equip-ping
eq-ui-ta-ble
eq-uity
equiv-a-lence
equiv-a-lent
equiv-o-cal
equiv-o-cate
erad-i-cate
erad-i-ca-tion
erad-i-ca-tor
erase
eras-able
eraser
era-sure
erect
erec-tion
erec-tor
ergo
erode
Eros
ero-sion
erotic
erot-i-cism
er-rand
er-rant
er-ratic
er-ra-tum *(sing.)*
er-rata *(pl.)*
er-ro-ne-ous
er-ror
er-satz
erst-while
er-u-dite
er-u-di-tion
erupt
erup-tion (bursting forth)

cf. **ir-rup-tion** (violent invasion)
es-ca-late
es-ca-la-tion
es-ca-la-tor
es-ca-pade
es-cape
es-ca-pee
es-carp-ment
es-chew
es-cort
es-crow
es-o-teric
es-pe-cial
es-pi-o-nage
es-pla-nade
es-pouse
es-prit de corps
es-say (theme)
cf. **as-say** (analyze ore)
es-say-ist
es-sence
es-sen-tial
es-sen-ti-al-ity
es-tab-lish
es-tate
es-teem
es-thete
or es-thetic
or es-thet-ics
es-ti-ma-ble
es-ti-ma-tion
es-ti-ma-tor
es-tro-gen
es-tu-ary
et al

et-cet-era
etch
eter-nal
eter-nity
ether
ethe-real
ethic
eth-i-cal
eth-nic
et-i-quette
Eu-cha-rist
eu-lo-gize
eu-logy
eu-phe-mism
eu-pho-ni-ous
eu-phony
Eur-asian
eu-reka
eu-tha-na-sia
evac-u-ate
evac-u-a-tion
evac-uee
evade
evad-able
evader
eval-u-ate
eval-u-a-tion
eval-u-a-tor
evan-ge-lism
evan-ge-list
evap-o-rate
evap-o-ra-tion
evap-o-ra-tor
eva-sion
eva-sive
eve

Plural, past tense, adverbial, and noun derivatives formed by adding
s, d or *ed, ly, ness, ment, ful, less,* or *ing* to an unchanged root word are
not listed, nor are words formed by dropping the final *e* and adding *ing*.

evec-tion (moon's orbital motion)
cf. **evic-tion** (put out)
eve-ning
even-tide
event
even-tual
even-tu-al-ity
ev-er-last-ing
ev-er-more
ev-ery
ev-ery-body
ev-ery-day
ev-ery-thing
ev-ery-where
evict
evic-tion (put out)
cf. **evec-tion** (moon's orbital motion)
ev-i-dence
ev-i-dent
evil
evil-doer
evil eye *(n.)*
evil—minded *(adj.)*
evoke
evo-lu-tion
evo-lu-tion-ary
evolve
ewe (female sheep)
cf. **yew** (shrub)
cf. **you** (pronoun)
ex-ac-er-bate
ex-act
ex-ag-ger-ate
ex-ag-ger-a-tion

ex-ag-ger-a-tor
ex-alt
ex-al-ta-tion
ex-alter
ex-am-i-na-tion
ex-am-ine
ex-am-iner
ex-am-ple
ex-as-per-ate
ex-as-per-a-tion
ex-ca-vate
ex-ca-va-tion
ex-ca-va-tor
ex-ceed (go beyond)
cf. **ac-cede** (give consent)
ex-cel
ex-celled
ex-cel-lence
ex-cel-lency
ex-cel-lent
ex-cel-ling
ex-cept (other than)
cf. **ac-cept** (receive)
ex-cep-tion
ex-cep-tion-able
ex-cerpt
ex-cess (too much)
cf. **ac-cess** (entry)
ex-ces-sive
ex-change
ex-change-able
ex-cise
ex-cit-able
ex-cite
ex-citer

ex-claim
ex-cla-ma-tory
ex-clud-able
ex-clude
ex-cluder
ex-clu-sion
ex-clu-sive
ex-com-mu-ni-cate
ex-com-mu-ni-ca-tion
ex-creta
ex-cre-tion
ex-cru-ci-ate
ex-cru-ci-at-ing
ex-cru-sion
ex-cus-able
ex-cuse
ex-e-cra-ble
ex-e-crate
ex-e-cra-tion
ex-e-cra-tive
ex-e-cute
ex-e-cu-tion
ex-e-cu-tioner
ex-ec-u-tive
ex-ec-u-tor
ex-ec-u-trix
ex-ec-u-tri-ces
or **ex-ec-u-trix-es**
ex-em-plary
ex-em-plify
ex-empt
ex-emp-tion
ex-er-cise (practice)
cf. **ex-or-cise** (drive out)
ex-ert
ex-er-tion

Do not divide one-syllable words. Divide words by syllables, but leave at least two letters of the word on the first line and three letters on the following line. For additional guidelines, see page ix.

ex-hale	ex-panse	ex-per-i-menter
ex-ha-la-tion	ex-pan-si-ble	ex-pert
ex-haust	ex-pan-sion	ex-per-tise
ex-haust-ible	ex-pan-sive (wide)	ex-pert-ism
ex-haus-tion	*cf.* ex-pen-sive (costly)	ex-pi-ate
ex-haus-tive	ex-pa-tri-ate	ex-pi-a-tion
ex-hibit	ex-pa-tri-a-tion	ex-pi-ra-tion
ex-hi-bi-tion	ex-pect	ex-pi-ra-tory
ex-hi-bi-tion-ism	ex-pect-ance	ex-pire
ex-hi-bi-tion-ist	ex-pect-ant	ex-plain
ex-hib-i-tor	ex-pec-ta-tion	ex-pla-na-tion
ex-hil-a-rate	ex-pe-di-ency	ex-plan-a-tory
ex-hil-a-ra-tion	ex-pe-di-ence	ex-ple-tive
ex-hort	ex-pe-di-ent	ex-pli-ca-ble
ex-hor-ta-tion	ex-pe-dite	ex-plicit
ex-horter	ex-pe-diter	ex-plode
ex-hume	*or* ex-pe-di-tor	ex-ploit
ex-i-gence	ex-pe-di-tion	ex-ploit-able
ex-i-gency	ex-pe-di-tion-ary	ex-ploi-ta-tion
ex-i-gent	ex-pe-di-tious	ex-ploiter
ex-ist	ex-pel	ex-plo-ra-tion
ex-ist-ence	ex-pel-la-ble	ex-plor-a-tory
ex-ist-ent	ex-pelled	ex-plore
ex-is-ten-tial	ex-pel-ler	ex-plorer
ex-is-ten-tial-ism	ex-pel-ling	ex-plo-sion
ex-is-ten-tial-ist	ex-pend	ex-plo-sive
ex-o-dus	ex-pend-able	ex-po-nent
ex of-fi-cio	ex-pender	ex-port
ex-on-er-ate	ex-pen-di-ture	ex-port-able
ex-on-er-a-tion	ex-pense	ex-por-ta-tion
ex-or-bi-tance	ex-pen-sive (costly)	ex-porter
ex-or-bi-tant	*cf.* ex-pan-sive (wide)	ex-pose *(v.)*
ex-or-cise (drive out)	ex-pe-ri-ence	ex-posé *(n.)*
cf. ex-er-cise (practice)	ex-per-i-ment	*or* ex-pose
ex-otic	ex-per-i-men-tal	ex-poser
ex-pand	ex-per-i-men-ta-tion	ex-po-si-tion

Plural, past tense, adverbial, and noun derivatives formed by adding *s*, *d* or *ed*, *ly*, *ness*, *ment*, *ful*, *less*, or *ing* to an unchanged root word are not listed, nor are words formed by dropping the final *e* and adding *ing*.

ex-pos-i-tive
ex post facto
ex-pos-tu-late
ex-po-sure
ex-pound
ex-pounder
ex-press
ex-press-age
ex-press-ible
ex-pres-sion
ex-pres-sion-ism
ex-pres-sive
ex-press-way
ex-pro-pri-ate
ex-pro-pri-a-tion
ex-pro-pri-a-tor
ex-pul-sion
ex-pul-sive
ex-punge
ex-pur-gate
ex-qui-site
ex-scind
ex-tant
  (in existence)
  cf. **ex-tent** (length)
ex-tem-po-ral
ex-tem-po-ra-ne-ous
ex-tem-po-rary
ex-tem-pore
ex-tem-po-ri-za-tion
ex-tem-po-rize
ex-tem-po-rizer
ex-tend
ex-tend-ible
ex-ten-sible
ex-ten-sion
ex-ten-sive

ex-tent (length)
  cf. **ex-tant** (in existence)
ex-ten-u-ate
ex-ten-u-a-tion
ex-ten-u-a-tor
ex-te-rior
ex-ter-mi-nate
ex-ter-mi-na-tion
ex-ter-mi-na-tor
ex-ter-nal
ex-tinct
ex-tinc-tion
ex-tin-guish
ex-tin-guish-able
ex-tin-guisher
ex-tir-pate
ex-tol
  or ex-toll
ex-tolled
ex-tol-ler
ex-tor-sion (rotation)
  cf. **ex-tor-tion**
  (demanding money)
ex-tort
ex-tor-tion
  (demanding money)
  cf. **ex-tor-sion** (rotation)
ex-tor-tioner
ex-tor-tion-ist
ex-tra
ex-tract
ex-tract-able
  or ex-tract-ible
ex-trac-tion
ex-trac-tive
ex-trac-tor
ex-tra-cur-ric-u-lar

ex-tra-dit-able
ex-tra-dite
ex-tra-di-tion
ex-tra-ne-ous
ex-traor-di-nary
ex-trap-o-late
ex-tra-sen-sory
ex-tra-ter-res-trial
ex-trav-a-gance
ex-trav-a-gant
ex-trav-a-ganza
ex-treme
ex-trem-ism
ex-trem-ist
ex-trem-ity
ex-tri-cate
ex-tri-ca-ble
ex-tri-ca-tion
ex-trin-sic
ex-tro-vert
ex-trude
ex-tru-sion
ex-u-ber-ance
ex-u-ber-ant
ex-u-ber-ate
ex-ude
ex-ult
ex-ult-ant
ex-ul-ta-tion
eye (organ of sight)
  cf. **aye** (yes)
eyeball—to—eyeball
  (adj.)
eye bank *(n.)*
eye-let
eye-sore
eye-wit-ness

Do not divide one-syllable words. Divide words by syllables, but leave at least two letters of the word on the first line and three letters on the following line. For additional guidelines, see page ix.

60

F

fa-ble
fab-ric
fab-ri-cate
fab-ri-ca-tion
fab-ri-ca-tor
fab-u-lous
fa-cade
or fa-çade
facet (surface)
cf. fau-cet (valve)
face
face—lifting *(n.)*
face—saver *(n.)*
fa-ce-tious
face—to—face
   (adj.)
fa-cial
fac-ile
fa-cil-i-tate
fa-cil-i-ta-tion
fa-cil-i-ties
fa-cil-ity
fac-sim-ile
fac-tion
fac-tual
fac-to-ries
fac-tory
fac-ul-ties
fac-ulty
fad
fad-dish
fad-dist
fade
fagot

or fag-got
Fahr-en-heit
fail
fail—safe *(adj.)*
fail-ure
faint (swoon)
   cf. feint (pretense)
faint-hearted
fair
   (pleasant weather)
   cf. fare (fee)
fair—minded *(adj.)*
fair-way
fair-ies
fairy
fairy-land
fait ac-com-pli *(n.)*
faith
fake
fak-ery
fal-la-cious
fal-lacy
fal-la-cies
fal-li-ble
fal-li-bil-ity
fall-out *(n.)*
fall out *(v.)*
false
false-hood
fal-setto
fal-si-fi-ca-tion
fal-si-fied
fal-sify
fal-ter
fa-mil-ial
fa-mil-iar
fa-mil-iar-ity

fa-mil-iar-iza-tion
fa-mil-iar-ize
fam-i-lies
fam-ily
fam-ine
fam-ish
fa-mous
fa-natic
fa-nat-i-cal
fa-nat-i-cism
fan-cied
fan-cier
fancy
fancy—free *(adj.)*
fan-cy-work *(n.)*
fan-fare
fan-fold
fan—jet
fan-ta-sia
fan-ta-sies
fan-ta-size
fan-tasy
far
far-away
far-fetched
far—flung
far—off
far-sighted
far-ther
farce
far-ci-cal
fare (fee)
   cf. fair
   (pleasant weather)
fare-well
farm
farmer

Plural, past tense, adverbial, and noun derivatives formed by adding
s, d or *ed, ly, ness, ment, ful, less,* or *ing* to an unchanged root word are
not listed, nor are words formed by dropping the final *e* and adding *ing*.

farm-hand	fat-ter	fed-er-a-tion
farm-house	fatty	fe-dora
farm-yard	fat-u-ous	fee-ble
far—off *(adj.)*	fau-cet (valve)	fee-ble-minded *(adj.)*
far—out *(adj.)*	*cf.* **facet** (surface)	fee-bly
far-ther	fault	feed-back *(n.)*
far-ther-most	fault-finder	feet *(pl.* of foot)
far-thest	fault-ier	*cf.* **feat** (unusual deed)
fas-ci-nate	faun (deity)	feign
fas-ci-na-tion	*cf.* **fawn** (deer)	feint (pretense)
fas-cism	faux pas	*cf.* **faint** (swoon)
fas-cist	fa-vor	fe-lic-i-tate
fash-ion	fa-vor-able	fe-lic-i-ta-tion
fash-ion-able	fa-vor-ite	fe-lic-i-ties
fas-ten	fa-vor-it-ism	fe-lic-i-tous
fast—food *(adj.)*	faze (disturb)	fe-line
fas-tid-i-ous	*cf.* **phase** (aspect)	fel-low
fast—talk *(v.)*	fe-alty	fel-low-ship
fa-tal	fear	felon
fa-tal-ism	fear-some	fel-o-nies
fa-tal-ist	fea-si-ble	fe-lo-ni-ous
fa-tal-is-tic	fea-si-bil-ity	fel-ony
fa-tal-i-ties	feast	felt
fa-tal-ity	feat (unusual deed)	fe-male
fate (destiny)	*cf.* **feet** *(pl.* of foot)	fem-i-nine
cf. fete	feather	fem-i-nin-ity
or fête (festival)	feath-er-weight	femme fa-tale *(n.)*
fa-ther	fea-ture	fence
fa-ther-hood	fe-cund	fend
fa-ther-land	fe-cun-dity	fender
fathers—in—law	fed-eral	fer-ment
fathom	fed-er-al-ism	fer-men-ta-tion
fath-om-able	fed-er-al-ist	fe-ro-cious
fa-tigue	fed-er-al-iza-tion	fer-ret
fat—soluble *(adj.)*	fed-er-al-ize	fer-ried
fat-ten	fed-er-ate	ferry

Do not divide one-syllable words. Divide words by syllables, but leave at least two letters of the word on the first line and three letters on the following line. For additional guidelines, see page ix.

fer-ry-boat
fer-tile
fer-til-ity
fer-til-iza-tion
fer-til-ize
fer-til-izer
fer-vent
fer-vid
fer-vor
fes-cue
fes-ti-val
fes-tive
fes-tiv-i-ties
fes-tiv-ity
fes-toon
fe-tal
fetch
fete
or **fête** (festival)
  cf. **fate** (destiny)
fetid
fe-tish
or fe-tich
fe-tish-ism
or fe-tich-ism
fe-tus
feud
feu-dal
feu-dal-ism
fe-ver
fe-ver-ish
fi-ancé (betrothed man)
fi-an-cée (betrothed woman)
fi-asco
fi-as-coes
(or) fi-as-chi

fiat
fib
fibbed
fib-ber
fib-bing
fi-ber
or fi-bre
fi-brous
fiche (microfilm)
  cf. fish (tuna, etc.)
fickle
fic-tion
fic-tional
fic-ti-tious
fi-del-i-ties
fi-del-ity
fidget
fidg-et-i-ness
fid-gety
fi-du-cia-ries
fi-du-ciary
fief
fief-dom
field
fielder
field goal *(n.)*
fiend
fiend-ish
fierce
fiercer
fierc-est
fi-ery
fi-esta
fif-teen
fif-teenth
fif-ti-eth

fif-ties
fifty
fifty—fifty *(adj.)*
fig-ment
fig-ur-a-tive
fig-ure
fig-ure-head
fil-a-ment
fil-ial
fil-i-bus-ter
film
film-strip
fil-ter
fil-ter-able
or fil-tra-ble
filth
filth-ier
filth-i-ness
filthy
fil-trate
fil-tra-tion
fi-na-gle
fi-na-gler
fi-nal
fi-nale
fi-nal-ist
fi-nal-ity
fi-nal-ize
fi-nance
fi-nan-cial
fin-an-cier
finder
fin-er-ies
fin-ery
fi-nesse
fin-est

Plural, past tense, adverbial, and noun derivatives formed by adding
s, d or *ed, ly, ness, ment, ful, less,* or *ing* to an unchanged root word are
not listed, nor are words formed by dropping the final *e* and adding *ing*.

63

fine—tooth comb *(n.)*	fish *(pl.)*	flame
fin-ger	*or* fishes	flam-ma-ble
fin-ger-nail	fish—and—chips	flange
fin-ger-print	*(n. pl.)*	flank
fin-i-cal	fish-er-man	flare (flame)
or fin-icky	fish-ery	*cf.* **flair** (talent)
fin-ish	fis-sion	flare—up *(n.)*
fin-isher	fis-sion-able	flan-nel
fi-nite	fis-sure	flash
fir (tree)	fist	flash-bulb
cf. **fur** (soft hair)	fist-i-cuffs	flash-cube
fire	five—and—ten *(n.)*	flash flood
fire-arm	fix	flash-gun
fire-ball	fix-ate	flash-ier
fire-bomb	fix-a-tion	flash-i-ness
fire-cracker	fix-ture	flash-light
fire en-gine *(n.)*	fiz-zle	flask
fire es-cape *(n.)*	flab-ber-gast	flat
fire ex-tin-guisher *(n.)*	flab-bier	flat-boat
fire-fly	flab-bi-ness	flat-car
fire-man	flabby	flat—footed *(adj.)*
fire-place	flac-cid	flat-ten
fire-power	flag	flat-ter
fire-proof	flag-el-late	flat-tish
fire-side	flagged	flat-top
fire-trap	flag-ging	flat-tery
fire-wood	flagon	flaunt
first	flag-stone	fla-vor
first aid *(n.)*	**flair** (talent)	flaw
first base *(n.)*	*cf.* **flare** (flame)	**flea** (small insect)
first-born	flak	*cf.* **flee**
first class *(n.)*	flake	(run away)
first—rate *(adj.)*	flak-ier	flea market *(n.)*
fis-cal	flak-i-ness	fleet
fish (tuna, etc.)	flaky	flesh
cf. **fiche**	flam-boy-ance	flesh and blood *(n.)*
(microfilm)	flam-boy-ant	flesh—colored

Do not divide one-syllable words. Divide words by syllables, but leave at least two letters of the word on the first line and three letters on the following line. For additional guidelines, see page ix.

flesh-ier
flesh-i-ness
flew
 (to have flown)
 cf. **flu** (influenza)
 cf. **flue** (tube, pipe for
 carrying smoke)
flex
flex-i-ble
flex-ion
flib-ber-ti-gib-bet
flick
flier
or **flyer**
flies
flight
flight-ier
flight-i-ness
flighty
flim-flam
flim-sier
flim-si-ness
flimsy
fling
flint
flip
flip—flop *(n.) (v.)*
flip-pancy
flip-pant
flipped
flip-per
flirt
flir-ta-tion
flir-ta-tious
flirter
flit-ter
float

flock
floe (floating ice)
 cf. **flow** (run like water)
flog
flood
flood-gate
flood-light
floor
floor show *(n.)*
floor-walker
flop
flop-house
flopped
flop-pier
flop-pi-ness
floppy
flora
flo-ral
floras
or **flo-rae** *(n. pl.)*
flo-rist
flo-res-cence
flo-res-cent
florid
floss
flo-ta-tion
flo-tilla
flot-sam
flounce
floun-der
flour
 (powdery substance)
 cf. **flower** (plant)
flour-ish
flout
flow (run like water)
 cf. **floe** (floating ice)

flow-chart
flow-diagram
flower (plant)
 cf. **flour**
 (powdery substance)
flow-er-pot
flow-ery
flown
flu (influenza)
 cf. **flew** (to have flown)
 cf. **flue** (tube, pipe for
 carrying smoke)
fluc-tu-ate
fluc-tu-a-tion
flu-ency
flu-ent
fluff
fluff-ier
fluff-i-ness
fluffy
fluid
flu-id-ity
fluke
fluky
or **flukey**
flume
flung
flunky
 or **flun-key**
flu-o-res-cence
flu-o-res-cent
fluor-i-date
flour-i-da-tion
flu-o-ride
flur-ries
flurry
flush

Plural, past tense, adverbial, and noun derivatives formed by adding
s, d or *ed, ly, ness, ment, ful, less,* or *ing* to an unchanged root word are
not listed, nor are words formed by dropping the final *e* and adding *ing*.   65

flus-ter	folk dance	foot sol-dier
flute	folk-lore	foot-sore
flut-ist	folk music	foot-stool
flut-ter	folk-sier	fop
flux	folk-singer	fop-pish
fly	folksy	fop-pish-ness
fly-able	folk-tale	for-age
fly ball *(n.)*	fol-li-cle	foray
fly—by—night *(adj.)*	fol-low	for-bid
flyer	follow—through *(n.)*	*or* for-bade
or flier	follow—up *(adj.) (n.)*	*or* for-bad
fly-wheel	fol-low up *(v.)*	for-bear
foal	fol-lies	*or* fore-bear
foam	folly	for-bear-ance
foam-ier	fo-ment	for-bid-den
fob	fond	for-bid-ding
fo-cal	fon-dle	for-bore
fo-cus	fon-due	for-borne
or foci	food stamp	force
fod-der	fool	for-ceps
foe	fool-har-di-ness	forc-ing
fog	fool-hardy	ford
fogged	fool-proof	fore (at the front)
fog-gier	fool's gold	*cf.* four (number)
fog-gi-ness	fool's par-a-dise	fore-arm
fog-ging	foot	fore-bear
fog-horn	foot-age	*or* for-bear
foi-ble	foot-ball	fore-bode
foil	foot-can-dle	*or* for-bode
foist	foot—drag-ging *(n.)*	fore-cast
fold	foot-hold	fore-clo-sure
fol-de-rol	foot-lights	fore-fa-ther
fo-li-age	foot-loose	forego
fo-li-ate	foot-note	fore-ground
fo-lio	foot-path	fore-head
folk	foot-print	for-eign

Do not divide one-syllable words. Divide words by syllables, but leave at least two letters of the word on the first line and three letters on the following line. For additional guidelines, see page ix.

for-eign af-fairs
for-eign—born *(adj.)*
for-eigner
fore-man
fore-most
fore-noon
fo-ren-sic
fore-see
fore-sight
for-est
fore-stall
for-ester
for-estry
fore-tell
for-ever
for-ever-more
fore-warn
fore-word
for-feit
for-fei-ture
for-gave
forge
for-ger-ies
for-gery
for-get
forget—me—not
for-get-ta-ble
for-get-ting
for-giv-able
for-give
for-giver
forgo
or forego
for-lorn
for-mal
form-al-de-hyde

for-mal-ism
for-mal-ist
for-mal-i-ties
for-mal-ity
for-mal-iza-tion
for-mal-ize
for-mat
for-ma-tion
for-ma-tive
for-mer
for-mi-da-ble
for-mula
for-mu-las
or for-mu-lae
for-mu-late
for-sake
for-saken
for-sook
fort (army post)
    cf. **forte** (strong point)
for-ti-fi-ca-tion
for-tify
forth (forward)
    cf. **fourth** (number)
forth-right
forth-with
for-ti-eth
for-ti-tude
fort-night
FOR-TRAN
    (or) For-tran
for-tu-i-tous
for-tu-ity
for-tu-nate
for-tune
for-tune—teller

forty
forty—niner
fo-rum
for-ward
fos-sil
fos-ter
fought
foul (containing filth)
    cf. **fowl** (any bird)
foul line *(n.)*
foul—up *(n.)*
foul up *(v.)*
found
foun-da-tion
founder
found-ries
foundry
foun-tain
foun-tain-head
foun-tain pen *(n.)*
four (number)
    cf. **fore** (at the front)
four—dimensional *(adj.)*
four-fold
four—footed *(adj.)*
four—poster
four-score
four-some
four-teen
fourth (number)
    cf. **forth** (forward)
fowl (any bird)
    cf. **foul** (containing filth)
fox
foxes *(n. pl.)*
    or **fox**

Plural, past tense, adverbial, and noun derivatives formed by adding
s, d or *ed, ly, ness, ment, ful, less,* or *ing* to an unchanged root word are
not listed, nor are words formed by dropping the final *e* and adding *ing*.

fox-ier
fox-hole
fox-tail
fox—trot *(n.)* *(v.)*
foxy
foyer
fra-cas
frac-tion
frac-ture
frag-ile
fra-gil-ity
frag-ment
frag-men-tary
frag-men-ta-tion
fra-grance
fra-grant
frail
frail-ties
frailty
frame
frame—up *(n.)*
frame-work
franc
(unit of money)
cf. **frank** (open)
fran-chise
fran-chi-see
frank-furter
or frank-forter
fran-tic
fra-ter-nal
fra-ter-nity
fra-ter-ni-za-tion
fra-ter-nize
frat-ri-cide
fraud
fraud-u-lence

fraud-u-lent
fraught
fray
fraz-zle
freak
freak-ish
freak—out *(n.)*
freak out *(v.)*
freckle
free
free-dom
free enterprise
free—fall *(n.)*
free—for—all *(n.)*
free-hand
free—lance *(v.)*
  (adj.)
freer
free love
free-thinker
free-way
free-will *(adj.)*
freeze
freezer
freight
fren-zied
frenzy
fre-quence
fre-quency
fre-quent
fresh
freshen
fresh-man
fresh-wa-ter *(adj.)*
fret
fret-ted
fret-ting

friar
(member of religious order)
cf. **fryer** (one who fries)
fric-as-see
fric-tion
friend
friend-lier
friend-li-ness
fright
frighten
frigid
fri-gid-ity
frilly
fringe
fringe benefit *(n.)*
Fris-bee
frisk
frisk-ier
frisk-i-ness
frisky
frit
frit-ter
fri-vol-ity
friv-o-lous
frock
frog-man
frolic
frol-icked
frol-ick-ing
frol-ic-some
front
front-age
fron-tal
fron-tier
fron-tiers-man
fron-tis-piece
front office

Do not divide one-syllable words. Divide words by syllables, but leave at least two letters of the word on the first line and three letters on the following line. For additional guidelines, see page ix.

68

frost
frost-bite
frost-ier
frosty
froth
froth-ier
frown
frowsy
or frowzy
froze
fro-zen
fruc-tose
fru-gal
fruit
fruit fly
fru-i-tion
fruity
frump
frus-trate
frus-tra-tion
fuch-sia
fuddy—duddy *(n.)*
fudge
fuel
fu-gi-tive
ful-crum
ful-fill
or ful-fil
full
full-back
full—blooded
(adj.)
full—dress *(adj.)*
fum-ble
fu-mi-gate
fu-mi-ga-tion
fu-mi-ga-tor

func-tion
func-tional
fun-da-men-tal
fun-da-men-tal-ism
fun-da-men-tal-ist
fu-neral
fu-ne-real
fun-gi-cide
fun-gus
fungi *(n. pl.)*
or fun-guses
fun-nel
fun-nier
funny
funny bone
fur
(soft hair)
cf. fir (tree)
fu-ri-ous
furl
fur-long
fur-lough
fur-nace
fur-nish
fur-ni-ture
fu-ror
furred
fur-rier
fur-row
furry
fur-ther
fur-ther-ance
fur-ther-more
fur-ther-most
fur-thest
fur-tive
fury

fuse (part of circuit)
cf. fuze
(slow-burning wick)
fu-se-lage
fu-sil-lade
fu-sion
fuss
fuss-ier
fussy
fu-tile
fu-til-ity
fu-ture
fu-tur-is-tic
fu-tu-rity
fuze (slow-burning wick)
cf. fuse (part of circuit)
fuzz
fuzz-ier
fuzz-i-ness
fuzzy

G

gab-ar-dine
gab-fest
ga-ble
gad-get
gad-ge-teer
gage (pledge)
cf. gauge (measure)
gai-ety
gaily
gain
gait (step)
cf. gate (entranceway)

Plural, past tense, adverbial, and noun derivatives formed by adding
s, d or *ed, ly, ness, ment, ful, less,* or *ing* to an unchanged root word are
not listed, nor are words formed by dropping the final *e* and adding *ing*.   69

gala
gal-axy
gale
gall
gal-lant
gal-lantry
gal-leon
gal-ler-ies
gal-lery
gal-ley
gal-lon
gal-lop
gal-lows
ga-lore
gal-va-ni-za-tion
gal-va-nize
gam-bit
gam-ble (risk)
  cf. gam-bol (caper)
gam-bler
game
gamut
gang
gang-plank
gan-grene
gan-gre-nous
gang-ster
gant-let
gap
gape
ga-rage
garb
gar-bage
gar-ble
gar-çon
gar-den

gar-dener
gar-de-nia
gar-gle
gar-goyle
gar-ish
gar-land
gar-lic
gar-ment
gar-ner
gar-nish
gar-nishee
gar-ri-son
gar-rot
gar-ru-lous
gas
gas-eous
gases (n. pl.)
  or gas-ses
gash
gas-ket
gas mask
gas-o-line
  or gas-o-lene
gasp
gassed
gas-sing
gas sta-tion
gassy
gas-tric
gas-tro-in-tes-ti-nal
gas-tro-nomic
gate (entranceway)
  cf. gait (step)
gate-way
gather
gath-erer

gaudy
gaud-ier
gaud-i-ness
gauge (measure)
  cf. gage (pledge)
gauge-able
gauger
gaunt
gaunt-let
gauze
gave
gavel
gawk
gawk-ier
gawk-i-ness
gay
gayer
gaze
ga-zebo
ga-zelle
gazer
ga-zette
gaz-et-teer
gear
gear-shift
gee
geese
gee—whiz (adj.)
Gei-ger counter
gei-sha
gel-a-tin
  or gel-a-tine
geld
gem
Gem-ini
gen-darme

Do not divide one-syllable words. Divide words by syllables, but leave at least two letters of the word on the first line and three letters on the following line. For additional guidelines, see page ix.

gen-der
gen-eral
gen-er-al-ist
gen-er-al-ity
gen-er-al-iza-tion
gen-er-al-ize
gen-er-ate
gen-er-a-tion
gen-er-a-tive
gen-er-a-tor
ge-neric
gen-e-sis
ge-netic
ge-nius
gen-o-cide
gen-teel
gen-tile
gen-til-ity
gen-tle
gen-tle-man
gen-tle-woman
gen-try
gen-u-flect
gen-u-ine
ge-nus
geo-desic
ge-og-ra-pher
geo-graphic
geo-graph-i-cal
ge-o-graphy
ge-ol-o-gist
ge-ol-ogy
geo-met-ric
geo-met-ri-cal
ge-om-e-try
geo-phys-ics

geo-phys-i-cist
ge-ri-at-ric
germ
germ cell
ger-mi-cidal
ger-mi-cide
ger-mi-nate
ger-mi-na-tion
germ warfare
ge-stalt
ge-stapo
ges-tate
ges-ta-tion
ges-ture
ge-sund-heit
get
get-a-way
get—to-geth-er *(n.)*
get-up *(n.)*
get up *(v.)*
gey-ser
ghast-lier
ghast-li-ness
ghastly
ghetto
ghet-tos *(n. pl.)*
or ghet-toes
ghost
ghost-lier
ghost write *(v.)*
ghoul
gi-ant
gib-ber
gib-ber-ish
gib-bet
gid-di-ness

giddy
gift
gi-gan-tic
gig-gle
gig-gler
gig-gly
gig-olo
gild (cover)
   cf. guild (society)
gilt (layer of gold)
   cf. guilt (blame)
gilt—edged
or gilt—edge *(adj.)*
gim-mick
gin-ger
gin-ger ale
gin-ger-bread
gin-ger-li-ness
gin-gerly
ging-ham
gi-raffe
gird
gir-dle
girded
or girt
girder
girl
girl Friday
girl-ish
girl friend
girl scout
girth
gist
give
give—and—take *(n.)*
give-a-way *(n.)*

Plural, past tense, adverbial, and noun derivatives formed by adding
s, d or *ed, ly, ness, ment, ful, less,* or *ing* to an unchanged root word are
not listed, nor are words formed by dropping the final *e* and adding *ing.*

give away *(v.)*	glit-ter	gnat
given	glit-tery	gnaw
gla-cial	gloat	gnome
gla-cier	gloater	go—ahead *(n.)*
glad	global	goal
glad—hand *(v.)*	globe	goat
glad-i-a-tor	globe—trotter *(n.)*	go—between
glam-or-ize	glob-u-lar	gob-ble
or glam-our-ize	glob-ule	gob-let
glam-or-ous	gloom	gob-lin
glam-our	gloom-ier	god-child
or glamor	gloom-i-ness	god-dess
glance	gloomy	god-fa-ther
gland	glo-ri-fi-ca-tion	god-for-saken
glan-du-lar	glo-ri-fied	god-mother
glare	glo-rify	god-parent
glass	glo-ri-ous	god-send
glass-ier	gloss	god-son
glass-i-ness	glos-sa-ries	goi-ter
glass-ware	glos-sary	*or* goi-tre
glassy	gloss-i-est	gold
glau-coma	glossy	golden
glaze	*or* gloss-ies	golden rule
gleam	glow	gold—filled *(adj.)*
glean	glue	gold-fish
glee	gluey	gold leaf
glee club *(n.)*	glum	gold rush
glen	glum-mer	golf
glib	glut	gon-dola
glide	glut-ted	gone
glider	glut-ting	gong
glide path *(n.)*	glut-tony	gon-or-rhea
glim-mer	glyc-erin	good—by
glimpse	*or* glyc-er-ine	*or* good—bye
glint	gnarl	good—for—nothing *(adj.)*
glis-ten	gnash	good—hearted

Do not divide one-syllable words. Divide words by syllables, but leave at least two letters of the word on the first line and three letters on the following line. For additional guidelines, see page ix.

good—looking *(adj.)*
goof
goose
goose-flesh
gore
gor-geous
gor-i-est
gory
gos-ling
gos-pel
gos-sip
gos-sipy
got
got-ten
gouge
gouger
gourd
gour-met
gov-ern
gov-er-nance
gov-ern-ess
gov-er-nor
gown
grab
grabbed
grab-bing
grabby
grace
gra-cious
gra-da-tion
grade
grade school
grad-ual
grad-u-ate
grad-u-a-tion
graf-fiti *(n. pl.)*

graf-fito *(n. sing.)*
graft
grain
gram
gram-mar
gram-mar-ian
gram-mar school
gram-mat-i-cal
grand
grand-child
grand-daugh-ter
grand-duch-ess
gran-dee
grand-fa-ther
gran-dil-o-quence
grand jury
grand-mother
gran-deur
gran-di-ose
grange
gran-ite
grant
gran-u-lar
gran-u-late
gran-u-la-tion
gran-ule
grape
grape-fruit
grape-shot
grape-vine
graph
graphic
graph-ite
grap-nel
grap-ple
grasp

grasp-able
grasper
grass
grass-hop-per
grass-ier
grass-land
grass roots
grassy
grate (framework)
cf. **great** (important)
grat-i-fi-ca-tion
grat-i-fied
grat-ify
gra-tis
grat-i-tude
gra-tu-itous
gra-tu-ity
grave
gravel
graven
grave-stone
grave-yard
grav-i-tate
grav-i-ta-tion
grav-ity
gra-vies
gravy
gray
gray-ish
graze
grease
greas-ier
greas-i-ness
greasy
great (important)
cf. **grate** (framework)

Plural, past tense, adverbial, and noun derivatives formed by adding
s, d or *ed, ly, ness, ment, ful, less,* or *ing* to an unchanged root word are
not listed, nor are words formed by dropping the final *e* and adding *ing*.　　73

great—aunt	grin	grotto
great cir-cle	grinned	grouch
greed	grin-ning	grouch-i-est
greed-ier	grind	grouchy
greed-ily	grinder	ground
greed-i-ness	grind-stone	ground floor
greedy	gringo	ground rule
green	grip (firm hold)	ground-work
green-back	cf. grippe (contagious	group
green-house	disease)	group therapy
green thumb (n.)	gripe	grouse
greet	gripped	grout
greeter	grip-ping	grove
gre-gar-i-ous	gris-li-est	grovel
grem-lin	grisly	growl
gre-nade	gris-tle	grown—up (adj.) (n.)
gren-a-dier	grit	growth
grew	griz-zled	grub
grey	griz-zly	grubbed
grey-hound	griz-zly bear	grub-bier
grid	groan	grub-bi-ness
grid-dle	gro-cer	grub-bing
grid-i-ron	gro-cer-ies	grubby
grief	gro-cery	grub-stake
griev-ance	grog	grudge
grieve	grog-gier	gruel
griev-ous	grog-gi-ness	gru-el-ling
grill (cooking utensil)	groggy	grue-some
cf. grille (openwork	groin	gruff
metal screen)	grom-met	grum-ble
grim	groom	grum-bler
gri-mace	groove	grump-ier
grime	groovy	grump-i-ness
grim-ier	grope	grumpy
grim-i-ness	gross	grunt
grimy	gro-tesque	guar-an-tee

Do not divide one-syllable words. Divide words by syllables, but leave at least two letters of the word on the first line and three letters on the following line. For additional guidelines, see page ix.

guar-an-teed
guar-an-ties
guar-an-tor
guar-anty
guard-house
guard-ian
gu-ber-na-to-rial
guess
guess-work
guest
guf-faw
guid-ance
guide
guide-book
guild (society)
cf. gild (cover)
guile
guil-lo-tine
guilt (blame)
cf. gilt (layer of gold)
guilt-ier
guilt-i-ness
guilty
guinea pig
gui-tar
gulf
gull
gul-let
gull-ible
gul-lies
gully
gulp
gump-tion
gun
gun-boat
gun-fire

gung ho *(adj.)*
gun-ner
gun-nery
gun-pow-der
gur-gle
guru
gush
gusher
gush-ier
gushy
gust-ier
gusto
gusty
gut
gut-ter
gut-tural
guz-zle
gym-na-sium
gym-nast
gym-nas-tic
gy-ne-col-ogy
gyp-sum
gyp-sies
gypsy
gy-rate
gy-ra-tion
gy-ro-scope

H

ha-beas cor-pus
hab-er-dasher
hab-er-dash-ery

habit
hab-it-able
ha-bi-tant
ha-bi-tat
hab-i-ta-tion
habit—forming *(adj.)*
ha-bit-ual
ha-bit-u-ate
hab-i-tude
ha-bi-tué
hack-saw
Ha-des
hag
hag-gard
hag-gle
hag-gler
hail (shout in welcome)
cf. hale (strong and well)
Hail Mary
hail-stone
hail-storm
hair (fur)
cf. hare (small animal)
hair-breadth
hair-cut
hair-dresser
hair-ier
hair-line
hair-piece
hair-pin
hair—raising *(adj.)*
hair-split-ting
hair-spring
hair-styl-ist
hair—trigger *(adj.)*
hair trigger *(n.)*

Plural, past tense, adverbial, and noun derivatives formed by adding
s, d or *ed, ly, ness, ment, ful, less,* or *ing* to an unchanged root word are
not listed, nor are words formed by dropping the final *e* and adding *ing*.

hairy	hal-ter	hangar (shed)
hale (strong and well)	halve	*cf.* hanger (hook)
cf. hail (shout in welcome)	ham-burger	hang—up (*n.*)
half	ham-let	hang up (*v.*)
half—and—half (*n.*)	ham-mer	hank
half-back	hammer–and–tongs (*adj.*)	han-ker
half—baked (*adj.*)	ham-mock	hanky—panky (*n.*)
half—breed (*n.*)	ham-per	Ha-nuk-kah
half brother (*n.*)	ham-string	*or* Cha-nu-kah
half—caste (*n.*)	hand	hap-haz-ard
half—cocked (*adj.*)	hand-bag	hap-less
half—dollar (*n.*)	hand-ball	hap-pen
half-hearted (*adj.*)	hand-bill	hap-pier
half hour	hand-book	hap-pily
half nel-son	hand-cuff	hap-pi-ness
half note	hand-i-cap	happy
half sis-ter	hand-i-craft	happy—go—lucky (*adj.*)
half-way	hand-i-work	hara—kiri
half—wit (*n.*)	hand-ker-chief	ha-rangue
hal-i-to-sis	hand-ker-chiefs	ha-rass
hall (passageway)	*or* hand-ker-chieves	har-bin-ger
cf. haul (pull)	han-dle	har-bor
hal-le-lu-jah	hand-made (made by hand)	hard
or al-le-luia	*cf.* hand-maid (servant)	hard—and—fast (*adj.*)
hall-mark	hand—me—down (*adj.*)	hard—bitten (*adj.*)
hall-way	hand-shake	hard—boiled (*adj.*)
hal-low	hand-some	hard—core (*adj.*)
Hal-low-een	hand—to—mouth (*adj.*)	harden
hal-lu-ci-nate	hand-work	hard—headed (*adj.*)
hal-lu-ci-na-tion	hand-writ-ing	hard—hearted (*adj.*)
hal-lu-ci-na-tory	hand-writ-ten	hard—hitting (*adj.*)
hal-lu-ci-no-gen	hand-wrote	har-dier
hal-lu-ci-no-sis	hand-ier	hard-ship
halo	handy	hard-ware
halt	handy-man	hard-wood
	hang	hardy

Do not divide one-syllable words. Divide words by syllables, but leave at least two letters of the word on the first line and three letters on the following line. For additional guidelines, see page ix.

hare (small animal)
cf. hair (fur)
hare-brained
harem
har-lot
har-lotry
harm
har-monic
har-mon-ica
har-mo-ni-ous
har-mo-nize
har-mo-nizer
har-mony
har-ness
harp
harp-ist
har-poon
har-pooner
har-ried
harsh
har-vest
has
has—been *(n.)*
hash
hash-ish
has-sle
haste
has-ten
hast-ier
hast-ily
hast-i-ness
hasty
hatch
hatcher
hatch-er-ies
hatchet

hatch-way
hate
ha-tred
haugh-tier
haugh-tily
haughty
haul (pull)
cf. hall (passageway)
haunch
haunt
ha-ven
havoc
hawk
hawk-eye
haw-ser
hay
hay fe-ver
hay-loft
hay-stack
hay-wire
haz-ard
haz-ard-ous
haze
hazer
ha-zier
ha-zi-ness
hazy
H—bomb
head
head-ache
head-dress
header
head-first
head-hunter
head—hunting *(n.)*
head-light

head-line
head-long
head-mas-ter
head-mis-tress
head—on *(adj.)*
head-quar-ters
head-strong
head-waiter
head-way
heady
heal (cure)
cf. heel (part of foot)
health
health-ier
health-i-est
health-i-ness
healthy
heap
hear (perceive by the ear)
cf. here (in this place)
heard (perceived by the ear)
cf. herd (group of animals)
hear-say
hearse
heart
heart-ache
heart-beat
heart-break
heart-burn
hearten
heart-felt
heart-ier
heart-rend-ing
heart-sick
heart—to—heart *(adj.)*
hearty

Plural, past tense, adverbial, and noun derivatives formed by adding
s, d or *ed, ly, ness, ment, ful, less,* or *ing* to an unchanged root word are
not listed, nor are words formed by dropping the final *e* and adding *ing*.

heat	heirs ap-par-ent	herd (group of animals)
heater	(n. pl.)	cf. heard
hea-then	heir-ess	(perceived by the ear)
hea-then-ish	heir-loom	herder
heat wave (n.)	heist	herds-man
heave	he-li-cop-ter	here (in this place)
heaven	he-li-port	cf. hear (perceive by the ear)
heav-en-li-ness	he-lium	here-af-ter
heav-ier	hell	hereby
heav-ily	hell—bent (adj.)	he-red-i-tary
heav-i-ness	hell-cat	he-red-ity
heavy	hel-lion	herein
heavy-weight	hell-ish	hereon
He-brew	helm	her-e-sies
heckle	hel-met	her-esy
heck-ler	help-ful	her-e-tic
hec-tic	helter—skelter (adj.)	he-ret-i-cal
hedge	hem	her-i-tage
he-do-nism	hemmed	her-mit
he-do-nist	hem-ming	her-mit-age
he-do-nis-tic	hemi-sphere	her-nia
hee-bie—jee-bies	hem-line	hero
heed	he-mo-glo-bin	he-roic
heel (part of foot)	hem-or-rhage	her-oin (drug)
cf. heal (cure)	hence	cf. her-o-ine (brave girl)
heft	hence-forth	hero worship (v.)
heft-ier	hence-for-ward	her-self
hefty	hench-man	hes-i-tance
he-ge-mony	hen party	hes-i-tancy
heifer	hep-a-ti-tis	hes-i-tant
height	her-ald	hes-i-tate
heighten	her-aldry	hes-i-ta-tion
hei-nous	herb	het-er-o-ge-ne-ity
heir	her-ba-ceous	het-er-o-ge-ne-ous
(one who inherits)	herb-age	het-ero-sex-ual
cf. air (atmosphere)	her-biv-o-rous	hew (cut)
heir ap-par-ent	Her-cu-lean (adj.)	cf. hue (color)

Do not divide one-syllable words. Divide words by syllables, but leave
at least two letters of the word on the first line and three letters on the
following line. For additional guidelines, see page ix.

78

hex	high school	hip-po-pot-a-muses
hex-a-gon	high—sounding	*or* hip-po-pot-a-mi
hex-ag-o-nal	*(adj.)*	*(n. pl.)*
hi-a-tus	high—spirited *(adj.)*	hire
hi-ba-chi	high—strung *(adj.)*	hir-sute
hi-ber-nate	high—toned *(adj.)*	hiss
hi-ber-na-tion	high-way	hist
hic-cup	high-way-man	his-to-gram
or hic-cough	hi-jack	his-to-rian
hid-den	*or* high—jack	his-toric
hide	hike	his-tor-i-cal
hid-eous	hiker	his-tory
hide-out	hi-lar-i-ous	his-tri-onic
hie (hurry)	hi-lar-ity	hit—and—miss *(adj.)*
cf. **high** (altitude)	hill	hit—and—run *(adj.) (v.)*
hi-er-ar-chi-cal	hill-billy	hitch
hi-er-ar-chies	hill-side	hitch-hike
hi-er-ar-chy	hill-top	hither
hi-ero-glyphic	hilly	hith-erto
high (altitude)	hilt	hit—or—miss *(adj.)*
cf. **hie** (hurry)	him (pronoun)	hives
high—and—mighty	*cf.* **hymn** (song)	hoard (amass)
(adj.)	him-self	*cf.* **horde** (crowd)
high-born	hind	hoarder
high-brow	hin-der	hoarse
higher—up	hind-most	hoax
high fi-del-ity	hind-quar-ter	hob-bies
high—frequency	hin-drance	hob-ble
high—grade *(adj.)*	hind-sight	hobby
high—handed *(adj.)*	Hindu	hob-by-horse
high—hat *(v.)*	*or* Hindoo	hob-by-ist
high jump	hinge	hob-gob-lin
high-light	hint	hob-nail
high mass	hip-pie	hob-nob
high-ness	*or* hippy	hob-nobbed
high—pitched *(adj.)*	hip-po-drome	hob-nob-bing
high—pressure *(adj.)*	hip-po-pot-a-mus	hobo

Plural, past tense, adverbial, and noun derivatives formed by adding *s, d* or *ed, ly, ness, ment, ful, less,* or *ing* to an unchanged root word are not listed, nor are words formed by dropping the final *e* and adding *ing.*

79

ho-bos	**hol-low**	**Ho-meric**
or **ho-boes**	**hol-low-ware**	**home run**
hock	*or* **hol-lo-ware**	**home-sick**
hockey	**holly**	**home-site**
hock-shop	**ho-lo-caust**	**home-spun**
ho-cus	**ho-log-a-mous**	**home-stead**
hocus—pocus *(n.)*	**ho-lo-gram**	**home-stretch**
hod	**ho-lo-graph**	**home-ward**
hodge-podge	**ho-lo-phras-tic**	**home-work**
Hodg-kin's disease	**ho-lo-zoic**	**homey**
hoe	**hol-stein**	*or* **homy**
hoe-down	**hol-ster**	**ho-mi-cidal**
hog	**holy**	**homi-cide**
hogged	**Holy Com-mu-nion**	**hom-ier**
hog-ging	**holy day**	**hom-i-est**
hog-gish	**Holy Father**	**ho-mog-e-ne-ity**
hogs-head	**Holy Ghost**	**ho-mo-ge-neous**
hog—tie *(n.)*	**Holy Ro-man Em-pire**	**ho-mog-e-ni-za-tion**
hog-wash	**Holy See**	**ho-mol-o-gous**
hoi pol-loi	**Holy Week**	**hom-o-lo-graphic**
hoist	**hom-age**	**hom-onym**
hoity—toity *(n.)*	**hom-bre**	**ho-mo-phone**
hokey	**hom-burg**	**ho-moph-o-nous**
hokum	**home**	**Ho-mo sa-pi-ens**
hold	**home-com-ing**	**hone**
holder	**home eco-nom-ics**	**hon-est**
hold off *(v.)*	**home econ-o-mist**	**hon-esty**
hold on *(v.)*	**home-land**	**honey**
hold-out *(n.)*	**home-lier**	**hon-ey-bee**
hold-over *(n.)*	**home-li-est**	**hon-ey-comb**
holdup	**home-like**	**hon-ey-dew**
hole (opening	**home-made**	**hon-ey-moon**
cf. **whole** (entire)	**home-maker**	**honk**
hol-i-day	**ho-meo-path**	**honky—tonk** *(n.) (adj.)*
ho-li-ness	**ho-me-op-a-thy**	**honor**
Hol-ler-ith *(n.)*	**ho-meo-pathic**	**hon-or-able**

Do not divide one-syllable words. Divide words by syllables, but leave at least two letters of the word on the first line and three letters on the following line. For additional guidelines, see page ix.

hon-o-rar-i-um	horse-hair	hot-house
hon-o-rar-i-ums	horse-hide	hot line *(n.)*
or hon-o-raria	horse-man	hour (60 minutes)
hon-or-ary	horse-power	*cf.* our (us)
hon-or-ific	horse-shoe	hour-long *(adj.)*
hood	horse-whip	house
hood-lum	horse-woman	house-boat
hood-wink	horsey	house-breaker
hooey	*or* horsy	house-bro-ken
hoo-ray	hor-ti-cul-ture	house-clean
hop	hor-ti-cul-tural	house-coat
hopped	hor-ti-cul-tur-ist	house-fly
hop-ping	ho-sanna	house-hold
horde (crowd)	hose	house-keep-er
cf. hoard (amass)	ho-siery	house-maid
ho-ri-zon	hos-pi-ta-ble	house party
hor-i-zon-tal	hos-pi-ta-bly	house-top
hor-monal	hos-pi-tal	house-wares
hor-mone	hos-pi-tal-ity	house-warm-ing
horn	hos-pi-tal-iza-tion	house-wife
hor-net	hos-pi-tal-ize	house-wives
hor-o-scope	host	house-work
hor-ren-dous	hos-tage	hovel
hor-ri-ble	hos-tel	hover
hor-ri-bly	host-ess	how-ever
hor-rid	hos-tile	how-it-zer
hor-ri-fied	hos-til-i-ties	howl
hor-rify	hos-til-ity	how—to *(adj.)*
hor-ror	hot	hub
hor-ror struck *(adj.)*	hot air *(n.)*	hub-bub
hors d'oeuvre	hot-bed	huck-le-berry
hors d'oeuvres *(n. pl.)*	hot—blooded *(adj.)*	huck-ster
or hors d'oeuvre	hot-cake	hud-dle
horse	hot dog	hue (color)
horse-back	ho-tel	*cf.* hew (cut)
horse-fly	hot-head	huff

Plural, past tense, adverbial, and noun derivatives formed by adding
s, d or *ed, ly, ness, ment, ful, less,* or *ing* to an unchanged root word are
not listed, nor are words formed by dropping the final *e* and adding *ing*.

huffy
hug
hugged
hug-ging
huge
hulk
hull
hul-la-ba-loo
hum
hu-man
hu-mane
hu-man-ism
hu-man-is-tic
hu-man-i-tar-ian
hu-man-i-tar-i-an-ism
hu-man-ity
hum-ble
hum-bly
hum-bug
hum-drum
hu-mid
hu-mid-i-fied
hu-mid-i-fier
hu-mid-ify
hu-mid-ity
hu-mil-i-ate
hu-mil-i-a-tion
hu-mil-ity
hummed
hum-ming
hu-mor
hu-mor-esque
hu-mor-ist
hu-mor-ous
hump
hump-back

hump-ier
humpty—dumpty
humpy
hu-mus
hunch
hunch-back
hun-dred
hun-dreds (n. pl.)
or hun-dred
hun-dred-weight
hun-ger
hun-ger strike
hun-grily
hun-gry
hunk
hunt
hunter
hunts-man
hur-dle
hurdy—gurdy
hurl
hurler
hur-rah
or hur-ray
hur-ri-cane
hur-ried
hur-ries
hurry
hurt
hus-band
hus-bandry
hush
hush—hush (adj.)
husk
husker
hus-kier

hus-ki-ness
hus-kies (n. pl.)
husky
hus-tle
hut
hutch
huz-zah
or huzza
hy-brid
hy-drant
hy-drate
hy-drau-lic
hy-dro-dy-nam-ics
hy-dro-elec-tric
hy-dro-gen
hy-dro-gen bomb
hy-drom-eter
hy-dro-pon-ics
hy-ena
hy-giene
hy-gienic
hy-gien-ist
hymn (song)
 cf. him (pronoun)
hym-nal
hymn-book
hy-per-ac-tive
hy-per-bola
hy-per-bole
hy-per-bolic
hy-per-crit-i-cal
hy-phen
hy-phen-ate
hy-phen-ation
hyp-no-ses (n. pl.)
hyp-no-sis

Do not divide one-syllable words. Divide words by syllables, but leave
at least two letters of the word on the first line and three letters on the
following line. For additional guidelines, see page ix.

82

hyp-notic	ice-breaker	id-iom
hyp-no-tism	ice—cold *(adj.)*	id-i-o-matic
hyp-no-tist	ice cream *(n.)*	id-io-syn-cra-sy
hyp-no-tize	Ice-lan-dic *(adj.)*	id-iot
hy-po-chon-dria	ice—skate *(v.)*	id-i-otic
hy-po-chon-driac	ice skate *(n.)*	**idle** (doing nothing)
hy-poc-ri-sies	ici-cle	*cf.* **idol** (image)
hy-poc-risy	icon	idler
hyp-o-crite	icon-o-clasm	**idol** (image)
hyp-o-crit-i-cal	icon-o-clast	*cf.* **idle** (doing nothing)
hy-po-der-mic	icon-o-clas-tic	idol-a-ter
hy-pos-ta-tize	icy	idol-a-trous
hy-pot-e-nuse	ID card	idol-a-try
or hy-poth-e-nuse	ideal	idol-ize
hy-poth-e-sis	ide-al-ism	idyll
hy-poth-e-ses *(n. pl.)*	ide-al-ist	*or* idyl
hy-poth-e-size	ide-al-is-tic	idyl-lic
hy-po-thet-i-cal	ide-al-ity	ig-loo
hys-te-ria	ide-al-iza-tion	ig-ne-ous
hys-teric	ide-al-ize	ig-nit-able
hys-ter-ical	idem	*or* ig-nit-ible
	iden-ti-cal	ig-nite
	iden-ti-fi-a-ble	ig-no-ble
	iden-ti-fi-a-bly	ig-no-min-i-ous
I	iden-ti-fi-ca-tion	ig-no-miny
	iden-ti-fied	ig-no-ra-mus
	iden-ti-fier	ig-no-rance
	iden-ti-ties	ig-no-rant
	iden-tity	ig-nore
ibid	ide-o-log-i-cal	ikon
ibi-dem	ide-ol-o-gies	ill
ice	ide-ol-o-gist	ill—advised *(adj.)*
ice age *(n.)*	ide-ol-ogy	ill-bred
ice-berg	*or* ide-al-ogy	il-le-gal
ice-boat	id-i-o-cies	il-le-gal-ity
ice-bound	id-iocy	il-le-gal-ize
ice-box		

Plural, past tense, adverbial, and noun derivatives formed by adding
s, d or *ed, ly, ness, ment, ful, less,* or *ing* to an unchanged root word are
not listed, nor are words formed by dropping the final *e* and adding *ing.*

il-leg-i-ble	imag-i-nary	im-men-si-ty
il-leg-i-bil-i-ty	imag-i-na-tion	im-men-su-ra-ble
il-leg-i-bly	imag-i-na-tive	im-merge
il-le-git-i-macy	imag-ine	im-mer-gence
il-le-git-i-mate	im-bal-ance	im-merse
ill—fated *(adj.)*	im-be-cile	im-mers-ible
ill—favored *(adj.)*	im-be-cilic	im-mer-sion
ill—gotten *(adj.)*	im-be-cil-i-ties	im-mi-grant (one entering
il-licit (forbidden)	im-be-cil-i-ty	a country)
cf. **elicit** (draw forth)	im-bibe	*cf.* **em-i-grant** (one leaving
il-lit-er-acy	im-bi-bi-tion	a country)
il-lit-er-ate	im-bri-cate	im-mi-grate
ill—mannered	im-bri-ca-tion	im-mi-gra-tion
il-logic	im-bro-glio	im-mi-nent (about to happen
il-log-i-cal	im-brue	*cf.* **em-i-nent** (distinguished
il-lu-mi-nate (light up)	im-brute	im-mit-i-ga-ble
cf. **alu-mi-nate**	im-bue	im-mo-bile
(metallic oxide)	im-i-ta-ble	im-mo-bil-ity
il-lu-mi-na-tion	im-i-tate	im-mo-bi-li-za-tion
il-lu-sion (false	im-i-ta-tion	im-mo-bi-lize
impression)	im-i-ta-tive	im-mod-er-acy
cf. **al-lu-sion**	im-i-ta-tor	im-mod-er-ate
(indirect reference)	im-mac-u-lacy	im-mod-er-a-tion
cf. **elu-sion** (escape)	im-mac-u-late	im-mod-est
il-lu-sion-ary	**Im-mac-u-late Con-cep-tion**	im-mod-esty
il-lu-sive	im-ma-nent	im-mo-late (kill as a sacrifice
il-lu-sory	im-ma-te-rial	*cf.* **em-u-late** (try to equal)
il-lus-trate	im-ma-ture	im-mo-la-tion
il-lus-tra-tion	im-ma-tu-rity	im-mo-la-tor
il-lus-tra-tive	im-mea-sur-able	im-moral
il-lus-tra-tor	im-me-di-acy	im-mor-al-ist
il-lus-tri-ous	im-me-di-ate	im-mo-ral-ity
ill will *(n.)*	im-med-i-ca-ble	im-mor-tal
im-age	im-me-mo-rial	im-mor-tal-ity
im-ag-ery	im-mense	im-mor-tal-ize
imag-in-able	im-men-si-ties	im-mov-able

Do not divide one-syllable words. Divide words by syllables, but leave at least two letters of the word on the first line and three letters on the following line. For additional guidelines, see page ix.

im-mov-a-bil-ity
im-mune
im-mu-ni-ties
im-mu-nity
im-mu-ni-za-tion
im-mu-nize
im-mu-nol-ogy
im-mure
im-mu-ta-ble
imp
im-pact
im-pac-tion
im-pac-tor
or im-pacter
im-pair
im-pala
im-pale
im-part
im-par-tial
im-par-ti-al-ity
im-pass
im-pass-a-ble (not passable)
cf. **im-pas-si-ble** (unable
to feel pain)
im-pass-abil-ity
im-passe
im-pas-si-bil-ity
im-pas-sioned
im-pas-sive
im-pas-siv-ity
im-pa-tience
im-pa-tient
im-peach
im-peach-able
im-pec-ca-bil-ity
im-pec-ca-ble

im-pec-ca-bly
im-pe-cu-nious
im-pe-cu-ni-os-ity
im-pede
im-ped-i-ment
im-ped-i-menta
im-pelled
im-pel-ler
or im-pel-lor
im-pel-ling
im-pend
im-pen-dent
im-pen-e-tra-bil-ity
im-pen-e-tra-ble
im-pen-e-tra-bly
im-pen-i-tence
im-pen-i-tent
im-per-a-tive
im-per-ceiv-able
im-per-cep-ti-bil-ity
im-per-cep-ti-ble
im-per-cep-ti-bly
im-per-cep-tive
im-per-fect
im-per-fec-tion
im-pe-rial
im-pe-ri-al-ism
im-pe-ri-al-ist
im-peril
im-per-ish-able
im-pe-rium
im-per-ma-nence
im-per-ma-nency
im-per-ma-nent
im-per-me-abil-ity
im-per-me-able

im-per-meably
im-per-mis-si-bil-ity
im-per-mis-si-ble
im-per-mis-si-bly
im-per-sonal
im-per-son-ate
im-per-son-ation
im-per-son-ator
im-per-ti-nence
im-per-ti-nen-cies
im-per-ti-nency
im-per-ti-nent
im-per-turb-abil-ity
im-per-turb-able
im-per-turb-ably
im-per-vi-ous
im-pet-u-os-i-ties
im-pet-u-os-ity
im-pet-u-ous
im-pi-eties
im-pi-ety
im-pinge
im-pi-ous
imp-ish
im-pla-ca-bil-ity
im-pla-ca-ble
im-pla-ca-bly
im-plant
im-plau-si-bil-ity
im-plau-si-ble
im-plau-si-bly
im-ple-ment
im-pli-cate
im-pli-ca-tion
im-pli-ca-tive
im-plicit

Plural, past tense, adverbial, and noun derivatives formed by adding
s, d or *ed, ly, ness, ment, ful, less,* or *ing* to an unchanged root word are
not listed, nor are words formed by dropping the final *e* and adding *ing*.

im-plode
im-plore
im-plied
im-ply
im-po-lite
im-pol-i-tic
im-po-lit-i-cal
im-pon-der-a-ble
im-pon-der-ably
im-pone
im-port
im-por-tance
im-por-tant
im-por-ta-tion
im-porter
im-por-tune
im-pose
im-po-si-tion
im-pos-si-bil-ity
im-pos-si-ble
im-pos-si-bly
im-pos-tor
or im-pos-ter
im-pos-ture
im-po-tence
im-po-tency
im-po-tent
im-pound
im-pov-er-ish
im-prac-ti-ca-bil-ity
im-prac-ti-ca-ble
im-prac-ti-ca-bly
im-prac-ti-cal
im-prac-ti-cal-ity
im-pre-cate
im-pre-ca-tion

im-pre-ca-tory
im-pre-cise
im-preg-na-bil-ity
im-preg-na-ble
im-preg-na-bly
im-preg-nate
im-press-ibil-ity
im-press-ible
im-press-ibly
im-pres-sion
im-pres-sion-abil-ity
im-pres-sion-able
im-pres-sion-ably
im-pres-sion-ism
im-pres-sion-ist
im-pres-sion-is-tic
im-pres-sive
im-press-ment
im-prest
im-pri-ma-tur
im-pri-mis
im-print
im-prison
im-pris-on-able
im-prob-a-bil-ity
im-prob-a-ble
im-prob-a-bly
im-promptu
im-proper
im-pro-pri-eties
im-pro-pri-ety
im-prov-abil-ity
im-prov-able
im-prov-ably
improve
im-prov-i-dence

im-prov-i-dent
im-pro-vi-sa-tion
im-pro-vise
im-pru-dence
im-pru-dent
im-pu-dent
im-pu-dic-ity
im-pugn
im-puis-sance
im-puis-sant
im-pulse
im-pul-sion
im-pul-sive
im-pu-nity
im-pure
im-pu-ri-ties
im-pu-rity
im-put-abil-ity
im-put-able
im-pute
in (inside)
cf. inn (hotel)
in-abil-ity
in ab-sen-tia
in-ac-ces-si-bil-ity
in-ac-ces-si-ble
in-ac-ces-si-bly
in-ac-cu-ra-cies
in-ac-cu-racy
in-ac-cu-rate
in-ac-tion
in-ac-ti-vate
in-ac-tive
in-ad-e-qua-cies
in-ad-e-quacy
in-ad-e-quate

Do not divide one-syllable words. Divide words by syllables, but leave at least two letters of the word on the first line and three letters on the following line. For additional guidelines, see page ix.

in-ad-mis-si-bil-ity
in-ad-mis-si-ble
in-ad-mis-si-bly
in-ad-ver-tence
in-ad-ver-ten-cies
in-ad-ver-tency
in-ad-ver-tent
in-ad-vis-a-bil-ity
in-ad-vis-a-ble
in-ad-vis-a-bly
in-alien-abil-ity
in-alien-able
in-alien-ably
in-al-ter-abil-ity
in-al-ter-able
in-al-ter-ably
in-amo-rata
in-ane
in-an-i-mate
in-a-ni-tion
inan-i-ties
inan-ity
in-ap-pli-ca-bil-ity
in-ap-pli-ca-ble
in-ap-pli-ca-bly
in-ap-pre-cia-tive
in-ap-proach-able
in-ap-pro-pri-ate
in-apt
in-ar-tic-u-late
in-ar-tis-tic
in-as-much as *(conj.)*
in-at-ten-tion
in-at-ten-tive
in-au-di-bil-ity
in-au-di-ble

in-au-di-bly
in-au-gu-ral
in-au-gu-rate
in-au-gu-ra-tion
in-aus-pi-cious
in-bred
Inca
in-cal-cu-la-ble
in-can-des-cence
in-can-des-cent
in-can-ta-tion
in-can-ta-tory
in-ca-pa-bil-ity
in-ca-pa-ble
in-ca-pa-bly
in-ca-pac-i-tate
in-ca-pac-i-ta-tion
in-ca-pac-i-ta-tor
in-ca-pac-i-ties
in-ca-pac-ity
in-car-cer-ate
in-car-cer-a-tion
in-car-nate
in-car-na-tion
in-cau-tion
in-cau-tious
in-cen-di-ary
in-cense
in-cen-tive
in-cep-tion
in-ces-sant
in-cest
in-ces-tu-ous
inch
in-ci-dence (extent)
cf. **in-ci-dents** (events)

in-ci-dent
in-ci-den-tal
in-cin-er-ate
in-cin-er-a-tor
in-cip-i-ent
in-ci-pit
in-cise
in-ci-sion
in-ci-sive
in-ci-sor
in-ci-ta-tion
in-cite (rouse)
cf. **in-sight** (wisdom)
in-clem-ency
in-clem-ent
in-clin-able
in-cli-na-tion
in-cline
in-close
in-clud-able
or in-clud-ible
in-clu-sion
in-clu-sive
in-co-erc-ible
in-cog-i-tant
in-cog-nita (female)
in-cog-nito
in-cog-ni-zance
in-cog-ni-zant
in-co-her-ence
in-co-her-ent
in-com-bus-ti-bil-ity
in-com-bus-ti-ble
in-com-bus-ti-bly
in-come
in-com-men-su-ra-bil-ity

Plural, past tense, adverbial, and noun derivatives formed by adding
s, d or *ed, ly, ness, ment, ful, less,* or *ing* to an unchanged root word are
not listed, nor are words formed by dropping the final *e* and adding *ing*.

in-com-men-su-ra-ble	in-con-sid-er-ate	in-crim-i-nate
in-com-men-su-ra-bly	in-con-sis-tence	in-crim-i-na-tion
in-com-men-su-rate	in-con-sis-tency	in-crim-i-na-tory
in-com-mu-ni-ca-bil-ity	in-con-sis-tent	in-crus-ta-tion
in-com-mu-ni-ca-ble	in-con-sol-able	in-cu-bate
in-com-mu-ni-ca-bly	in-con-sol-ably	in-cu-ba-tion
in-com-mu-ni-cado	in-con-so-nance	in-cu-ba-tor
in-com-mu-ni-ca-tive	in-con-so-nant	in-cul-cate
in-com-mut-able	in-con-stancy	in-cul-ca-tion
in-com-mut-ably	in-con-stant	in-cul-ca-tor
in-com-pa-ra-bil-ity	in-con-sol-able	in-cul-pa-ble
in-com-pa-ra-ble	in-con-spic-u-ous	in-cum-ben-cies
in-com-pa-ra-bly	in-con-test-able	in-cum-bency
in-com-pat-i-bil-i-ties	in-con-tro-vert-ible	in-cum-bent
in-com-pat-i-bil-ity	in-con-ve-nience	in-cum-ber
in-com-pat-i-ble	in-con-ve-niency	in-cur
in-com-pat-i-bly	in-con-ve-nient	in-cur-able
in-com-pe-tence	in-con-tro-vert-ibil-ity	in-curred
in-com-pe-tency	in-con-tro-vert-ible	in-cur-ring
in-com-pe-tent	in-con-tro-vert-ibly	in-cur-sion
in-com-plete	in-con-vinc-ible	in-debted
in-com-pre-hen-si-bil-ity	in-cor-po-rate	in-de-cency
in-com-pre-hen-si-ble	in-cor-po-ra-tion	in-de-cent
in-com-pre-hen-si-bly	in-cor-rect	in-de-ci-pher-able
in-com-pre-hen-sion	in-cor-ri-gi-bil-ity	in-de-ci-sion
in-com-put-able	in-cor-ri-gi-ble	in-de-ci-sive
in-con-ceiv-abil-ity	in-cor-ri-gi-bly	in-de-co-rum
in-con-ceiv-able	in-cor-rupt-ible	in-deed
in-con-ceiv-ably	in-crease	in-de-fa-ti-ga-bil-ity
in-con-clu-sive	in-cred-i-bil-ity	in-de-fat-i-ga-ble
in-con-gru-ity	in-cred-i-ble	in-de-fat-i-ga-bly
in-con-gru-ous	in-cred-i-bly	in-de-fin-able
in-con-se-quence	in-cre-du-lity	in-def-i-nite
in-con-se-quen-tial	in-cred-u-lous	in-del-i-ble
in-con-sid-er-able	in-cre-ment	in-del-i-cacy
in-con-sid-er-ably	in-cre-men-tal	in-dem-ni-fi-ca-tion

Do not divide one-syllable words. Divide words by syllables, but leave at least two letters of the word on the first line and three letters on the following line. For additional guidelines, see page ix.

in-dem-ni-fied
in-dem-ni-fy
in-dem-ni-ties
in-dem-ni-ty
in-dent
in-den-ta-tion
in-den-ture
in-de-pen-dence (freedom)
  cf. in-de-pen-dents (self-
  governing)
in-de-scrib-able
in-de-struc-ti-ble
in-de-struc-ti-bly
in-de-ter-min-able
in-de-ter-min-ably
in-de-ter-mi-nacy
in-de-ter-mi-nate
in-de-ter-mi-na-tion
in-dex
in-dexes
or in-di-ces
in-di-cate
in-di-ca-tion
in-dic-a-tive
in-di-ca-tor
in-di-cia
in-dict (charge with
  an offense)
  cf. in-dite (put in
  words or writing)
in-dict-able
in-dicter
or in-dictor
in-dif-fer-ence
in-dif-fer-ent
in-di-gence

in-dig-e-nous
in-di-gent
in-di-gest-ibil-ity
in-di-gest-ible
in-di-ges-tion
in-dig-nant
in-dig-na-tion
in-dig-ni-ties
in-dig-nity
in-digo
in-di-rect
in-dis-cern-ible
in-dis-creet (not prudent)
  cf. in-dis-crete (not
  separate)
in-dis-cre-tion
in-dis-crim-i-nate
in-dis-pens-abil-ity
in-dis-pens-able
in-dis-pens-ably
in-dis-pose
in-dis-po-si-tion
in-dis-put-able
in-dis-put-ably
in-dis-sol-u-ble
in-dis-tinct
in-dis-tinc-tive
in-dis-tin-guish-abil-ity
in-dis-tin-guish-able
in-dis-tin-guish-ably
in-dite (put in words
  or writing)
  cf. in-dict (charge
  with an offense)
in-diter
in-di-vert-ible

in-di-vert-ibly
in-di-vid-ual
in-di-vid-u-al-ism
in-di-vid-u-al-ist
in-di-vid-u-al-ity
in-di-vid-u-al-iza-tion
in-di-vid-u-al-ize
in-doc-ile
in-do-cil-ity
in-doc-tri-nate
in-doc-tri-na-tion
in-doc-tri-na-tor
in-do-lence
in-do-lent
in-dom-i-ta-bil-ity
in-dom-i-ta-ble
in-dom-i-ta-bly
In-do-nesian
in-door *(adj.)*
in-doors *(adv.)*
in-du-bi-ta-bil-ity
in-du-bi-ta-ble
in-du-bi-ta-bly
in-duce
in-duc-ibil-ity
in-duc-ible
in-duct
in-duc-tance
in-ductee
in-duc-tion
in-duc-tive
in-duc-tor
in-dulge
in-dulger
in-dul-gence
in-du-rate

Plural, past tense, adverbial, and noun derivatives formed by adding
s, d or *ed, ly, ness, ment, ful, less,* or *ing* to an unchanged root word are
not listed, nor are words formed by dropping the final *e* and adding *ing*.

in-du-ra-tion
in-du-ra-tive
in-dus-trial
in-dus-tri-al-ism
in-dus-tri-al-ist
in-dus-tri-al-iza-tion
in-dus-tri-al-ize
in-dus-tries
in-dus-tri-ous
in-dus-try
ine-bri-ant
ine-bri-ate
ine-bri-a-tion
in-ebri-ety
in-ed-i-ble
in-ed-ited
in-ed-u-ca-bil-ity
in-ed-u-ca-ble
in-ef-fa-bil-ity
in-ef-fa-ble
in-ef-fa-bly
in-ef-fec-tive
in-ef-fec-tual
in-ef-fec-tu-al-ity
in-ef-fi-ca-cious
in-ef-fi-cacy
in-ef-fi-ciency
in-ef-fi-cient
in-elas-tic
in-el-i-gi-bil-ity
in-el-i-gi-ble
in-ept
in-ep-ti-tude
in-equal-ity
in-eq-ui-ta-ble
in-eq-ui-ta-bly

in-eq-ui-ty (injustice)
 cf. **in-iq-uity** (wicked act)
in-erad-i-ca-bil-ity
in-erad-i-ca-ble
in-erad-i-ca-bly
in-er-rancy
in-er-rant
in-ert
in-er-tia
in-es-cap-able
in-es-cap-ably
in-es-ti-ma-ble
in-es-ti-ma-bly
in-ev-i-ta-bil-ity
in-ev-i-ta-ble
in-ev-i-ta-bly
in-ex-act
in-ex-cus-able
in-ex-haust-ible
in-ex-haust-ibly
in-ex-o-ra-ble
in-exp-en-sive
in-ex-pe-ri-ence
in-ex-pi-a-ble
in-ex-pli-ca-bil-ity
in-ex-tin-guish-able
in-ex-tri-ca-ble
in-fal-li-bil-ity
in-fal-li-ble
in-fa-mies
in-fa-mous
in-famy
in-fancy
in-fant
in-fan-ti-cide
in-fan-tile

in-fan-til-ity
in-fan-til-ism
in-fan-try
in-fan-try-man
in-fat-u-ate
in-fat-u-a-tion
in-fect
in-fec-tor
in-fec-tion
in-fec-tious
in-fec-tive
in-fe-lic-i-tous
in-fe-lic-i-ties
in-fe-lic-ity
in-fer
in-fer-ence
in-fer-en-tial
in-ferred
in-fer-ring
in-fe-rior
in-fe-ri-or-ity
in-fer-nal
in-ferno
in-fer-tile
in-fest
in-fes-ta-tion
in-fi-del
in-fi-del-i-ties
in-fi-del-ity
in-field *(n.)*
in-fight-ing *(n.)*
in-fil-trate
in-fil-tra-tion
in-fil-tra-tive
in-fil-tra-tor
in-fi-nite

Do not divide one-syllable words. Divide words by syllables, but leave at least two letters of the word on the first line and three letters on the following line. For additional guidelines, see page ix.

in-fin-i-tes-i-mal
in-fin-ity
in-firm
in-fir-ma-ries
in-fir-mary
in-fix
in-flame
in-flam-ma-bil-ity
in-flam-ma-ble
in-flam-ma-bly
in-flam-ma-tion
in-flam-ma-tory
in-flat-able
in-flate
in-fla-tion-ary
in-fla-tion-ism
in-flect
in-flec-tion
in-flex-i-ble
in-flict
in-flic-tion
in-flu-ence
in-flu-en-tial
in-flu-enza
in-flux
in-form
in-for-mal
in-for-mal-i-ties
in-for-mal-ity
in-form-ant
in-form-a-tive
in-former
in-frac-tion
in-fra-red
in-fre-quency
in-fre-quent

in-fringe
in-fu-ri-ate
in-fuse
in-fus-ible
in-fu-sion
in-ge-nious
in-ge-nue
or in-gé-nue
in-ge-nu-i-ties
in-ge-nu-ity
in-gen-u-ous
in-gest
in-gest-ible
in-ges-tive
in-got
in-grain
in-grate
in-gra-ti-ate
in-gra-ti-a-tion
in-gra-tia-tory
in-grat-i-tude
in-gre-di-ent
in-gress
in—group *(n.)*
in-growth
in-grown
in-gur-gi-tate
in-gur-gi-ta-tion
in-habit
in-hab-it-able
in-hab-it-ant
in-hal-ant
in-ha-la-tion
in-ha-la-tor
in-hale
in-her-ent

in-herit
in-her-it-able
in-her-it-ance
in-her-i-tor
in-her-i-tress
or in-her-i-trix
in-hibit
in-hi-bi-tion
in-hib-i-tor
or in-hib-it-er
in-hos-pi-ta-ble
in—house *(adj.)*
in-hu-man (not human)
cf. in-hu-mane (brutal)
in-hu-man-ity
in-im-i-cal
in-im-i-ta-ble
in-im-i-ta-bly
in-iq-ui-tous
in-iq-uity(wicked act)
cf. in-eq-uity (injustice)
ini-tial
ini-tial-ize
ini-ti-ate
ini-ti-a-tion
ini-tia-tive
ini-ti-a-tor
ini-tia-tory
in-ject
in-jec-tion
in-jec-tor
in-ju-di-cious
in-junc-tion
in-jure
in-ju-ries
in-ju-ri-ous

Plural, past tense, adverbial, and noun derivatives formed by adding
s, d or *ed, ly, ness, ment, ful, less,* or *ing* to an unchanged root word are
not listed, nor are words formed by dropping the final *e* and adding *ing*.

in-ju-ry
in-jus-tice
ink
in-kling
ink-stand
ink-well
in-laid
in-land
in—law *(n.)*
in-lay
in-let
in lo-co pa-ren-tis
in-mate
in me-mo-riam *(prep.)*
in—migrant
in—migrate *(v.)*
in-most
inn (hotel)
 cf. in (inside)
in-nards
in-nate
in-ner
inner city *(n.)*
in-ner-most *(n.)*
in-ner-spring
in-ner-vate
in-ner-va-tion
in-ning
inn-keeper
in-no-cence
in-no-cen-cies
in-no-cency
in-no-cent
in-noc-u-ous
in-no-vate
in-no-va-tion

in-no-va-tive
in-no-va-tor
in-no-va-tory
in-nu-endo
in-nu-en-dos
 or in-nu-en-does
in-nu-mer-a-ble
in-nu-mer-a-bly
in-oc-u-late
in-oc-u-la-tion
in-of-fen-sive
in-op-er-a-ble
in-op-er-a-tive
in-op-por-tune
in-or-di-nate
in-or-ganic
in-os-cu-late
in-os-cu-la-tion
in-pa-tient
in—per-son *(adj.)*
in per-so-nam
in—print *(adj.)*
in—process *(adj.)*
in pro-pria per-sona *(adv.)*
in-put
in-quest
in-quire
in-quirer
in-qui-ries
in-quiry
in-qui-si-tion
in-quis-i-tive
in-road *(n.)*
in-sa-lu-bri-ous
in-sa-lu-brity

in-san-i-tary
in-san-i-ta-tion
in-san-i-ties
in-san-ity
in-sa-tia-bil-ity
in-sa-tia-ble
in-sa-tia-bly
in-sa-tiate
in-scribe
in-scriber
in-scrip-tion
in-scrip-tive
in-scroll
in-scru-ta-bil-ity
in-scru-ta-ble
in-scru-ta-bly
in-seam
in-sect
in-sec-ti-cidal
in-sec-ti-cide
in-sec-ti-fuge
in-sec-tiv-o-rous
in-se-cure
in-se-cu-rity
in-sem-inate
in-sem-i-na-tion
in-sen-si-bil-ity
in-sen-si-ble
in-sen-si-bly
in-sen-si-tive
in-sen-si-tiv-ity
in-sen-tient
in-sep-a-ra-bil-ity
in-sep-a-ra-ble
in-sep-a-ra-bly
in-sert

Do not divide one-syllable words. Divide words by syllables, but leave
at least two letters of the word on the first line and three letters on the
following line. For additional guidelines, see page ix.

in-ser-tion
in—ser-vice *(adj.)*
in-set
in-shore
in-side
in-sider
in-sid-i-ous
in-sight (wisdom)
cf. in-cite (rouse)
in-sig-nia
or in-signe
in-sig-nif-i-cance
in-sig-nif-i-cancy
in-sig-nif-i-cant
in-sin-cere
in-sin-cer-ity
in-sin-u-ate
in-sin-u-a-tion
in-sipid
in-si-pid-ity
in-sist
in-sis-tence
in-sis-ten-cies
in-sis-tency
in-so-bri-ety
in-so-cia-bil-ity
in-so-cia-ble
in-so-cia-bly
in-so-far *(adv.)*
in-so-late
in-so-la-tion
in-sole
in-so-lence
in-so-lent
in-sol-u-bi-li-za-tion
in-sol-u-bi-lize

in-sol-u-bil-ity
in-sol-u-ble
in-sol-u-bly
in-solv-able
in-solv-ably
in-sol-vency
in-sol-vent
in-som-nia
in-som-niac
in-so-much as *(conj.)*
in-sou-ci-ance
in-sou-ci-ant
in-spect
in-spec-tion
in-spec-tor
in-spi-ra-tion
in-spi-ra-tional
in-spire
in-sta-bil-ity
in-sta-ble
in-stall
or in-stal
in-stal-la-tion
in-stance
in-stancy
in-stant
in-stan-ta-neous
in-stead
in-step
in-sti-gate
in-sti-ga-tion
in-sti-ga-tor
in-still
or in-stil
in-stinct
in-stinc-tive

in-sti-tute
in-sti-tu-tion
in-sti-tu-tional
in-sti-tu-tion-al-iza-tion
in-sti-tu-tion-al-ize
in-struct
in-struc-tion
in-struc-tive
in-struc-tor
in-stru-ment
in-stru-men-tal
in-stru-men-tal-ism
in-stru-men-tal-ist
in-stru-men-tal-ity
in-stru-men-ta-tion
in-sub-or-di-nate
in-sub-or-di-na-tion
in-sub-stan-tial
in-suf-fer-able
in-suf-fi-cience
in-suf-fi-ciency
in-suf-fi-cient
in-su-lant
in-su-late
in-su-la-tion
in-su-la-tor
in-su-lin
in-sult
in-su-per-a-ble
in-su-per-a-bly
in-sup-port-able
in-sup-port-ably
in-sup-press-ible
in-sur-abil-ity
in-sur-able
in-sure

Plural, past tense, adverbial, and noun derivatives formed by adding
s, d or *ed, ly, ness, ment, ful, less,* or *ing* to an unchanged root word are
not listed, nor are words formed by dropping the final *e* and adding *ing.*

in-surer
in-sur-gence
in-sur-gen-cies
in-sur-gency
in-sur-gent
in-sur-mount-able
in-sur-mount-ably
in-sur-rec-tion
in-tact
in-take
in-te-ger
in-te-gral
in-te-grate
in-te-gra-tion
in-teg-rity
in-tel-lect
in-tel-lec-tion
in-tel-lec-tive
in-tel-lec-tual
in-tel-lec-tu-al-ism
in-tel-lec-tu-al-ity
in-tel-lec-tu-al-iza-tion
in-tel-lec-tu-al-ize
in-tel-li-gence
in-tel-li-gent
in-tel-li-gen-tsia
in-tel-li-gi-bil-ity
in-tel-li-gi-ble
in-tel-li-gi-bly
in-tem-per-ance
in-tem-per-ate
in-tend
in-tense
in-ten-si-fi-ca-tion
in-ten-si-fier
in-ten-sify

in-ten-sion (intensity)
cf. in-ten-tion (resolve)
in-ten-si-ties
in-ten-sity
in-ten-sive
in-tent
in-ten-tion (resolve)
cf. in-ten-sion (intensity)
in-ten-tional
in-ter
in-ter-act
in-ter-ac-tant
in-ter-ac-tion
in-ter-ac-tive
in-ter-atomic
in-ter-breed
in-ter-ca-lary
in-ter-ca-late
in-ter-cede
in-ter-ceder
in-ter-cel-lu-lar
in-ter-cept
in-ter-cepter
in-ter-cep-tion
in-ter-cep-tor
in-ter-ces-sion
in-ter-ces-sional
in-ter-ces-sor
in-ter-ces-sory
in-ter-change
in-ter-changer
in-ter-change-able
in-ter-change-ably
in-ter-col-le-giate
in-ter-co-lum-ni-a-tion
in-ter-com

in-ter-com-mu-nion
in-ter-con-ti-nen-tal
in-ter-course
in-ter-de-nom-i-na-tional
in-ter-de-part-men-tal
in-ter-de-pen-dence
in-ter-de-pen-dency
in-ter-de-pen-dent
in-ter-dict
in-ter-dic-tion
in-ter-dis-ci-plin-ary
in-ter-est
in-ter-face
in-ter-faith
in-ter-fere
in-ter-fer-ence
in-terim
in-te-ri-or (inside)
cf. an-te-ri-or (toward the front)
in-ter-ject
in-ter-jec-tion
in-ter-jec-tor
in-ter-jec-tory
in-ter-lace
in-ter-leaf
in-ter-li-brary
in-ter-lo-cu-tion
in-ter-loc-u-tor
in-ter-loc-u-tory
in-ter-lope
in-ter-loper
in-ter-lude
in-ter-mar-riage
in-ter-marry
in-ter-me-di-acy

Do not divide one-syllable words. Divide words by syllables, but leave
at least two letters of the word on the first line and three letters on the
following line. For additional guidelines, see page ix.

in-ter-me-di-ary
in-ter-me-di-ate
in-ter-mezzo
in-ter-mi-na-ble
in-ter-mi-na-bly
in-ter-min-gle
in-ter-mis-sion
in-ter-mit
in-ter-mit-tence
in-ter-mit-tent
in-ter-mit-ter
in-ter-mix
in-tern
or in-terne
in-ternal
internal–combustion engine
in-ter-na-tional
or in-ter-na-tio-nale
in-ter-na-tion-al-ism
in-ter-na-tion-al-ist
in-ter-na-tion-al-iza-tion
in-ter-na-tion-al-ize
in-ter-ne-cine
in-ternee
in-ter-nist
in-ter-of-fice
in-ter-pel-late
in-ter-pen-e-trate
in-ter-pen-e-tra-tion
in-ter-per-sonal
in-ter-phase
in-ter-play
in-ter-po-late
in-ter-po-la-tion
in-ter-po-la-tive
in-ter-po-la-tor

in-ter-pret
in-ter-preter
in-ter-pre-tive
in-ter-ra-cial
in-ter-re-late
in-ter-re-la-tion
in-ter-ro-gate
in-ter-ro-ga-tion
in-ter-rog-a-tive
in-ter-ro-ga-tor
in-ter-rupt
in-ter-rupt-ible
in-ter-rupter
in-ter-rup-tion
in-ter-scho-las-tic
in-ter-sect
in-ter-sec-tion
in-ter-ses-sion
in-ter-space
in-ter-sperse
in-ter-state
in-ter-twine
in-ter-val
in-ter-vene
in-ter-ve-nor
or in-ter-vener
in-ter-ven-tion
in-ter-view
in-ter-weave
in-ter-wo-ven
in-ter-zonal
in-tes-tacy
in-tes-tate
in-tes-ti-nal
in-tes-tine
in-ti-macy

in-ti-mate
in-ti-mater
in-ti-ma-tion
in-tim-i-date
in-tim-i-da-tion
in-tim-i-da-tor
in-tol-er-a-bil-ity
in-tol-er-a-ble
in-tol-er-a-bly
in-tol-er-ance
in-tol-er-ant
in-to-nate
in-to-na-tion
in-to-na-tional
in-tone
in toto
in-tox-i-cant
in-tox-i-cate
in-tox-i-ca-tion
in-trac-ta-bil-ity
in-trac-ta-ble
in-trac-ta-bly
in-tra-mu-ral
in-tra-mus-cu-lar
in-tran-si-gence
in-tran-si-gent
in-tra-state
in-tra-ve-nous
in-trepid
in-tri-ca-cies
in-tri-cacy
in-tri-cate
in-tri-gant
or in-tri-guant
in-trigue
in-trin-sic

in-tro-duce	in-ven-tory	in-vo-ca-tion
in-tro-duc-tion	in-verse	in-voice
in-tro-duc-tory	in-ver-sion	in-voke
in-tro-spect	in-vert	in-vol-un-tarily
in-tro-spec-tion	in-ver-te-brate	in-vol-un-tar-i-ness
in-tro-spec-tive	in-verter	in-vol-un-tary
in-tro-ver-sion	in-vert-ible	in-volve
in-tro-vert	in-vest	in-vul-ner-able
in-trude	in-ves-ti-gate	in-ward
in-truder	in-ves-ti-ga-tion	*or* in-wards
in-tru-sion	in-ves-ti-ga-tional	io-dine
in-tru-sive	in-ves-ti-ga-tive	*or* io-din
in-tu-itive	in-ves-ti-ga-tor	ion
in-un-date	in-ves-ti-ga-tory	ion-o-sphere
in-un-da-tion	in-ves-ti-ture	ipso facto
in-ure	in-vet-er-acy	iras-ci-bil-ity
in-vade	in-vet-er-ate	iras-ci-ble
in-va-lid	in-vi-a-bil-ity	iras-ci-bly
in-val-i-date	in-vi-a-ble	irate
in-val-i-da-tion	in-vid-i-ous	ire
in-val-i-da-tor	in-vig-o-rate	ir-i-des-cence
in-valu-able	in-vig-o-ra-tion	ir-i-des-cent
in-var-i-ance	in-vig-o-ra-tor	irk
in-vari-ant	in-vin-ci-bil-ity	irk-some
in-va-sion	in-vin-ci-ble	iron
in-va-sive	in-vin-ci-bly	Iron Age *(n.)*
in-vec-tive	in-vi-o-la-ble	iron-bound
in-veigh	in-vi-o-la-bly	iron-clad
in-veigher	in-vi-o-lacy	iron cur-tain
in-vei-gle	in-vi-o-late	ironic
in-vei-gler	in-vis-i-bil-ity	iron-stone
in-vent	in-vis-i-ble	iron-ware
in-ven-tion	in-vi-ta-tion	iron-work
in-ven-tive	in-vi-ta-tional	iro-nies
in-ven-tor	in-vite	irony
in-ven-to-ries	in-vi-tee	Ir-o-quois

Do not divide one-syllable words. Divide words by syllables, but leave
at least two letters of the word on the first line and three letters on the
96   following line. For additional guidelines, see page ix.

ir-ra-di-ate
ir-ra-di-a-tion
ir-ra-di-a-tive
ir-ra-di-a-tor
ir-rad-i-ca-ble
ir-rad-i-ca-bly
ir-ra-tio-nal
ir-ra-tio-nal-ism
ir-ra-tio-nal-ist
ir-ra-tio-nal-is-tic
ir-ra-tio-nal-i-ty
ir-re-al-i-ty
ir-re-claim-able
ir-rec-on-cil-abil-ity
ir-rec-on-cil-able
ir-rec-on-cil-ably
ir-re-cov-er-able
ir-re-cov-er-ably
ir-re-deem-able
ir-re-deem-ably
ir-re-duc-ibil-ity
ir-re-duc-ible
ir-re-duc-i-bly
ir-re-fut-abil-ity
ir-re-fut-able
ir-re-fut-ably
ir-re-gard-less
ir-reg-u-lar
ir-reg-u-lar-i-ties
ir-reg-u-lar-ity
ir-rel-a-tive
ir-rel-e-vance
ir-rel-e-van-cies
ir-rel-e-cancy
ir-rel-e-vant
ir-re-li-gion

ir-re-li-gious
ir-re-mov-able
ir-rep-a-ra-ble
ir-rep-a-ra-bly
ir-re-place-abil-ity
ir-re-place-able
ir-re-place-ably
ir-re-press-ible
ir-re-proach-able
ir-re-proach-ably
ir-re-sist-ible
ir-res-o-lute
ir-re-spec-tive
ir-re-spon-si-ble
ir-re-spon-si-bly
ir-re-spon-sive
ir-rev-er-ence
ir-rev-er-ent
ir-re-vers-ible
ir-rev-o-ca-ble
ir-rev-o-ca-bly
ir-ri-gate
ir-ri-ga-tion
ir-ri-ga-tor
ir-ri-ta-bil-i-ties
ir-ri-ta-bil-ity
ir-ri-ta-ble
ir-ri-tant
ir-ri-tate
ir-ri-ta-tion
ir-rupt
ir-rup-tion (violent
  invasion)
  cf. **erup-tion** (bursting
  forth)
Is-lam

Is-lam-ic
is-land
is-lander
isle (island)
  cf. **aisle** (pathway)
iso-bar
iso-late
iso-la-tion
iso-la-tion-ism
iso-la-tion-ist
iso-met-ric
iso-therm
iso-tope
iso-topic
Is-rael
Is-raeli
Is-raelis *(n. pl.)*
Is-ra-el-ite
is-su-ance
is-sue
isth-mus
italic
ital-i-cize
itch
item
item-iza-tion
item-ize
it-er-ate
it-er-a-tion
itin-er-ant
itin-er-ary
it-self
ivied
ivo-ries
ivory
ivy

J

jab
jabbed
jab-bing
jab-ber
jab-ber-wocky
jack
jackal
jacket
Jack Frost *(n.)*
jack-ham-mer
jack—in—the—box *(n.)*
jack—in—the—boxes
or jacks—in—the—box *(n. pl.)*
jack-knife
jack—of—all—trades *(n.)*
jacks–of–all–trades *(n. pl.)*
jack—o'—lantern
jack-pot
jack-rab-bit
Jack-so-nian
jack-straw
jade
jag
jagged
jag-ging
jag-uar
jai alai
jail
jail-bird
jail-break
jailer
or jailor

Jain
Jain-ism
ja-lopy
jal-ou-sie
jam (press closely)
   cf. jamb (side of opening)
jam-ba-laya
jam-bo-ree
jammed
jam-mer
jam-ming
jam session
jan-gle
jan-gled
jan-gling
jan-is-sary
or jan-i-zary
jan-is-saries *(n. pl.)*
jan-i-tor
jan-i-to-rial
jan-i-tress
Jan-sen-ism
Jan-sen-ist
Jan-sen-is-tic
Jap-a-nese
jape
jar
jar-di-niere
jar-gon
jar-gon-ize
jarred
jar-ring
jas-mine
jaun-dice
jaunt
jaun-tier

jaun-ti-est
jaun-tily
jaun-ti-ness
jav-e-lin
jaw
Jay-cee
jay-hawker
jay-vee
jay-walk
jazz
jazz-ier
jazz-i-est
jazz-ily
jazz-i-ness
J—bar lift *(n.)*
jeal-ous
jean
jeep
jeer
Jef-fer-son
Jef-fer-so-nian
Je-ho-vah
jell
jel-lied
jelly
jel-ly-fish
jeop-ar-dize
jeop-ardy
Jer-e-miah
jerk
jerk-ier
jerk-i-est
jerk-ily
jerk-i-ness
jerky
jer-ri-can

jer-sey	jiffy	job lot
Je-ru-sa-lem	jig	jockey
jest	jigged	jo-cose
jester	jig-ger	joc-u-lar
Je-suit	jig-ging	joc-u-lar-ity
Je-sus	jig-gle	jo-cund
jet air-plane	jig-gly	jodh-pur
jet—black	jig-saw	jog
jet engine	jilt	jogged
jet-port	Jim Crow *(n.)*	jog-ger
jet—propelled	jim—dandy	jog-ging
jet pro-pul-sion	jim-mies *(n. pl.)*	jog-gle
jet-sam	jimmy	john-ny-cake
jet set *(n.)*	jin-gle	Johnny—on—the—spot *(n.)*
jet stream	jin-gled	joie de vivre
jet-ti-son	jin-gler	join
jet-ti-son-able	jin-gling	joiner
jetty	jingo	joint
jeu-nesse do-rée	jin-go-ism	joist
Jew	jin-go-ist	joke
jewel	jin-go-is-tic	joker
jew-eled	jin-rik-i-sha	jol-lier
or jew-elled	jinx	jol-li-est
jew-eler	jit-ney	jol-li-fi-ca-tion
or jew-el-ler	jit-ter	jol-li-ties
jew-elry	jit-ter-bug	jolly
Jew-ess	jit-tery	jolt
Jew-ish	jiu-jitsu	jot
Jew's harp	*or* ju-jitsu	jot-ted
or Jews' harp	jive	jot-ter
Jez-e-bel	job	jot-ting
jib	jobbed	jounce
jibbed	job-ber	jounc-ier
job-ber	job-bing	jounc-i-est
jib-bing	job-holder	jouncy
jibe	job—hopping	jour-nal

Plural, past tense, adverbial, and noun derivatives formed by adding *s, d* or *ed, ly, ness, ment, ful, less,* or *ing* to an unchanged root word are not listed, nor are words formed by dropping the final *e* and adding *ing*.

99

jour-nal-ese
jour-nal-ism
jour-nal-ist
jour-nal-is-tic
jour-ney
jour-ney-man
joust
jo-vial
jo-vi-al-ity
jowl
joy
joy-ous
joy-ride
ju-bil-ant
ju-bi-la-tion
ju-bi-lee
Ju-dah
Ju-daic
or Ju-da-ical
Ju-da-ism
Judas
Judeo—Christian
judge
judg-ment
or judge-ment
ju-di-ca-tory
ju-di-ca-ture
ju-di-cial
ju-di-ciary
ju-di-cious
judo
jug
jug-gle
jug-gler
jug-gling
jug-u-lar

juice
juic-ier
juic-i-est
juic-i-ness
juicy
ju-jitsu
or ju-jutsu
juke box *(n.)*
ju-li-enne
jum-ble
jumbo
jump
jump suit *(n.)*
jumpy
junc-tion
junc-ture
jun-gle
ju-nior
junk
jun-ket
junkie
or junky
junk mail *(n.)*
junk-yard
junta
Ju-pi-ter
ju-rid-i-cal
or ju-ridic
juries
ju-ris-dic-tion
ju-ris-dic-tional
ju-ris-pru-dence
ju-ris-pru-dent
ju-ris-pru-den-tial
ju-rist
ju-ris-tic

ju-ror
jury
ju-ry-man
jus-tice
jus-tice of the peace *(n.)*
jus-ti-cia-bil-ity
jus-ti-cia-ble
jus-ti-fi-abil-ity
jus-ti-fi-able
jus-ti-fi-ably
jus-ti-fi-ca-tion
jus-ti-fi-ca-tory
jus-ti-fied
jus-ti-fier
jus-tify
jut
jut-ted
jut-ting
ju-ve-nile
jux-ta-pose
jux-ta-po-si-tion

K

kaf-fee-klatsch
kaf-tan
kai-ser
kale
ka-lei-do-scope
ka-lei-do-scopic
or ka-lei-do-scop-i-cal
ka-mi-kaze
kan-ga-roo

Do not divide one-syllable words. Divide words by syllables, but leave at least two letters of the word on the first line and three letters on the following line. For additional guidelines, see page ix.

karat (weight)
   cf. **car-rot** (vegetable)
   cf. **caret** (printer's mark)
ka-rate
kat-zen-jam-mer
kava
kayak
kayo (knockout)
kayoed
ka-zoo
keel
keel-boat
keel-haul
keep
keeper
keep-sake
ke-loid
kelp
ken-nel
kept
ker-chief
ker-chiefs
  or **ker-chieves** *(n. pl.)*
ker-nel (nut)
   cf. **colo-nel** (officer)
ker-o-sine
  or **ker-o-sene**
ketchup
  or **cat-sup**
ket-tle
ket-tle-drum
Kew-pie
key
key-board
key club *(n.)*

key-hole
key-note
key-stroke
key word
khaki
kib-butz *(sing.)*
kib-but-zim *(pl.)*
kib-butz-nik
ki-bitz
ki-bitzer
ki-bosh
kick
kick-back
kicker
kick-off
kick-stand
kick-up *(n.)*
kick up *(v.)*
kid
kid-ded
kid-der
kid-ding
kid-nap
kid-napped
kid-nap-per
  or **kid-naper**
kid-nap-ping
kid-ney
kid-skin
kill
killer
kill-joy
kiln
kilo
kilo-cy-cle
ki-lo-gram

ki-lo-hertz
ki-lo-me-ter
kilo-watt
kilowatt—hour *(n.)*
kilt
kil-ter
ki-mono
kin
kind
kin-der-gar-ten
kin-der-gart-ner
kind-hearted
kin-dle
kind-lier
kind-li-est
kind-li-ness
kin-dling
kin-dred
ki-ne-mat-ics
kin-e-scope
ki-ne-sics
ki-net-ics
kin-folk
king
king-bird
king-dom
king-fish
king-lier
king-li-est
king-li-ness
king-maker
king-pin
king—size
  or **king—sized** *(adj.)*
kink
kink-ier

Plural, past tense, adverbial, and noun derivatives formed by adding
s, d or *ed, ly, ness, ment, ful, less,* or *ing* to an unchanged root word are
not listed, nor are words formed by dropping the final *e* and adding *ing.*

101

kins-folk *(n. pl.)*
kin-ship
kins-man
kins-woman
ki-osk
kis-met
kiss
kit
kitchen
kitch-en-ette
kitch-en-ware
kith
kit-ten
kit-ten-ish
kitty
kitty—corner
or kitty—cornered
kiwi
klatch
or klatsch
klep-to-ma-nia
klep-to-ma-niac
kludge
knack
knap (crest of hill)
  cf. nap (short sleep)
knap-sack
knave (dishonest person)
  cf. nave (part of a
    church)
knavery
knavish
knead (mix)
  cf. need (desire)
knee (leg joint)
  cf. née or nee (name)

knee action *(n.)*
knee-cap
knee—deep *(adj.)*
knee-hole
kneel
knell
knew (understood)
  cf. new (not old)
knick-ers
knick-knack
knife
knife—edge
knight (lord)
  cf. night (darkness)
knight—errant
knight-hood
knit (tie together)
  cf. nit (louse egg)
knob
knock
knock-down
knocker
knock—knee
knock—out *(n.)*
knock out *(v.)*
knock-wurst
or knack-wurst
knoll
knot (fastener)
knot-hole
knot-ted
knot-ting
knotty
know
know-how
know—it—all *(n.)*

knowl-edge-abil-ity
knowl-edge-able
knowl-edge-ably
known
know—nothing *(n.)*
knuckle
ko-peck
or ko-pek
Ko-ran
ko-sher
kow-tow
kraal
krem-lin
Krishna
Krish-na-ism
Kriss Krin-gle
krona
krone
or kro-nen
kudo
kum-quat
kung fu
kwash-i-or-kor

L

la-bel
la-beled
or la-belled
la-bel-ing
or la-bel-ling
la-bor
la-borer
lab-o-ra-to-ries

Do not divide one-syllable words. Divide words by syllables, but leave
at least two letters of the word on the first line and three letters on the
102 following line. For additional guidelines, see page ix.

lab-o-ra-tory
la-bo-ri-ous
la-bor-sav-ing
lab-y-rinth
lace
lac-er-ate
lac-er-a-tion
lac-ier
lac-i-est
lack
lack-a-dai-si-cal
lackey
la-conic
lac-quer
la-crosse
lac-tate
lad-der
lad-der—back
lade
laden
la-dies
ladies—in—waiting
ladies man
or lady's man
la-dle
lady
la-dy-bug
lady—in—waiting
la-dy-like
la-dy-ship
lag
la-ger
lagged
lag-ging
lag-gard
la-goon

laid
lair
laissez—faire *(n.)*
la-ity
lake
lamb
lam-baste
or lam-bast
lamb-skin
lame
lame-brain
lame-duck
lamer
lam-est
la-ment
la-men-ta-ble
la-men-ta-bly
lam-en-ta-tion
lam-i-nate
lam-i-na-tion
lamp
lamp-black
lam-poon
lam-prey
lance
lancer
land
land-fall
land-fill
land grant
land-holder
land-ing craft
land-ing gear
land-ing strip
land-lady
land-locked

land-lord
land-lub-ber
land-mark
land-owner
land-scape
land-slide
lan-guage
lan-guid
lan-guish
lan-guor
lank
lank-ier
lank-i-est
lank-i-ness
lanky
lan-o-lin
lan-tern
lan-yard
lap
la-pel
lapped
lap-ping
lapse
lar-ce-nist
lar-ce-nous
lar-ceny
lard
larder
large
large—scale *(adj.)*
lar-iat
lark
larva
lar-vae
or lar-vas *(n. pl.)*
lar-vi-cide

Plural, past tense, adverbial, and noun derivatives formed by adding
s, d or *ed, ly, ness, ment, ful, less,* or *ing* to an unchanged root word are
not listed, nor are words formed by dropping the final *e* and adding *ing*.

la-ryn-geal
lar-yn-gitic
lar-yn-gi-tis
la-ryn-ges (n. pl.)
lar-ynx
la-sa-gna
las-civ-i-ous
lase
la-ser
lash
lass
lasso
las-sos
or las-soes (n. pl.)
last
last—ditch (adj.)
last straw
last word
latch
latch-key
latch-string
late
late-comer
later
lat-est
la-ten-cies
la-tency
lat-erad
lat-eral
lat-est
la-tex
lath (wood strip)
cf. lathe (machine)
lather
lat-i-tude
lat-i-tu-di-nal

la-trine
lat-ter
Latter—Day Saint (n.)
lat-tice
lat-tice-work
laud
laud-able
lau-da-num
lau-da-tion
lau-da-tive
laud-a-tory
laugh
laugh-able
laugh-a-bly
laugh-ing-stock
laugh-ter
launch
launcher
laun-der
laun-derer
laun-der-ette
laun-dress
laun-dro-mat
laun-dries
laundry
laun-dry-man
laun-dry-woman
lau-re-ate
lau-rel
lava
la-va-liere
or la-val-liere
la-va-tion
lav-a-to-ries
lav-a-tory
lave

lav-en-der
lav-ish
law
law—abiding (adj.)
law-breaker
law-maker
law-man
lawn
lawn mower
law-suit
law-yer
lax
lax-a-tive
lax-ity
lay (bring down)
cf. lei (wreath)
lay-away
lay down
layer
lay-ette
lay-man
lay-off
lay-out
la-zier
la-zi-est
la-zily
la-zi-ness
lazy
la-zy-ish
la-zy Su-san
lea (meadow)
cf. lee (shelter)
leach
lead
leaden
leader

Do not divide one-syllable words. Divide words by syllables, but leave at least two letters of the word on the first line and three letters on the following line. For additional guidelines, see page ix.

leaf
leaf-age
leaf-ier
leaf-i-est
leaf-let
league
leak
leak-age
leak-ier
leak-i-est
leak-i-ness
leaky
lean (slant; thin)
cf. **lien** (legal claim)
lean—to *(n.)*
leap
leaped
or **leapt**
leap-frog
leap year
learn
learned
or **learnt**
learner
lease
leash
least
least-ways
least-wise
leather
leath-er-like
leath-ery
leave
leaven
leaves *(n. pl.)*
le-bens-raum

lecher
lech-er-ous
lech-ery
lec-i-thin
lec-tern
lec-tor
lec-ture
le-der-ho-sen
ledge
led-ger
lee (shelter)
cf. **lea** (meadow)
leech
leer
leery
lee-ward
lee-way
left
left—handed *(adj.)*
left—hander *(n.)*
left-ism
left-over *(adj.) (n.)*
left wing *(n.)*
left—winger *(n.)*
leg
leg-a-cies
leg-acy
le-gal
legal age *(n.)*
le-gal-ese
le-gal-ism
le-gal-ist
le-gal-i-ties
le-gal-ity
le-gal-iza-tion
le-gal-ize

leg-ate
leg-a-tee
le-ga-tion
le-ga-tor
leg-end
leg-en-darily
leg-end-ary
leg-er-de-main
legged
leg-ging
or **leg-gin**
leg-horn
leg-i-bil-ity
leg-i-ble
leg-i-bly
le-gion
le-gion-ar-ies
le-gion-ary
le-gion-naire
leg-is-late
leg-is-la-tion
leg-is-la-tive
leg-is-la-tor
leg-is-la-to-rial
leg-is-la-tress
leg-is-la-trix
leg-is-la-ture
le-git-i-macy
le-git-i-mate
le-git-i-ma-tion
le-git-i-ma-tize
le-git-i-mism
le-git-i-mist
leg
leg-room
le-gume

Plural, past tense, adverbial, and noun derivatives formed by adding
s, d or *ed, ly, ness, ment, ful, less,* or *ing* to an unchanged root word are
not listed, nor are words formed by dropping the final *e* and adding *ing*.

le-gu-mi-nous
leg-work
lei (wreath)
cf. lay (bring down)
lei-sure
lemon
lem-on-ade
lend
lender
lend—lease *(n.)*
length
lengthen
length-ier
length-ways
length-wise
lengthy
le-nience
le-nien-cies
le-niency
le-nient
Le-nin-ism
len-i-tive
len-ity
lens
or lense
len-til
leop-ard
le-o-tard
leper
lep-re-chaun
lep-ro-sar-ium
lep-rosy
lep-rous
le-sion
less
les-see

lessen (decrease)
cf. les-son (that learned)
lesser (smaller)
cf. les-sor (person)
lest
let
let-down
le-thal
le-thar-gic
leth-argy
let-ter
let-terer
let-ter-head
letter—perfect *(adj.)*
let-ter-press
let-tuce
leu-ke-mia
leu-ke-mic
levee (river bank)
cf. levy (order to
be paid)
level
lev-eled
or lev-elled
level—headed
lev-el-ing
or lev-el-ling
lever
lev-er-age
le-vi-a-than
lev-ied
lev-i-tate
lev-i-ta-tion
lev-ity
levy (order to be paid)
cf. levee (river bank)

lewd
lex-i-cog-ra-pher
lex-i-cog-ra-phy
lex-i-con
li-a-bil-i-ties
li-a-bil-ity
li-a-ble
li-ais-ing
li-ai-son
liar
li-ba-tion
li-bel
li-bel-ant
or li-bel-lant
li-beled
or li-belled
li-belee
or li-bel-lee
li-bel-ing
or li-bel-ling
li-bel-ous
or li-bel-lous
lib-eral
lib-er-al-ism
lib-er-al-ist
lib-er-al-is-tic
lib-er-al-i-ties
lib-er-al-ity
lib-er-al-iza-tion
lib-er-al-ize
lib-er-al-izer
lib-er-ate
lib-er-a-tion
lib-er-a-tor
lib-er-tar-ian
lib-er-tine

Do not divide one-syllable words. Divide words by syllables, but leave
at least two letters of the word on the first line and three letters on the
following line. For additional guidelines, see page ix.

lib-er-tin-ism
lib-er-ties
lib-erty
li-bid-i-nous
li-bido
li-bra
li-brar-ian
li-brar-ies
li-brary
lice
li-cense
or li-cence
li-cens-able
li-cense
or li-cence
li-censer
or li-cencer
li-cen-tious
licit
lie (falsehood)
  cf. lye (strong
  alkaline solution)
lief
liege
lien (legal claim)
  cf. lean (slanting; thin)
lieu
lieu-ten-an-cies
lieu-ten-ancy
lieu-ten-ant
life
life—and—death
or life—or—death
life belt
life-blood
life-boat

life buoy
life-guard
life-like
life-long
life pre-server
lifer
life-saver
life—size
or life—sized *(adj.)*
life-time
life-work
lift
lift—off *(n.)*
lift truck
lig-a-ment
li-gate
li-ga-tion
lig-a-ture
light
lighted
or lit
light bulb
lighten
ligh-ter
lighter—than—air *(adj.)*
light-face
light—fingered
light—footed
light—handed
light—headed
light-ning (flash)
  cf. light-en-ing (reduce)
light-weight
lig-ne-ous
lig-nite
lik-able

or like-able
like
like-lier
like-li-est
like-li-hood
like-wise
li-lac
lil-li-put
lil-li-pu-tian *(adj.)*
lilt
lily
lily—livered
lily of the val-ley
lily—white
limb
lim-ber
limbo
lime
lime-ade
lime-light
lim-er-ick
lime-stone
limey
limit
lim-i-ta-tion
limp
lim-pid
lin-age
Lin-coln-ian
line
lin-eage
lin-eal
lin-ear
line-backer
line-man
linen

Plural, past tense, adverbial, and noun derivatives formed by adding
s, d or *ed, ly, ness, ment, ful, less,* or *ing* to an unchanged root word are
not listed, nor are words formed by dropping the final *e* and adding *ing*.

liner
lines-man
lineup
lin-ger
lin-gerer
lin-ge-rie
lingo
lin-gual
lin-guist
lin-guis-tic
lin-i-ment
link
link-age
linkup
li-no-leum
Li-no-type
lin-seed
lint
lin-tel
linter
lion
li-on-ess
li-on-hearted
li-on-iza-tion
li-on-ize
li-on-izer
lion's share
lip
li-pase
lipped
lip-ping
lippy
lip—read
lip—reader
lip service
lip-stick

li-quate
li-qua-tion
liq-ue-fac-tion
liq-ue-fi-abil-ity
liq-ue-fi-able
liq-ue-fier
liq-ue-fy
li-queur (sweet,
  alcoholic drink)
cf. li-quor (any
  alcoholic drink)
liq-uid
liq-ui-date
liq-ui-da-tion
liq-ui-da-tor
li-quid-ity
liq-uid-ize
li-quor (any
  alcoholic drink)
  cf. li-queur (sweet,
  alcoholic drink)
lira
lisp
lis-some
or lis-som
list
lis-ten
lis-tener
lit
lit-any
li-ter
lit-er-acy
lit-eral
lit-er-al-ism
lit-er-ar-i-ness
lit-er-ary

lit-er-ate
lit-er-a-tion
lit-er-a-ture
lithe
lithe-some
litho-graph
li-tho-gra-pher
litho-graphic
li-thog-ra-phy
litho-sphere
lit-i-gant
lit-i-ga-ble
lit-i-gate
lit-i-ga-tion
li-ti-gious
lit-mus
lit-ter
lit-ter-a-teur
lit-ter-bag
lit-ter-bug
lit-terer
lit-ter-mate
lit-tle
lit-tler
lit-tlest
or least
Little League
lit-to-ral
li-tur-gi-cal
lit-ur-gist
liv-abil-ity
or live-abil-ity
liv-able
or live-able
live
live—in *(adj.)*

Do not divide one-syllable words. Divide words by syllables, but leave at least two letters of the word on the first line and three letters on the following line. For additional guidelines, see page ix.

live-lier	lobe	loft-i-ness
live-li-est	lo-bot-omy	lofty
live-li-hood	lob-ster	log
live-long	lo-cal *(adj.)*	log-a-rithm
liver	*cf.* lo-cale *(n.)*	logged
liv-er-ies	lo-cal-ism	log-ger
liv-er-wurst	lo-cal-i-ties	log-ger-head
liv-ery	lo-cal-ity	log-ging
live-stock	lo-cal-iza-tion	logic
live wire	lo-cal-ize	log-i-cal
livid	lo-cate	lo-gi-cian
li-vid-ity	lo-ca-tion	lo-gis-tic
liv-ing room	lo-ca-tor	loin
liv-ing stan-dard	loc cit	loin-cloth
living wage	loci	loi-ter
liz-ard	lock	loll
llama	locked—in *(adj.)*	lol-li-pop
load (pile on)	locker	*or* lol-ly-pop
cf. lode (vein of metal)	locket	lone
loader	lock jaw	lone-lier
loaf	lock-out	lone-li-est
loafer	lock-smith	lone-li-ness
loam	lockup	loner
loan	loco	lone wolf
loath	lo-co-mo-tion	long
or loathe (unwilling)	lo-co-mo-tive	longer
cf. loathe (hate)	lo-cus	long—distance
loather	lo-cust	lon-gev-ity
loath-some	lode (vein of metal)	long-hair *(n.)*
loaves *(n. pl.)*	*cf.* load (pile on)	long—hair
lob	lodge	*or* long—haired *(adj.)*
lobbed	lodger	long-hand
lob-bied	loess	long haul *(n.)*
lob-bing	loft	long—haul *(adj.)*
lobby	loft-ier	long-horn
lob-by-ist	loft-i-est	long-house

Plural, past tense, adverbial, and noun derivatives formed by adding *s, d* or *ed, ly, ness, ment, ful, less,* or *ing* to an unchanged root word are not listed, nor are words formed by dropping the final *e* and adding *ing*.

109

long-ish	lo-qua-cious	love
lon-gi-tude	lo-quac-ity	love affair
lon-gi-tu-di-nal	lo-ran	love beads
long johns *(n.)*	lord	love-bird
long—lived *(adj.)*	lore	love feast
long—playing *(adj.)*	lor-gnette	love—in *(n.)*
long—range *(adj.)*	lor-ries	love knot
long-shore-man	lorry	love-lier
long shot *(n.)*	lose (fail to keep)	love-li-est
lòng—standing *(adj.)*	*cf.* loose (not tight)	love-li-ness
long—suffering *(n.) (adj.)*	los-a-ble	lover
long—term *(adj.)*	loser	love seat
long—winded *(adj.)*	loss	love-sick
look	lost	loving cup
look—alike *(n.)*	lot	loving—kindness
looker—on	lo-thario	low
look-out	lo-tion	low-born
loom	lot-ter-ies	low-brow
loon	lot-tery	low—down *(adj.)*
loony	lo-tus	lower
or loo-ney	loud	low-est
loop	loud-mouth	low—grade *(adj.)*
loop-hole	loud-speaker	low—key
loose (not tight)	lounge	*or* low—keyed *(adj.)*
cf. lose (fail to keep)	lounger	low-land
loose—jointed *(adj.)*	louse	low-lier
loose—leaf *(adj.)*	lous-ier	low-li-est
loosen	lous-i-est	low-li-ness
looser	lousy	loyal
loot	lout	loy-al-ist
lop	lout-ish	loy-al-ties
lope	lou-ver	loy-alty
lop—eared *(adj.)*	*or* lou-vre	loz-enge
lopped	lov-able	lub-ber
lop-ping	*or* love-able	lu-bri-cant
lop-sided	lov-ably	lu-bri-cate

110   Do not divide one-syllable words. Divide words by syllables, but leave at least two letters of the word on the first line and three letters on the following line. For additional guidelines, see page ix.

lu-bri-ca-tion	**lu-mi-nes-cence**	**lurk**
lu-bri-ca-tor	**lu-mi-nes-cent**	**lurker**
lu-bri-cious	**lu-mi-nif-er-ous**	**lus-cious**
lu-bri-to-rium	**lu-mi-nist**	**lush**
lu-cent	**lu-mi-nos-i-ties**	**lust**
lu-cid	**lu-mi-nos-ity**	**lus-ter**
lu-cid-ity	**lu-mi-nous**	*or* **lus-tre**
Lu-ci-fer	**lum-mox**	**lus-ter-ware**
luck	**lump**	**lus-trate**
luck-ier	**lump-ier**	**lus-tra-tion**
luck-i-est	**lump-i-est**	**lus-trous**
luck-ily	**lump-i-ness**	**lute**
luck-i-ness	**lumpy**	**lu-te-nist**
lucky	**lu-na-cies**	*or* **lu-ta-nist**
lu-cra-tive	**lu-nacy**	**Lu-theran**
lu-cre	**lu-nar**	**lux**
lu-di-crous	**lu-nar eclipse** *(n.)*	**lux-ate**
lug	**lu-nate**	**lux-a-tion**
lug-gage	**lu-na-tic**	**lux-u-ri-ance**
lugged	**lu-na-tion**	**lux-u-ri-ant**
lug-ging	**lunch**	**lux-u-ri-ate**
lu-gu-bri-ous	**lun-cheon**	**lux-u-ri-ous**
luke-warm	**lun-cheon-ette**	**lux-u-ries**
lull	**lunch-room**	**lux-ury**
lul-la-bied	**lunch-time**	**ly-cée**
lul-laby	**lu-nette**	**ly-ceum**
lum-bago	**lung**	**lye** (strong alkaline solution)
lum-bar	**lunge**	*cf.* **lie** (falsehood)
lum-ber	**lung-fish**	**lymph**
lum-berer	**lu-ni-so-lar**	**lym-phoid**
lum-ber-jack	**lu-ni-tidal**	**lynch**
lum-ber-man	**lurch**	**lynch law**
lu-men	**lurcher**	**lynx**
lu-mi-naire	**lure**	**lyre** (stringed instrument)
lu-mi-nance	**lurer**	*cf.* **liar** (fibber)
lu-mi-nary	**lu-rid**	**lyric**

Plural, past tense, adverbial, and noun derivatives formed by adding *s*, *d* or *ed*, *ly*, *ness*, *ment*, *ful*, *less*, or *ing* to an unchanged root word are not listed, nor are words formed by dropping the final *e* and adding *ing*. 111

lyr-i-cal
lyr-i-cism
lyr-i-cist
lyr-ist

M

ma-ca-bre
mac-adam
mac-ad-am-ize
mac-a-roni
mace
mac-er-ate
mac-er-a-tion
mac-er-a-tor
mach
ma-chete
Ma-chi-a-vel-lian
mach-i-nate
mach-i-na-tion
mach-i-na-tor
ma-chine
ma-chine gun
ma-chinery
ma-chine shop
ma-chine tool
ma-chin-ist
mack-erel
mack-i-naw
mack-in-tosh
or mac-in-tosh
mac-rame

macro
mac-ro-cosm
mac-ro-cos-mic
mac-ro-eco-nom-ics
mac-ro-scopic
mad
madam
ma-dame
mad-cap
mad-den
mad-der
made (built)
   cf. **maid** (servant)
mad-e-moi-selle
ma-de-moi-selles
   or mes-de-moi-selles
   (n. pl.)
made—up *(adj.)*
mad-house
mad-man
Ma-donna
mad-ri-gal
ma-dri-lene
mad-woman
mael-strom
maestros
   or mae-stri *(n. pl.)*
Ma-fia
ma-fi-oso
mag-a-zine
mag-got
magic
mag-i-cal
mag-is-te-rial
mag-is-trate
Magna Charta
   or **Magna Carta**

magna cum laude
mag-na-nim-i-ties
mag-na-nim-ity
mag-nan-i-mous
mag-nate (important person)
   cf. **mag-net** (attracts)
mag-ne-sia
mag-ne-sium
mag-net (attracts)
   cf. **mag-nate**
   (important person)
mag-netic
mag-ne-tism
mag-ne-ti-za-tion
mag-ne-tize
mag-ne-tizer
mag-neto
mag-ne-tom-e-ter
mag-nific
mag-ni-fi-ca-tion
mag-nif-i-cence
mag-nif-i-cent
mag-nif-ico
mag-nif-i-coes
   or mag-nif-i-cos *(n. pl.)*
mag-ni-fied
mag-ni-fier
mag-nify
mag-ni-tude
mag-num
ma-ha-raja
   or ma-ha-ra-jah (male)
ma-ha-rani
   or ma-ha-ra-nee (female)
ma-hog-any
maid (servant)
   cf. **made** (built)

Do not divide one-syllable words. Divide words by syllables, but leave at least two letters of the word on the first line and three letters on the following line. For additional guidelines, see page ix.

maiden
maid-en-hood
maid—in—waiting
maids—in—waiting
 (n. pl.)
maid-ser-vant
mail (letters)
 cf. male (man)
mail-abil-ity
mail-able
mailbag
mail-box
mail-man
mail or-der *(n.)*
mail—order house
maim
main (chief)
 cf. mane (horse hair)
main-land
main-line
main-mast
main-spring
main-stay
main-stream
main-tain
main-tain-abil-ity
main-tain-able
main-tainer
main-te-nance
main-top
mai-son-ette
mai-tre d'
mai-tre d'hô-tel
maitres d'hô-tel *(n. pl.)*
ma-jes-tic
maize (corn)
 cf. maze (passage)

maj-es-ties
maj-esty
ma-jor
major—domo
ma-jor-i-ties
ma-jor-ity
make
make—do *(adj.)*
make-ready
make-shift
make-up *(n.)*
mal-ad-ap-ta-tion
mal-adapted
mal-adap-tive
mal-ad-justed
mal-ad-jus-tive
mal-ad-just-ment
mal-a-dies
mal-adroit
mal-ady
mal-aise
mal-ap-ro-pos
ma-laria
ma-lar-key
mal-con-tent
mal de mer
male (man)
 cf. mail
 (letters)
male-dic-tion
male-dic-tory
male-fac-tion
male-fac-tor
ma-lefic
ma-lef-i-cence
ma-lef-i-cent
ma-lev-o-lence

ma-lev-o-lent
mal-fea-sance
mal-for-ma-tion
mal-formed
mal-func-tion
mal-ice
ma-li-cious
ma-lign
ma-lig-nance
ma-lig-nan-cies
ma-lig-nancy
ma-lig-nant
ma-lig-nity
ma-lin-ger
ma-lin-gerer
mall (shaded walk)
 cf. maul
 (handle roughly)
mal-lard
mal-lea-bil-ity
mal-lea-ble
mal-let
mal-nour-ished
mal-nu-tri-tion
mal-odor
mal-odor-ous
mal-po-si-tion
mal-prac-tice
mal-prac-ti-tio-ner
malt
Mal-thu-sian
malt-ose
mal-treat
mam-mal
mam-mary
mam-moth
man

Plural, past tense, adverbial, and noun derivatives formed by adding
s, d or *ed, ly, ness, ment, ful, less,* or *ing* to an unchanged root word are
not listed, nor are words formed by dropping the final *e* and adding *ing.*

113

man—about—town (n.)
man-a-cle
man-age
man-age-abil-ity
man-age-able
man-age-ably
man-ager
man-a-ge-rial
man—at—arms
man-da-rin
man-date
man-da-tor
man-da-tory
man-do-lin
man-drel
or man-dril
mane (horse hair)
 cf. main (chief)
man—eater
ma-nege
or ma-nège
ma-neu-ver
ma-neu-ver-abil-ity
ma-neu-ver-able
ma-neu-verer
man Friday (n.)
man-ga-nate
man-ga-nese
mange
man-ger
mang-ier
mang-i-est
man-gle
man-gler
man-han-dle
man-hole

man-hood
man—hour
man-hunt
ma-nia
ma-niac
ma-ni-a-cal
man-i-cure
man-i-cur-ist
man-i-fest
man-i-fes-tant
man-i-fes-ta-tion
man-i-festo
man-i-fes-tos
or man-i-fes-toes
man-i-fold
man-i-kin
or man-ni-kin
ma-nila
or ma-nilla
ma-nip-u-la-bil-ity
ma-nip-u-la-ble
ma-nip-u-lat-able
ma-nip-u-late
ma-nip-u-la-tion
ma-nip-u-la-tive
ma-nip-u-la-tor
ma-nip-u-la-tory
man-kind
man—made
man-ne-quin
man-ner
man-ner-ism
man—of—war (n.)
manor
man power (n.)
 or manpower

manse
man-ser-vant
man-sion
man—size
 or man—sized
man-slaugh-ter
man-tel
man-tel-piece
man-tilla
man-tle
man—to—man (adj.)
man-ual
man-u-fac-ture
man-u-fac-turer
manu-script
many
many-fold (adv.)
many—sided (adj.)
Mao-ism
Mao-ist
map
ma-ple
map-maker
map-ping
ma-raca
mar-a-schino
mar-a-thon
ma-raud
ma-rauder
mar-ble
mar-ble-ize
mar-bly
march
marcher
mar-chesa (female)
mar-chese (male)

Do not divide one-syllable words. Divide words by syllables, but leave at least two letters of the word on the first line and three letters on the following line. For additional guidelines, see page ix.

mar-chio-ness
Mardi Gras
mare
mar-ga-rine
mar-gin
mar-ginal
mar-i-juana
or mar-i-huana
ma-rimba
ma-rina
mar-i-nate
ma-rine
mar-i-ner
mar-i-o-nette
mar-i-tal
mar-i-time
mark
mark-down
marker
mar-ket
mar-ket-able
mar-keter
mar-ket-place
marks-man
markup
marl
mar-ma-lade
mar-mo-real
ma-roon
mar-quee
mar-quess
or mar-quis
mar-quesses
or mar-quises
mar-riage
mar-riage-able

mar-ried
mar-row
marry
Mars
marsh
mar-shal (sheriff)
  cf. mar-tial (warlike)
marsh-land
marsh-mal-low
marsh-ier
marsh-i-est
marshy
mar-su-pial
mart
mar-tial (warlike)
  cf. mar-shal (sheriff)
mar-tian
mar-ti-net
mar-tyr
mar-tyr-dom
mar-vel
mar-veled
or mar-velled
mar-vel-ous
or mar-vel-lous
Marx-ian
Marx-ism
Marx-ist
mas-cara
mas-cu-line
mas-cu-lin-ity
mash
mask (disguise)
  cf. masque (dramatic
  (play)
mas-och-ism

mas-och-ist
mas-och-is-tic
Mason—Dixon line
Ma-sonic
masque (dramatic play)
  cf. mask (disguise)
mas-quer-ade
mass
mas-sa-cre
mas-sa-crer
mas-sage
mass com-mu-ni-ca-tion
mas-seur (male)
mas-seuse (female)
mas-sive
mass me-dium
mass me-dia (n. pl.)
mast
mas-tec-tomy
mas-ter
master—at—arms
masters—at—arms (n. pl.)
mas-ter bath
mas-ter bed-room
mas-ter-piece
mas-ter plan
mas-tery
mas-tic
mas-ti-cate
mas-ti-ca-tion
mas-ti-ca-tor
mas-tiff
mast-odon
mas-toid
mat
mat-a-dor

Plural, past tense, adverbial, and noun derivatives formed by adding
s, d or *ed, ly, ness, ment, ful, less,* or *ing* to an unchanged root word are
not listed, nor are words formed by dropping the final *e* and adding *ing*.

match
matcher
match-book
match-maker
mate
ma-te-rial
ma-te-ri-al-ism
ma-te-ri-al-iza-tion
ma-te-ri-al-ize
ma-té-riel
or ma-te-riel
ma-ter-nal
ma-ter-ni-ties
ma-ter-nity
math
math-e-mat-ics
math-e-mat-i-cal
math-e-ma-ti-cian
math-e-ma-ti-za-tion
mat-i-nee
or mat-i-née
ma-tri-arch
ma-tri-ar-chal
ma-tri-ar-chies
ma-tri-ar-chy
ma-tri-cidal
ma-tri-cide
ma-tric-u-late
ma-tric-u-lant
ma-tric-u-la̧-tion
ma-tri-lin-eal
mat-ri-mo-nial
mat-ri-mony
ma-trix
ma-tri-ces *(n. pl.)*
ma-tron

mat-ted
mat-ter
matter—of—fact *(adj.)*
mat-ting
mat-tock
mat-tress
mat-u-rate
mat-u-ra-tion
mat-u-ra-tional
ma-tur-a-tive
ma-ture
ma-turer
ma-tu-rity
ma-tu-ti-nal
matzo
mat-zoth *(n. pl.)*
maud-lin
maul (handle roughly)
   cf. mall (shaded walk)
mau-so-leum
mav-er-ick
mawk-ish
maxi-coat
maxim
max-i-mi-za-tion
max-i-mize
max-i-mizer
max-i-mum
max-i-mums
   or max-ima *(n. pl.)*
maxi-skirt
may
maybe
May-day (S.O.S.)
   cf. May Day (May 1)
may-hem

may-on-naise
mayor
may-oral
may-or-alty
may-or-ess
may-pole
maze (passage)
   cf. maize (corn)
meadow
mead-ow-land
mead-ow-lark
mea-ger
   or mea-gre
meal
meal-time
mealy-mouthed
mean
me-an-der
meant
mean-time
mean-while
mea-sles
mea-slier
mea-sli-est
mea-sly
mea-sur-abil-ity
mea-sur-able
mea-sur-ably
mea-sure
mea-surer
meat (food)
   cf. meet (come face to face)
   cf. mete (allot)
meat-ball
meat by—product *(n.)*
meat-ier

Do not divide one-syllable words. Divide words by syllables, but leave at least two letters of the word on the first line and three letters on the following line. For additional guidelines, see page ix.

mecca
me-chanic
me-chan-i-cal
mech-a-ni-cian
mech-a-nism
mech-a-nist
mech-a-nis-tic
mech-a-ni-za-tion
mech-a-nize
medal (flat piece of metal)
  cf. med-dle (interfere)
med-al-ist
  or med-al-list
me-dal-lic
me-dal-lion
med-dle (interfere)
  cf. medal (flat piece of metal)
me-dia
me-dial
me-dian
me-di-ant
me-di-ate
me-di-a-tion
me-di-a-tive
me-di-a-tor
me-di-a-tory
me-di-a-tress
medic
med-i-cal
med-i-cate
med-i-ca-tion
med-i-care
me-dic-i-nal
med-i-cine
med-ico

me-di-eval
  or me-di-ae-val
me-di-eval-ism
me-di-eval-ist
me-di-o-cre
me-di-oc-ri-ties
me-di-oc-rity
med-i-tate
med-i-ta-tion
med-i-ta-tive
med-i-ta-tor
Med-i-ter-ra-nean
me-dium
me-di-ums (n. pl.)
  or me-dia
med-ley
meek
meer-schaum
meet (come face to face)
  cf. meat (food)
  cf. mete (allot)
mega-cy-cle
meg-a-lo-ma-nia
meg-a-lo-ma-niac
meg-a-lo-ma-ni-a-cal
meg-a-lop-o-lis
mega-phone
mega-ton
mel-an-cho-lia
mel-an-cho-liac
mel-an-cholic
mel-an-chol-ies
mel-an-choly
mel-a-noma
melba toast
meld

me-lee
me-lio-rate
me-lio-ra-tion
me-lio-ra-tive
me-lio-rism
me-lio-rist
mel-low
me-lo-deon
me-lodic
me-lo-di-ous
mel-o-dist
mel-o-dize
melo-drama
melo-dra-matic
melo-dra-ma-tize
mel-o-dies
mel-ody
melon
melt
melt-able
mem-ber
mem-ber-ship
mem-brane
mem-bra-nous
me-mento
me-men-tos (n. pl.)
  or me-men-toes
memo
mem-oir
mem-o-ra-bilia
mem-o-ra-bil-ity
mem-o-ra-ble
mem-o-ra-bly
mem-o-ran-dum
mem-o-randa (n. pl.)
  or mem-o-ran-dums

Plural, past tense, adverbial, and noun derivatives formed by adding
s, d or ed, ly, ness, ment, ful, less, or ing to an unchanged root word are
not listed, nor are words formed by dropping the final e and adding ing.

117

me-mo-rial	mer-ci-ful	mes-sage
me-mo-ri-al-ist	mer-ci-less	mes-sen-ger
me-mo-ri-al-ize	mer-cury	mess hall *(n.)*
mem-o-ri-za-tion	mercy	mes-siah
mem-o-ries	mere	mess kit *(n.)*
mem-o-rize	merge	Messrs. *(n. pl.)*
mem-o-rizer	merger	mess-mate
mem-ory	me-rid-ian	messy
men-ace	me-ringue	mes-tizo
me-nag-erie	me-rino	met
mend	merit	me-tab-o-lism
men-da-cious	mer-i-toc-racy	metal (substance)
men-dac-ity	mer-it-ocratic	*cf.* **met-tle** (courage)
mender	mer-i-to-ri-ous	me-tal-lic
me-nial	mer-maid	met-al-lur-gi-cal
men-in-gi-tis	mer-man	met-al-lur-gist
men-o-pause	mero-mor-phic	met-al-lurgy
men-strual	mer-rier	meta-mor-phic
men-stru-ate	mer-ri-est	meta-mor-phism
men-stru-a-tion	mer-rily	meta-mor-phose
men-tal	mer-ri-ment	meta-mor-pho-ses *(n. pl.)*
men-tal-i-ties	merry	meta-mor-pho-sis
men-tal-ity	merry—go—round *(n.)*	met-a-phor
men-tion	mer-ry-mak-ing *(n.)*	meta-physic
men-tion-able	mesa	meta-phys-i-cal
men-tor	mes-cal	meta-plasm
menu	mes-ca-line	meta-plas-mic
mer-can-tile	mes-dames *(n. pl.)*	meta-psy-chol-ogy
mer-can-til-ism	mesh	me-tas-ta-sis
mer-ce-nar-ies	mes-mer-ism	me-tas-ta-size
mer-ce-nary	mes-mer-ize	meta-tar-sus
mer-chan-dise	mes-mer-izer	meta-zoan
mer-chant	me-so-morph	mete (allot)
mer-cu-rial	me-so-mor-phic	*cf.* **meat** (food)
mer-cury	Me-so-zoic	*cf.* **meet** (come face to face)
mer-cies	mes-quite	me-teor

Do not divide one-syllable words. Divide words by syllables, but leave
at least two letters of the word on the first line and three letters on the
following line. For additional guidelines, see page ix.

118

me-te-oric	mica	mi-cro-reader
me-te-or-ite	mi-cro	mi-cro-scale
me-te-or-oid	mi-crobe	mi-cro-scope
me-te-o-ro-log-i-cal	mi-cro-beam	mi-cro-scopic
me-te-o-rol-o-gist	mi-cro-bi-o-logic	mi-cro-sec-ond
me-te-o-rol-ogy	mi-cro-bi-o-log-i-cal	mi-cro-spec-tro-pho-tom-e-*
me-ter	mi-cro-bi-ol-o-gist	mi-cro-sphere
me-ter maid *(n.)*	mi-cro-bi-ol-ogy	mi-cro-sur-gery
meth-a-done	mi-cro-bus	mi-cro-wave
meth-a-nol	mi-cro-cap-sule	mid
method	Mi-cro-card	mid-air
me-thod-i-cal	mi-cro-cir-cuit	Mi-das
or me-thodic	mi-cro-code	mid-day
meth-od-ism	mi-cro-copy	mid-dle
Meth-od-ist	mi-cro-cosm	mid-dle—aged *(adj.)*
meth-od-olog-i-cal	mi-cro-cos-mic	mid-dle—class *(adj.)*
meth-od-ol-o-gist	mi-cro-cul-ture	mid-dle ear *(n.)*
meth-od-ol-ogy	mi-cro-den-si-tom-e-ter	mid-dle-man
Me-thu-se-lah	mi-cro-eco-nom-ics	middle—of-the—road *(adj.)*
me-tic-u-lous	mi-cro-elec-trode	mid-dle-weight
met-ric	mi-cro-elec-tron-ics	middy
met-ri-cal	mi-cro-fiche	mid-field
met-ric sys-tem *(n.)*	mi-cro-fiche *(n. pl.)*	midget
met-ro-nome	*or* mi-cro-fiches	midi
me-trop-o-lis	mi-cro-film	mid-land
met-tle (courage)	mi-cro-groove	mid-night
cf. metal (substance)	mi-cro-inch	mid-point
mew	mi-crom-e-ter (instrument)	mid-riff
Mex-i-can	*cf.* mi-cro-me-ter (length)	mid-sec-tion
me-zu-zah	mi-cro-or-gan-ism	mid-ship-man
or me-zuza	mi-cro-phone	midst
mez-za-nine	mi-cro-phon-ics	mid-stream
mezza voce	mi-cro-pho-tog-ra-phy	mid-sum-mer
mezzo	mi-cro-phys-ics	mid-town
mezzo forte	mi-cro-print	mid-way
mezzo—soprano	mi-cro-pro-gram-ming	mid-week

Plural, past tense, adverbial, and noun derivatives formed by adding
s, d or *ed, ly, ness, ment, ful, less,* or *ing* to an unchanged root word are
not listed, nor are words formed by dropping the final *e* and adding *ing*.

mid-wife	mil-i-tary	mim-icked
mid-win-ter	mil-i-tate	mim-ic-ries
mid-year	mi-li-tia	mim-icry
might (power)	milk	min-able
cf. mite (anything very small)	milk-fish	*or* mine-able
	milk glass *(n.)*	mince
might-ier	milk-maid	mincer
might-i-est	milk-man	mince-meat
might-i-ness	milk shake *(n.)*	mince pie
mighty	milk-sop	mind
mi-graine	milk-weed	mind—blowing *(adj.)*
mi-grant	mill (grinder)	mind—expanding *(adj.)*
mi-grate	*cf.* mil (unit of length)	mine
mi-gra-tion	mil-le-nar-ian	miner
mi-gra-tional	mil-le-nary	mine-layer
mi-gra-tor	mil-len-nium	min-eral
mi-gra-tory	mil-len-nia *(n. pl.)*	min-er-al-iz-able
mi-kado	*or* mil-len-ni-ums	min-er-al-iza-tion
mike	miller	min-er-al-ize
mil (unit of length)	mil-let	min-er-al-izer
cf. mill (grinder)	mil-li-gram	min-er-al-og-i-cal
mild	mil-li-me-ter	min-er-al-o-gist
mil-dew	mil-li-mi-cron	min-er-al-ogy
mile	mil-li-nery	min-e-strone
mile-age	mil-lion	mine-sweeper
miler	mil-lions *(n. pl.)*	min-gle
mile-post	*or* mil-lion	mini
mile-stone	mil-lion-aire	min-ia-ture
mi-lieu	mil-lion-air-ess	min-ia-tur-iza-tion
mil-i-tant	mil-li-roent-gen	min-ia-tur-ize
mil-i-tancy	mil-li-sec-ond	mini-bike
mil-i-tarily	mill-pond	mini-bus
mil-i-ta-rism	mill-stone	mini-car
mil-i-ta-ris-tic	mill-wright	mini-com-puter
mil-i-ta-ri-za-tion	mim-eo-graph	min-i-mal
mil-i-ta-rize	mimic	mini-max

Do not divide one-syllable words. Divide words by syllables, but leave at least two letters of the word on the first line and three letters on the following line. For additional guidelines, see page ix.

min-i-mi-za-tion
min-i-mize
min-i-mizer
min-i-mum
min-i-ma *(n. pl.)*
or min-i-mums
min-i-mum wage
min-ion
min-is-cule
mini-skirt
mini-state
min-is-ter
min-is-te-rial
min-is-trant
min-is-tra-tion
min-is-tries
min-is-try
mini-track
mink
min-now
mi-nor
mi-nor-i-ties
mi-nor-ity
Mi-no-taur
min-strel
mint
mint-age
min-u-end
min-uet
mi-nus
mi-nus-cule
min-ute (time)
cf. mi-nute (small)
min-ute-man
mi-nu-tia
mi-nu-tiae *(n. pl.)*

minx
mir-a-cle
mi-rac-u-lous
mi-rage
mire
mirk
mir-ror
mirth
mis-ad-ven-ture
mis-aligned
mis-al-li-ance
mis-ap-pli-ca-tion
mis-ap-ply
mis-ap-pre-hend
mis-ap-pre-hen-sion
mis-ap-pro-pri-ate
mis-ap-pro-pri-a-tion
mis-be-got-ten
mis-be-have
mis-be-hav-ior
mis-be-lieve
mis-cal-cu-late
mis-cal-cu-la-tion
mis-car-riage
mis-car-ried
mis-carry
mis-cast
mis-ce-ge-na-tion
mis-cel-la-nea
mis-cel-la-neous
mis-cel-la-nies
mis-cel-lany
mis-chance
mis-chief
mis-chie-vous
mis-clas-sify

mis-con-ceive
mis-con-cep-tion
mis-con-duct
mis-con-struc-tion
mis-con-strue
mis-count
mis-cre-ant
mis-deal
mis-deed
mis-de-meanor
miser
mis-er-a-ble
mis-er-a-bly
mis-er-ies
mis-ery
mis-fea-sance
mis-file
mis-fire
mis-for-tune
mis-give
mis-gov-ern
mis-guide
mis-han-dle
mis-hap
mish-mash
mis-in-form
mis-in-ter-pret
mis-in-ter-pre-ta-tion
mis-judge
mis-la-bel
mis-lay
mis-man-age
mis-no-mer
mi-sog-a-mist
mi-sog-amy
mis-place

Plural, past tense, adverbial, and noun derivatives formed by adding
s, d or *ed, ly, ness, ment, ful, less,* or *ing* to an unchanged root word are
not listed, nor are words formed by dropping the final *e* and adding *ing*.

121

mis-play
mis-print
mis-pri-son
mis-pro-nounce
mis-pro-nun-ci-a-tion
mis-quote
mis-read
mis-rule
miss
mis-sal (book)
  cf. **mis-sile** (rocket)
missed (failed to find)
  cf. **mist** (fog)
mis-shape
mis-shapen
mis-sile·(rocket)
  cf. **mis-sal** (book)
mis-sion
mis-sion-ar-ies
mis-sion-ary
mis-sive
mis-spell
mis-spend
mis-spent
mis-state
mis-step
mist (fog)
  cf. **missed** (failed to find)
mis-tak-able
mis-take
mis-taken
mis-ter
mis-time
mis-tle-toe
mis-took

mis-trans-late
mis-treat
mis-tress
mis-trial
mis-trust
mis-un-der-stand
mis-us-age
mis-use
mite (anything very small)
  cf. **might** (power)
mi-ter
  or **mi-tre**
mit-i-gate
mit-i-ga-tion
mitt
mit-ten
mitz-vah
mitz-voth *(n. pl.)*
mix
mixed—media
mixed—up *(adj.)*
mixer
mix-ture
mne-monic
moan
moat
mob
mobbed
mo-bile
mo-bile home *(n.)*
mo-bil-ity
mo-bi-li-za-tion
mo-bi-lize
mob-ster
moc-ca-sin
mock

mocker
mock-ery
mock—up *(n.)*
mod
modal (statistical figure)
  cf. **model** (a plan)
mode
mod-er-ate
mod-er-a-tion
mod-er-a-tor
mod-ern
mod-ern-ist
mod-ern-is-tic
mod-ern-iza-tion
mod-ern-ize
mod-est
mod-esty
mod-i-cum
mod-i-fi-ca-tion
mod-i-fier
mod-ish
mod-u-la-bil-ity
mod-u-lar
mod-u-late
mod-u-la-tion
mod-u-la-tor
mod-u-la-tory
mod-ule
mo-dus ope-randi
modi ope-randi *(n. pl.)*
mo-hair
Mo-ham-medan
moist
moisten
mois-ture
mo-lar

Do not divide one-syllable words. Divide words by syllables, but leave
at least two letters of the word on the first line and three letters on the
following line. For additional guidelines, see page ix.

mo-las-ses
mold
mold-able
molder
mold-ier
mold-i-est
moldy
mole
mo-lec-u-lar
mo-lec-u-lar-ity
mol-e-cule
mole-hill
mo-lest
mo-les-ta-tion
mo-lester
mol-li-fi-ca-tion
mol-lify
mol-lusk
or mol-lusc
molly-cod-dle
molt
mol-ten
mo-lyb-de-num
mo-ment
mo-men-tarily
mo-men-tary
mo-mento
mo-men-tous
mo-men-tum
mo-menta *(n. pl.)*
or mo-men-tums
mon-arch
mo-nar-chal
or mo-nar-chial
mo-nar-chi-cal
or mo-nar-chic

mon-ar-chies
mon-ar-chist
mon-ar-chis-tic
mon-ar-chy
mon-as-te-rial
mon-as-tery
mo-nas-tic
mo-nas-ti-cism
mon-atomic
mon-au-ral
mon-ax-ial
mon-es-trous
mon-e-tar-ily
mon-e-tary
mon-e-ti-za-tion
mon-e-tize
money
moneys *(n. pl.)*
or mon-ies
mon-ey-lender
mon-ey—maker *(n.)*
mon-ger
Mon-gol
Mon-go-lian
mon-gol-ism
mon-goose
mon-gooses *(n. pl.)*
or mon-geese
mon-grel
mo-ni-tion
mon-i-tor
mon-i-to-rial
monk
mon-key
mon-key wrench *(n.)*
mono-chro-matic

mon-o-cle
mo-nog-a-mist
mo-nog-amy
mono-gram
mono-grammed
mono-graph
mo-nog-y-nous
mo-nog-yny
mono-lin-gual
mono-lith
mono-lithic
mono-logue
or mono-log
mono-logu-ist
or mo-no-lo-gist
mo-no-mial
mono-mor-phic
mono-nu-cle-o-sis
mono-pho-nic
mono-plane
mo-nop-o-list
mo-nop-o-lis-tic
mo-nop-o-lize
mo-nop-oly
mono-rail
mono-so-dium glu-ta-mate *(n.)*
mono-syl-labic
mono-syl-la-bic-ity
mono-syl-la-ble
mono-the-ism
mono-the-ist
mono-the-is-tic
or mono-the-is-ti-cal
mono-tone
mono-tonic
mo-not-o-nous

mo-not-ony	moose	Mor-mon
mono-type	moot	Mor-mon-ism
mon-ox-ide	mop	morn
mon-sei-gneur	mopped	morn-ing (dawn)
mes-sei-gneurs *(n. pl.)*	mop-pet	*cf.* mourn-ing (grief)
mon-sieur	mop-ping	mo-rocco
mon-si-gnor	mop—up *(n.)*	mo-ron
mon-si-gnors *(n. pl.)*	mop up *(v.)*	mo-rose
or mon-si-gnori	moral	mo-ros-ity
mon-soon	mo-rale	mor-phine
mon-ster	mor-al-ism	mor-row
mon-stros-i-ties	mor-al-ist	mor-sel
mon-stros-ity	mor-al-is-tic	mor-tal
mon-strous	mo-ral-i-ties	mor-tal-ity
mon-tage	mo-ral-ity	mor-tar
Mon-tes-so-rian	mor-al-iza-tion	mor-tar-board
month	mor-al-ize	mort-gage
mon-u-ment	mor-al-izer	mort-gagee
mon-u-men-tal	mor-a-to-rium	*or* mort-gager
mon-u-men-tal-ize	mor-a-to-ri-ums *(n. pl.)*	mor-ti-cian
mooch	*or* mor-a-to-ria	mor-ti-fi-ca-tion
mood	mo-ray	mor-ti-fied
mood-ier	mor-bid	mor-tify
mood-i-est	mor-bid-ity	mor-tise
moody	mor-da-cious	*or* mor-tice
moon	mor-dac-ity	mor-tu-ar-ies
moon-beam	mor-dancy	mor-tu-ary
moon-light	mor-dant	mo-saic
moon-lit	more (greater)	Mos-lem
moon shot *(n.)*	*cf.* moor (land)	mosque
or moon shoot	more or less *(adv.)*	mos-quito
moon-stone	more-over	mos-qui-toes *(n. pl.)*
moon-struck	mo-res	*or* mos-qui-tos
moor (land)	morgue	moss
cf. more (greater)	mor-i-bund	moss-back
moor-age	mor-i-bun-dity	

Do not divide one-syllable words. Divide words by syllables, but leave
at least two letters of the word on the first line and three letters on the
following line. For additional guidelines, see page ix.

124

moss-ier	mo-tor home	mouth
moss-i-est	mo-tor inn	mouth-piece
mossy	mo-tor-ist	mouth—to—mouth *(adj.)*
most	mo-tor-iza-tion	mou-ton
mote	mo-tor-ize	mov-able
mo-tel	mo-tor lodge	*or* move-able
moth	mo-tor-man	mover
moth-ball	mo-tor pool	movie
moth—eaten *(adj.)*	mo-tor scooter	mov-ie-dom
mother	mo-tor-truck	mov-ie-goer
moth-er-hood	mo-tor ve-hi-cle	mov-ie-maker
moth-er-house	mot-tle	mow
mother—in—law	motto	Mr.
mothers—in—law *(n. pl.)*	mot-toes *(n. pl.)*	Mrs.
moth-er-land	*or* mot-tos	Ms.
moth-er-li-ness	mound	much
mother—of—pearl *(n.)*	mount	mu-cif-er-ous
moth-proof	moun-tain	mu-ci-lage
mo-tif (subject)	moun-tain ash	mu-ci-lag-i-nous
cf. mo-tive (reason)	moun-tain dew	muck
mo-tile	moun-tain-eer	muck-rake
mo-tion	moun-tain-ous	mu-cous
mo-ti-vate	moun-tain-side	mud
mo-ti-va-tion	moun-tain-top	mud-dier
mo-ti-va-tor	moun-te-bank	mud-di-est
mo-tive (reason)	mourn	muddy
cf. mo-tif (subject)	mourn-ing (grief)	mud-guard
mot-ley	*cf.* morn-ing (dawn)	mud-slinger
mo-tor	mourner	muff
mo-tor-bike	mouse	muf-fin
mo-tor-boat	mouse-trap	muf-fle
mo-tor bus	mous-saka	muf-fler
mo-tor-cade	mousse	mug
mo-tor-car	mous-tache	mugged
mo-tor court	mousy	mug-ger
mo-tor-cy-cle	*or* mousey	Mu-ham-madan

Plural, past tense, adverbial, and noun derivatives formed by adding
s, d or *ed, ly, ness, ment, ful, less,* or *ing* to an unchanged root word are
not listed, nor are words formed by dropping the final *e* and adding *ing*.

Mu-ham-mad-an-ism
muk-luk
mu-latto
mu-lat-toes
or mu-lat-tos
mul-berry
mulch
mule
mu·le-teer
mul-ish
mull
mul-let
mul-ti-col-ored
mul-ti-cul-tural
mul-ti-di-men-sional
mul-ti-di-rec-tional
mul-ti-dis-ci-plin-ary
mul-ti-fac-eted
mul-ti-far-i-ous
mul-ti-lat-eral
mul-ti-lay-ered
mul-ti-level
or mul-ti-lev-eled
mul-ti-lin-gual
mul-ti-lin-gual-ism
mul-ti-me-dia
mul-ti-mil-lion-aire
mul-ti-nu-clear
mul-ti-par-tite
mul-ti-party
mul-ti-phase
mul-ti-pha-sic
mul-ti-ple
mul-ti-plex
mul-ti-pli-able
mul-ti-plic-a-ble

mul-ti-pli-cand
mul-ti-pli-cate
mul-ti-pli-ca-tion
mul-ti-pli-ca-tive
mul-ti-plic-i-ties
mul-ti-plic-ity
mul-ti-plier
mul-ti-ply
mul-ti-po-lar
mul-ti-pro-cess-ing
mul-ti-pro-ces-sor
mul-ti-pro-gram-ming
mul-ti-pronged
mul-ti-pur-pose
mul-ti-ra-cial
mul-ti-sen-sory
mul-ti-stage
mul-ti-sto-ried
mul-ti-story
mul-ti-syl-labic
mul-ti-tude
mul-ti-tu-di-nous
mul-tiv-a-lence
mul-ti-va-lent
mul-ti-val-ued
mul-ti-var-i-ate
mum
mum-ble
mum-bler
mumbo jumbo
mum-mer
mum-mi-fi-ca-tion
mum-mi-fied
mum-mify
munch
mun-dane

mu-nic-i-pal
mu-nic-i-pal-i-ties
mu-nic-i-pal-ity
mu-nif-i-cent
mu-ni-tion
mu-ral
mur-der
mur-der-ess
mur-der-ous
mu-ri-atic acid
murk
murk-ier
murk-i-est
murk-ily
murk-i-ness
mur-mur
mus-ca-tel
mus-cle (strength)
cf. mus-sel (mollusk)
muscle—bound *(adj.)*
mus-co-vite
mus-cu-lar
mus-cu-lar-ity
mus-cu-lar dys-tro-phy
muse
mu-seum
mush
mush-room
mu-sic
mu-si-cal
mu-si-cale
mu-si-cian
mu-si-co-log-i-cal
mu-si-col-o-gist
mu-si-col-ogy
mus-ket

Do not divide one-syllable words. Divide words by syllables, but leave
at least two letters of the word on the first line and three letters on the
following line. For additional guidelines, see page ix.

mus-ke-teer
mus-ketry
musk—ox *(n.)*
musk-rat
Mus-lim
mus-lin
mus-sel (mollusk)
  cf. mus-cle (strength)
must
mus-tache
mus-ta-chioed
mus-tang
mus-tard
mus-ter
mus-tier
mus-ti-est
mus-ti-ness
mu-ta-ble
mu-ta-bly
mu-tant
mu-tate
mu-ta-tion
mu-ta-tive
mute
mu-ti-late
mu-ti-la-tion
mu-ti-la-tor
mu-ti-neer
mu-ti-nous
mu-ti-nies
mu-tiny
mutt
mut-ter
mut-ton
mu-tual
mu-tu-al-ism

mu-tu-al-ist
mu-tu-al-is-tic
mu-tu-al-ity
mu-tu-al-iza-tion
mu-tu-al-ize
muu-muu
muz-zle
muz-zler
my
my-co-flora
my-col-ogy
my-co-plasma
my-co-sis
my-eli-tis
my-elo-fi-bro-sis
myo-car-dial
myo-car-dio-graph
my-o-pia
my-o-pic
myr-iad
myrrh
myr-tle
my-self
mys-te-ri-ous
mys-tery
mys-tic
mys-ti-cal
mys-ti-cism
mys-ti-fi-ca-tion
mys-ti-fied
mys-ti-fier
mys-tique
myth
myth-i-cal
myth-i-cize
my-thol-ogy

nab
nabbed
na-celle
na-cre
na-cre-ous
na-dir
nag
nagged
nag-ging
nail
nail-brush
nail file
na-ive
or na-ïve
na-ïveté
or na-ivete
na-ked
name
name—calling *(n.)*
name-plate
name-sake
nano-gram
nano-sec-ond
nap (short sleep)
  cf. knap (crest of hill)
na-palm
nape
naph-tha
naph-thene
nap-kin
nar-cism
nar-cist
nar-cis-sism

Plural, past tense, adverbial, and noun derivatives formed by adding *s, d* or *ed, ly, ness, ment, ful, less,* or *ing* to an unchanged root word are not listed, nor are words formed by dropping the final *e* and adding *ing*.

127

nar-cis-sist	nat-u-ral	neb-u-lous
nar-co-sis	nat-u-ral-ism	nec-es-sar-i-ly
nar-cotic	nat-u-ral-ist	nec-es-sary
nar-co-tize	nat-u-ral-iza-tion	ne-ces-si-tate
nar-rate	nat-u-ral-ize	ne-ces-si-ties
nar-ra-tion	na-ture	ne-ces-sity
nar-ra-tive	naugh-tier	neck
nar-ra-tor	naugh-ti-est	neck-er-chief
nar-row	naughty	neck-lace
na-sal	nau-sea	neck-line
na-scent	nau-se-ate	neck-tie
nas-tur-tium	nau-seous	ne-crol-o-gist
nas-tier	nau-ti-cal	nec-ro-mancy
nas-ti-est	nau-ti-lus	nec-ro-pha-gia
nasty	na-val (navy)	ne-crop-o-lis
na-tal	*cf.* na-vel (orange)	nec-ropsy
na-tal-i-ties	nave (part of a church)	ne-cro-sis
na-tal-ity	*cf.* knave (dishonest person)	nec-tar
na-tant	na-vel (orange)	née
na-ta-tion	*cf.* na-val (navy)	*or* nee (name)
na-tion	nav-i-ga-bil-ity	*cf.* knee (leg joint)
na-tional	nav-i-ga-ble	need (desire)
na-tion-al-ism	nav-i-gate	*cf.* knead (mix)
na-tion-al-ist	nav-i-ga-tion	need-ier
na-tion-al-is-tic	nav-i-ga-tor	need-i-est
na-tion-al-i-ties	navy	nee-dle
na-tion-al-ity	nay (negative vote)	ne'er–do–well *(adj.) (n.)*
na-tion-al-iza-tion	*cf.* neigh (horse sound)	ne-far-i-ous
na-tion-al-ize	nazi	ne-gate
na-tion-hood	Na-zism	ne-ga-tion
na-tion-wide	near	ne-ga-tor
na-tive	nearby	neg-a-tive
na-tiv-ism	near-sighted	neg-a-tiv-ism
na-tiv-i-ties	neat	neg-a-tiv-ist
na-tiv-ity	neb-ula	neg-a-tron
natty	neb-u-los-ity	*or* neg-a-ton

Do not divide one-syllable words. Divide words by syllables, but leave at least two letters of the word on the first line and three letters on the following line. For additional guidelines, see page ix.

ne-glect
ne-glecter
neg-li-gee
or neg-ligé
neg-li-gence
neg-li-gent
neg-li-gi-ble
neg-li-gi-bly
ne-go-tia-bil-ity
ne-go-tia-ble
ne-go-tiant
ne-go-tiate
ne-go-ti-a-tion
ne-go-ti-a-tor
neigh (horse sound)
  cf. nay (negative vote)
neigh-bor
neigh-bor-hood
nei-ther
nem-e-sis
neon
neo-phyte
neo-plasm
nephew
nep-o-tism
Nep-tune
nerve
nervier
nerv-i-est
nervy
nest
nester
nes-tle
nest-ling
net
net-ted

net-ting
net-tle
net-work
neu-ral
neu-rol-o-gist
neu-rol-ogy
neu-ron
neu-rop-a-thy
neu-ro-phys-i-ol-ogy
neu-ro-psy-chi-at-ric
neu-ro-sen-sory
neu-ro-sis
neu-ro-sur-geon
neu-ro-sur-gery
neu-ro-tic
neu-rot-i-cism
neu-ter
neu-tral
neu-tral-ity
neu-tral-iza-tion
neu-tral-ize
neu-tron
never
nev-er-the-less
new (not old)
  cf. knew (understood)
new-born
new-comer
new-fan-gled
news-boy
news-cast
news dealer
news-let-ter
news-mag-a-zine
news-man
news-pa-per

news-print
news-reel
news-room
news-stand
news-wor-thy
newsy
next
Ni-ag-ara
nib
nice
nice-ties
niche
nick
nickel
  or nickle
nick-nack
nick-name
nic-o-tine
niece
nifty
nig-gard
nigh
night (darkness)
  cf. knight (lord)
night-cap
night-clothes
night-club
night court
night-fall
night-gown
night-mare
night owl
night-time
ni-hil-ism
ni-hil-ist
Nike

Plural, past tense, adverbial, and noun derivatives formed by adding
s, d or ed, ly, ness, ment, ful, less, or ing to an unchanged root word are
not listed, nor are words formed by dropping the final e and adding ing.

nil	no-bly	non com-pos men-tis
nim-ble	nobody	non-con-duc-tor
nim-blest	noc-tur-nal	non-con-form-ist
nim-bus	noc-turne	non-con-form-ity
nin-com-poop	noc-u-ous	non-credit
nine	nod	non-de-script
nine-fold	node	none
nine-teen	nod-ule	non-en-force-able
nine-teenth	no—fault *(adj.)*	non-en-tity
nineties	nog-gin	none-the-less
ninety	noise	non-ex-is-tence
nip	noise-maker	non-fat
nip-ping	nos-ier	non-fic-tion
nip-ple	nos-i-est	non-flam-ma-ble
nippy	noisy	non—food *(adj.)*
nir-vana	no—load *(adj.)*	non-in-ter-ven-tion
ni-sei	nolo con-ten-dere	non-me-tal-lic
nit (louse egg)	no-mad	non-par-ti-san
cf. knit (tie together)	no-madic	non-plus
ni-trate	no—man's—land *(n.)*	non-pro-duc-tive
ni-tric	nom de plume	non-pro-fes-sional
nitro	no-men-cla-ture	non-profit
ni-tro-gen	nom-i-nal	non-pro-lif-er-a-tion
ni-tro-glyc-erin	nom-i-nate	non-re-fund-able
or ni-tro-glyc-er-ine	nom-i-na-tion	non-res-i-dent
ni-trous	nom-i-na-tive	non-re-sis-tance
nitty—gritty *(n.)*	nom-i-na-tor	non-re-stric-tive
nit-wit	nom-i-nee	non-re-turn-able
no (negative)	non-ad-di-tive	non-sched-uled
cf. know (understand)	no-na-ge-nar-ian	non-sec-tar-ian
Noah	non-aligned	non-sense
nob	non-bus-i-ness	non se-qui-tur
nob-bier	non-ca-lo-ric	non-skid
nob-bi-est	non-cha-lance	non-stop
no-bil-ity	non-com-ba-tant	non-union
no-ble	non-com-mit-tal	noo-dle

Do not divide one-syllable words. Divide words by syllables, but leave at least two letters of the word on the first line and three letters on the following line. For additional guidelines, see page ix.

nook	nota bene	nox-ious
noon	no-ta-ble	noz-zle
noon-day	no-ta-bly	nub
noon-time	no-ta-ri-za-tion	nu-bile
no—par	no-ta-rize	nu-clear
or no—par—value	no-tary pub-lic	nu-cleus
nor-mal	no-tate	nude
nor-malcy	notch	nug-get
nor-mal-iza-tion	note	nui-sance
nor-mal-ize	note-book	null
nor-ma-tive	note-pa-per	nul-li-fi-ca-tion
north	note-wor-thy	nul-lify
north-bound	noth-ing	numb
north-east	no-tice	num-ber
north-easter	no-tice-able	nu-mer-a-ble
north-east-ern	no-tice-ably	nu-meral
north-ern	no-ti-fi-ca-tion	nu-mer-ate
north-land	no-ti-fied	nu-mer-a-tion
north pole	no-tify	nu-mer-a-tor
North Star	no-tion	nu-meric
north-ward	no-to-ri-eties	nu-mer-i-cal
north-west	no-to-ri-ety	nu-mer-ol-ogy
nose	no-to-ri-ous	nu-mer-o-log-i-cal
nose-bleed	noun	nu-mer-ous
nose cone	nour-ish	nu-mis-matic
nose dive	novel	nu-mis-ma-tist
nose-gay	nov-el-ette	num-skull
nose—piece	nov-el-ist	nup-tial
no-show	nov-el-ize	nurse
nos-tal-gia	nov-el-ties	nurse-maid
nos-tal-gic	nov-elty	nurs-ery
nos-tril	no-vena	nurse's aide
nosy	nov-ice	nur-ture
or nosey	no-vi-tiate	nut
not (negative)	no-vo-caine	nu-tri-ent
cf. knot (fastener)	now-a-days	nu-tri-ment

Plural, past tense, adverbial, and noun derivatives formed by adding
s, d or *ed, ly, ness, ment, ful, less,* or *ing* to an unchanged root word are
not listed, nor are words formed by dropping the final *e* and adding *ing*.

nu-tri-tion
nu-tri-tional
nu-tri-tion-ist
nu-tri-tious
nu-tri-tive
nutty
nuz-zle
ny-lon
nymph

O

oaf
oak
oaken
oar (used in rowing)
cf. or (a choice)
cf. ore (rock)
oa-ses (*n. pl.*)
oa-sis
oat
oath
ob-bli-gato
ob-du-racy
ob-du-rate
obe-di-ence
obe-di-ent
obei-sance
obei-sant
obe-lisk
obese
obe-sity

obey
ob-fus-cate
ob-fus-ca-tion
obit
obit-u-ary
ob-ject
ob-jec-tion
ob-jec-tion-able
ob-jec-tive
ob-jec-tor
ob-late
ob-la-tion
ob-li-gate
ob-li-ga-tion
ob-lig-a-tory
oblige
oblique
oblit-er-ate
oblit-er-a-tion
oblit-er-a-tive
oblit-er-a-tor
obliv-ion
obliv-i-ous
ob-long
ob-lo-quy
ob-nox-ious
oboe
ob-scene
ob-scen-i-ties
ob-scen-ity
ob-scur-ant
ob-scure
ob-scu-ri-ties
ob-scu-rity
ob-se-qui-ous
ob-se-quies

ob-serv-able
ob-ser-vance
ob-ser-va-tion
ob-ser-va-tory
ob-serve
ob-server
ob-sess
ob-ses-sion
ob-ses-sive
ob-sid-ian
ob-so-lesce
ob-so-les-cence
ob-so-les-cent
ob-so-lete
ob-sta-cle
ob-stet-ric
ob-ste-tri-cian
ob-sti-nacy
ob-sti-nate
ob-strep-er-ous
ob-struct
ob-struc-tion
ob-struc-tor
ob-tain
ob-tain-able
ob-trude
ob-tru-sion
ob-tru-sive
ob-tund
ob-tu-rate
ob-tuse
ob-verse
ob-vert
ob-vi-ate
ob-vi-ous
oc-ca-sion

Do not divide one-syllable words. Divide words by syllables, but leave at least two letters of the word on the first line and three letters on the following line. For additional guidelines, see page ix.

oc-ca-sional
Oc-ci-dent
oc-ci-den-tal
oc-clude
oc-clu-sion
oc-cult
oc-cult-ism
oc-cu-pancy
oc-cu-pant
oc-cu-pa-tion
oc-cu-pa-tional
oc-cu-pied
oc-cupy
oc-cur
oc-curred
oc-cur-rence
oc-cur-rent
oc-cur-ring
ocean
ocean-ar-ium
ocean-front
oce-anic
ocean-og-ra-pher
ocean-og-ra-phy
oce-lot
ocher
or ochre
oc-ta-gon
oc-tag-o-nal
oc-tane
oc-tave
oc-tavo
oc-tet
oc-to-ge-nar-ian
oc-to-pod
oc-to-pus

oc-to-roon
oc-u-lar
oc-u-list
odd
odd-ball
odd-i-ties
odd-ity
ode (poem)
cf. owed (debt)
odi-ous
odium
odo-graph
odom-e-ter
odon-tol-o-gist
odon-tol-ogy
odor
odor-ant
odor-if-er-ous
odor-ize
odor-ous
Odys-seus
od-ys-sey
Oe-di-pus
off
of-fal
off and on *(adv.)*
off-beat
off—color
or off—colored *(adj.)*
of-fend
of-fense
or of-fence
of-fen-sive
of-fer
of-fer-tory
off-hand

of-fice
of-fice-holder
of-fi-cer
of-fi-cial
of-fi-cial-dom
of-fi-ci-ary
of-fi-ci-ate
of-fi-cious
off—key *(adj.)*
off—line *(adj.)*
off-set
off-shoot
off-shore
off-side
off-spring
off—the—record *(adj.)*
ogive
ogle
ogre
ohm
ohm-me-ter
oil
oil-can
oil-ier
oil-i-est
oily
oint-ment
old
olden
old—fashioned *(adj.)*
old—timer *(n.)*
oleo
oleo-mar-ga-rine
oleo-resin
ol-fac-tion
ol-fac-tive

Plural, past tense, adverbial, and noun derivatives formed by adding
s, d or *ed, ly, ness, ment, ful, less,* or *ing* to an unchanged root word are
not listed, nor are words formed by dropping the final *e* and adding *ing*.   133

ol-fac-tory
oli-gar-chic
oli-gar-chy
oli-gop-o-lis-tic
oli-gop-oly
ol-ive
olym-piad
Olym-pic
om-buds-man
om-elet
or om-elette
omen
om-i-nous
omis-si-ble
omis-sion
omit
omit-ted
omit-ting
om-ni-bus
om-nif-i-cent
om-nip-o-tence
om-nip-o-tent
om-niv-o-rous
on–again, off–again *(adj.)*
once
one (number)
 cf. won (victorious)
one—armed bandit
or one—arm bandit *(n.)*
one-night stand *(n.)*
oner-ous
one-self
one—sided *(adj.)*
one—way *(adj.)*
on-go-ing
on-ion

on-ion-skin
on—line *(adj.)*
on-looker
only
on-set
on-shore
on-side
on-slaught
on-stage
on—the—job *(adj.)*
on—the—scene *(adj.)*
onto
onus
on-ward
ool-o-gist
ool-ogy
ooze
opac-i-ties
opac-ity
opal
opaque
op cit
open
open—circuit *(adj.)*
open—ended *(adj.)*
opener
open-handed
open house *(n.)*
open—minded *(adj.)*
open—mouthed *(adj.)*
op-era
op-er-a-ble
op-er-a-bly
op-era-goer *(n.)*
op-er-and
op-er-ant

op-er-ate
op-er-atic
op-er-a-tion
op-er-a-tional
op-er-a-tive
op-er-a-tor
op-er-etta
ophid-ian
ophi-ol-ogy
ophi-oph-a-gous
oph-thal-mic
oph-thal-mol-o-gist
oph-thal-mol-ogy
opi-ate
opine
opin-ion
opin-ion-ated
opium
opos-sum
op-po-nent
op-por-tune
op-por-tun-ism
op-por-tun-ist
op-por-tun-is-tic
op-por-tu-ni-ties
op-por-tu-nity
op-pos-able
op-pose
op-po-site
op-po-si-tion
op-press
op-pres-sion
op-pres-sive
op-pres-sor
op-pro-brium
op-pugn

Do not divide one-syllable words. Divide words by syllables, but leave at least two letters of the word on the first line and three letters on the following line. For additional guidelines, see page ix.

op-ta-tive
op-tic
op-ti-cal
op-ti-cian
op-ti-mism
op-ti-mist
op-ti-mis-tic
or op-ti-mis-ti-cal
op-ti-mi-za-tion
op-ti-mize
op-ti-mum
op-tion
op-tion-al
op-tom-e-trist
op-tom-e-try
opt out *(v.)*
op-u-lence
op-u-lent
opus
opuses *(n. pl.)*
or opera
or (choice)
  cf. oar (used in rowing)
  cf. ore (rock)
or-a-cle (person)
  cf. au-ri-cle (heart)
orac-u-lar
oral (spoken)
  cf. au-ral (hearing)
or-ange
or-ang-ish
or-angy
or or-angey
orate
ora-tion
or-a-tor

or-a-tor-i-cal
or-a-tory
orb
or-bic-u-lar
or-bit
or-bital
or-biter
or-chard
or-ches-tra
or-ches-tral
or-ches-trate
or-ches-tra-tor
or or-ches-trater
or-ches-tra-tion
or-chid
or-dain
or-deal
or-der
or-derly
or-di-nal
or-di-nance (law)
  cf. ord-nance (weapons)
or-di-nary
or-di-nate
or-di-na-tion
ord-nance (weapons)
  cf. ord-i-nance (law)
ore (rock)
  cf. or (choice)
  cf. oar (used in rowing)
oreg-ano
or-gan
or-gandy
or or-gan-die
organ—grinder *(n.)*
or-ganic

or-gan-ism
or-gan-ist
or-ga-ni-za-tion
or-ga-ni-za-tional
or-gan-ize
or-ga-nizer
or-gi-as-tic
or-gies
orgy
ori-ent
ori-en-tal
ori-en-tate
ori-en-ta-tion
or-i-fice
or-i-gin
orig-i-nal
orig-i-nal-ity
orig-i-nate
orig-i-na-tion
orig-i-na-tive
orig-i-na-tor
or-na-ment
or-na-men-tal
or-na-men-ta-tion
or-nate
or-nery
or-nithic
or-ni-thol-o-gist
or-ni-thol-ogy
oro-graphic
orog-ra-phy
or-phan
or-phan-age
or-phrey
orth-odon-tics
orth-odon-tist

Plural, past tense, adverbial, and noun derivatives formed by adding
s, d or *ed, ly, ness, ment, ful, less,* or *ing* to an unchanged root word are
not listed, nor are words formed by dropping the final *e* and adding *ing*.

or-tho-dox	ot-ter	out-land-ish
or-tho-doxy	ot-to-man	out-law
or-tho-epist	**ought** (should)	out-lay
or-tho-epy	*cf.* **aught** (zero)	out-let
or-tho-graphic	ounce	out-line
or or-tho-graph-i-cal	**our** (us)	out-moded
or-tho-pe-dic	*cf.* **hour** (60 minutes)	out-num-ber
or or-tho-pae-dic	our-self	out—of—bounds *(adj.) (adv.)*
or-tho-pe-dist	our-selves	out—of—date *(adj.)*
os-cil-late	oust	out—of—doors *(n. pl.)*
os-cil-la-tion	ouster	out—of—the—way *(adj.)*
os-cil-la-tor	out	out-pa-tient
os-cil-la-tory	out—and—out *(adj.)*	out-post
os-cu-late	out-bid	out-put
os-cu-la-tion	out-board	out-rage
os-cu-la-tory	out-break	out-ra-geous
os-matic	out-burst	out-right
os-mo-sis	out-cast	out-side
os-motic	out-class	out-spo-ken
os-si-fi-ca-tion	out-come	out-ward
os-si-fied	out-crop	*or* out-wards
os-sify	out-cry	out-wit
os-ten-si-ble	out-dated	out-wore
os-ten-si-bly	out-dis-tance	out-worn
os-ten-ta-tion	outdo	oval
os-ten-ta-tious	out-door	ovary
os-te-ol-o-gist	out-doors-man	ova-tion
os-te-ol-ogy	out-doorsy	oven
os-teo-my-eli-tis	out-draw	over
os-tra-cism	outer	over-abun-dance
os-tra-cize	out-er-coat	over-achiever
os-trich	out-er-most	over-act
other	outer space *(n.)*	over-ac-tive
oth-er-wise	out-fit	over-all
oto-lar-yn-gol-o-gist	out-go-ing	over-bear-ing
oto-lar-yn-gol-ogy	out-growth	over-bid

Do not divide one-syllable words. Divide words by syllables, but leave
at least two letters of the word on the first line and three letters on the
136   following line. For additional guidelines, see page ix.

over-blown
over-board
over-bur-den
over-ca-pac-i-ty
over-cast
over-charge
over-coat
over-come
overdo (too much)
cf. **over-due** (late)
over-drawn
over-due (late)
cf. **overdo** (too much)
over-eat
over-em-pha-size
over-ex-pose
over-flow
over-grow
over-hang
over-head
over-in-dulge
over-kill
over-lap
over-lay
over-load
over-look
over-night
over-re-act
over-rule
over-seas
over-sight
over—the—counter *(adj.)*
over-throw
over-time
over-ture
over-turn

over-view
over-weight
over-whelm
over-wrought
ovu-late
ovum
ova *(n. pl.)*
owed (debt)
cf. ode (poem)
owl
own
ox
oxen *(n. pl.)*
ox-ford
ox-i-da-tion
ox-ide
ox-i-diz-able
ox-i-dize
ox-i-dizer
ox-y-gen
ox-y-gen-ate
oys-ter
ozone
ozo-no-sphere

P

pace
pace-maker
pacer
pace-set-ter
pachy-derm
pach-ys-an-dra

pa-cific
pac-i-fi-ca-tion
pa-cif-i-cism
pa-cif-i-ca-tor
pac-i-fier
pac-i-fism
pac-i-fist
pac-ify
pack (bundle)
pack-able
pack-age
pack-board
packed (bundled)
cf. **pact** (agreement)
packer
packet
pack-horse
pack-ing-house
pact (agreement)
cf. **packed** (bundled)
pad
pad-ded
pad-dle
pad-lock
pa-dre
pa-gan-ism
page
pag-eant
pag-eantry
page boy
pag-i-nate
pag-i-na-tion
pail (container)
cf. **pale**
(without much color)
pail-ful

Plural, past tense, adverbial, and noun derivatives formed by adding
s, d or *ed, ly, ness, ment, ful, less,* or *ing* to an unchanged root word are
not listed, nor are words formed by dropping the final *e* and adding *ing*.

pain (ache)
  cf. **pane** (glass)
pains-tak-ing
paint
painter
pair (two)
  cf. **pare** (trim)
  cf. **pear** (fruit)
pa-ja-mas
pal-ace
pal-at-able
pal-ate (roof of mouth)
  cf. **pal-let** (mattress)
  cf. **pal-ette** (artist's board)
pa-la-tial
pa-la-ver
pale (without much color)
  cf. **pail** (container)
Pa-leo-lithic
pa-le-on-to-lo-gist
pa-le-on-tol-ogy
Pa-leo-zoic
pal-ette (artist's board)
  cf. **pal-ate** (roof of mouth)
  cf. **pal-let** (mattress)
pal-i-sade
pal-la-dium
pal-let (mattress)
  cf. **pal-ate** (roof of mouth)
  cf. **pal-ette** (artist's board)
pal-lid
pal-lor
palm
palm-ist

palm-istry
pal-pa-bil-ity
pal-pa-ble
pal-pa-bly
pal-pate
pal-pi-tate
pal-pi-ta-tion
palsy
pal-try
pam-per
pam-phlet
pam-phle-teer
pan
pan-a-cea
pan-a-cean
pan-ama
Pan—Americanism
pan-cake
pan-chro-matic
pan-creas
panda (animal)
  cf. **pan-der** (exploiter)
pan-de-mo-nium
pan-der (exploiter)
  cf. **panda** (animal)
Pan-do-ra's box *(n.)*
pane (glass)
  cf. **pain** (ache)
panel
pan-el-ist
pang
pan-han-dle
Pan-hel-lenic
panic
pan-icked
pan-orama

pansy
pant
pan-ta-loon
  or pan-ta-lone
pan-the-ism
pan-theon
pan-ther
pan-to-mime
pan-to-mimic
pan-to-mim-ist
pan-try
pant-suit
panty hose
pan-zer
pap
pa-pacy
pa-pal
pa-paya
pa-per
pa-per-back
pa-per-boy
pa-per-hanger
pa-per-weight
pa-per-work
papier—mâché
pa-pilla
pa-pist
pa-poose
pa-prika
Pap smear *(n.)*
pa-py-rus
par
par-a-ble
pa-rab-ola
par-a-bolic
pa-rab-o-loid

Do not divide one-syllable words. Divide words by syllables, but leave
at least two letters of the word on the first line and three letters on the
following line. For additional guidelines, see page ix.
138

para-chute
para-chut-ist
pa-rade
par-a-dise
par-a-dox
par-a-dox-i-cal
par-af-fin
para-gen-e-sis
par-a-gon
para-graph
par-a-keet
par-al-de-hyde
par-al-lel
par-al-lel-epi-ped
par-al-lel-ism
par-al-lel-o-gram
pa-ral-o-gism
pa-ral-y-sis
par-a-lytic
par-a-lyze
para-medic
para-med-i-cal
pa-ram-e-ter
para-met-ric
or para-met-ri-cal
pa-ram-e-ter-ize
para-mil-i-tary
par-a-mount
para-noia
para-noid
par-a-pet
par-a-pher-na-lia
para-phrase
para-phras-tic
para-ple-gia
para-pro-fes-sional

para-psy-chol-o-gist
para-psy-chol-ogy
par-a-site
par-a-sitic
or par-a-sit-i-cal
par-a-sit-ism
para-sol
para-trooper
par-boil
par-cel
par-cel post
parch
par-don
par-don-able
pare (trim)
    cf. pair (two)
    cf. pear (fruit)
par-e-go-ric
par-ent
pa-ren-tal
par-ent-age
pa-ren-the-sis
par-en-thetic
or par-en-thet-i-cal
pa-ren-the-size
par-ent-hood
pa-re-sis
par ex-cel-lence *(adj.)*
par-fait
pari—mu-tuel *(n.)*
par-ish
pa-rish-io-ner
par-ity
park
parka
Par-kin-son's Law

park-land
park-way
par-lay (bet)
    cf. par-ley (talk)
par-ley (talk)
    cf. par-lay (bet)
par-lia-ment
par-lia-men-tar-ian
par-lia-men-tary
par-lor
pa-ro-chial
pa-ro-chi-al-ism
par-o-dist
par-ody
pa-role
pa-rolee
par-quet
par-ri-cide
par-rot
parry
par-si-mo-ni-ous
par-si-mony
pars-ley
pars-nip
par-son
par-son-age
part
par-take
Par-the-non
par-tial
par-tic-i-pant
par-tic-i-pate
par-tic-i-pa-tion
par-tic-i-pa-tive
par-tic-i-pa-tor
par-tic-i-pa-tory

par-ti-cip-ial	pass-port	**pa-tience** (calm endurance)
par-ti-ci-ple	past (ended)	*cf.* **pa-tients**
par-ti-cle	*cf.* **passed**	(doctors' clients)
par-tic-u-lar	(moved)	pa-tina
par-tic-u-lar-ize	paste	pa-tio
par-ti-san	paste-board	pa-tri-arch
or par-ti-zan	pas-tel	pa-tri-ar-chal
par-tite	pas-teur-iza-tion	pa-tri-cian
par-ti-tion	pas-teur-ize	pat-ri-cide
par-ti-tion-ist	pas-time	pat-ri-lin-eal
part-ner	pas-tor	pa-triot
part-ner-ship	pas-to-ral	pa-tri-otic
par-tridge	pas-tor-ate	pa-tri-o-tism
part—time *(adj.)*	pastry	pa-trol
par-tu-ri-tion	pas-tur-age	pa-trol-man
par value	pas-ture	pa-tron
pass	pat	pa-tron-age
pass-able	patch	pa-tron-ize
pass-ably	patch-board	pa-troon
pas-sage	patch cord	pat-ter
pas-sage-way	patch test	pat-tern
pass-book	patch-work	pau-city
passé	pate	paunch
passed	pâté	pau-per
(moved)	pâté de foie gras	**pause** (stop)
cf. **past** (ended)	pa-tent	*cf.* **paws** (feet)
pas-sen-ger	pa-ter-nal	pave
pass-erby	pa-ter-nal-ism	pa-vil-ion
pass—fail *(n.)*	pa-ter-nal-is-tic	pawl
pas-si-ble	pa-ter-nity	pawn
pas-sion	path	pawn-bro-ker
pas-sion-ate	pa-thetic	pawn-shop
pas-sive	pa-thet-i-cal	**paws** (feet)
pas-siv-ism	path-o-log-i-cal	*cf.* **pause** (stop)
pass-key	pa-thol-o-gist	pay-able
pass out *(v.)*	pa-thol-ogy	pay—as—you—go *(adj.)*
Pass-over *(n.)*	path-way	pay-check

Do not divide one-syllable words. Divide words by syllables, but leave
at least two letters of the word on the first line and three letters on the
following line. For additional guidelines, see page ix.

pay-day
payee
pay-load
pay-roll
pea
peace (order)
 cf. piece
  (fragment)
peace-able
peace-ably
peace corps *(n.)*
peace-time
pea-cock
peak (summit)
 cf. peek (look)
 cf. pique (anger)
peal (toll)
 cf. peel (strip)
pea-nut
pearl (gem)
 cf. purl (knit)
peas-ant
peat
peb-ble
pe-can
peck
pe-cu-liar
pe-cu-liar-ity
pe-cu-ni-ary
ped-a-gogic
ped-a-gog-i-cal
ped-a-gogue
 or ped-a-gog
ped-a-gogy
pedal (foot lever)
 cf. ped-dle (sell)
ped-ant

ped-dle (sell)
 cf. pedal
  (foot lever)
ped-dler
 or ped-lar
ped-es-tal
pe-des-trian
pe-di-at-ric
pe-di-a-tri-cian
ped-i-gree
pe-dom-e-ter
peek (look)
 cf. peak (summit)
 cf. pique (anger)
peek-a-boo
peel (strip)
 cf. peal (toll)
peep
peer (look)
 cf. pier (dock)
peer-age
peeve
pee-vish
peg
peg-board
pel-i-can
pel-let
pell—mell *(adv.)*
pelt
pel-vic
pel-vis
pen
pe-nal
pe-nal-ize
pen-alty
pen-ance
pen-chant

pen-cil (writing tool)
 cf. pen-sile (hanging)
pen-dant
pen-du-lous
pen-du-lum
pen-e-trate
pen-e-tra-tion
pen-i-cil-lin
pen-in-sula
pen-i-tence
pen-i-tent
pen-i-ten-tial
pen-i-ten-tiary
pen-knife
pen-light
 or pen-lite
pen-man-ship
pen-nant
penny
penny ar-cade *(n.)*
pen-ny-weight
pe-nol-o-gist
pe-nol-ogy
pen pal *(n.)*
pen-sile (hanging)
 cf. pen-cil
  (writing tool)
pen-sion
pen-sioner
pen-sive
pen-ta-gon
pen-tath-lon
Pen-te-cost
Pen-te-cos-tal
pent-house
pe-nult
pen-ul-ti-mate

Plural, past tense, adverbial, and noun derivatives formed by adding
s, d or *ed, ly, ness, ment, ful, less,* or *ing* to an unchanged root word are
not listed, nor are words formed by dropping the final *e* and adding *ing*. 141

pe-nu-ri-ous	per-fect	per-ma-nent
pen-ury	per-fec-tion	per-me-able
peon	per-fec-tion-ist	per-me-ate
pe-on-age	per-fid-i-ous	per-mis-si-bil-ity
peo-ple	per-fidy	per-mis-sible
pep-per-mint	per-fo-rate	per-mis-si-bly
pep-pery	per-fo-ra-tion	per-mis-sion
pep talk (n.)	per-force	per-mis-sive
pep-tic	per-form	per-mit
per-am-bu-late	per-for-mance	per-mu-ta-tion
per-am-bu-la-tion	per-former	per-ni-cious
per-am-bu-la-tor	per-fume	per-ox-ide
per-cale	per-func-tory	per-pen-dic-u-lar
per cap-ita	per-fuse	per-pe-trate
per-ceiv-able	per-fu-sion	per-pe-tra-tion
per-ceiv-ably	per-haps	per-pe-tra-tor
per-ceive	pe-rim-e-ter	per-pet-ual
per-cent	pe-riod	per-pet-u-ate
per-cent-age	pe-ri-od-ic	per-pe-tu-ity
per-cen-tile	pe-ri-od-i-cal	per-plex
per cen-tum	peri-odon-tal	per-plex-ity
per-cept	peri-odon-tics	per-qui-site
per-cep-ti-bil-ity	peri-pa-tetic	per se
per-cep-ti-ble	pe-riph-er-al	per-se-cute (annoy)
per-cep-tion	pe-riph-ery	cf. pros-e-cute (bring
per-cep-tive	peri-scope	into court)
per-cep-tual	per-ish	per-se-cu-tion
perch	per-ish-able	per-se-ver-ance
per-chance	per-i-win-kle	per-se-vere
per-co-late	per-jure	per-si-flage
per-co-la-tor	per-jurer	per-sist
per-cus-sion	per-jury	per-sis-tence
per diem	perky	per-sis-tent
per-di-tion	per-ma-frost	per-son
pe-remp-tory	per-ma-nence	per-sona
pe-ren-nial	per-ma-nency	per-son-able

Do not divide one-syllable words. Divide words by syllables, but leave at least two letters of the word on the first line and three letters on the following line. For additional guidelines, see page ix.

per-sonal (individual)
  cf. per-son-nel
  (employees)
per-son-al-ity
per-son-al-iza-tion
per-son-al-ize
per-sona non grata
per-son-i-fi-ca-tion
per-son-ify
per-son-nel (employees)
  cf. per-sonal (individual)
per-spec-tive (visual)
  cf. pro-spec-tive
  (expected)
per-spic-u-ous
per-spi-ra-tion
per-spire
per-suade
per-sua-sion
per-sua-sive
pert
per-tain
per-ti-na-cious
per-ti-nent
per-turb
pe-ruse
per-vade
per-va-sion
per-verse
per-ver-sion
per-vert
pes-si-mism
pes-si-mis-tic
pes-ter
pes-ti-cide
pes-ti-lence

pes-tle (tool)
  cf. pis-til (flower)
  cf. pis-tol (weapon)
pet
petal
petit
pe-ti-tion
pet-rify
pet-ro-chem-i-cal
pet-rol
pe-tro-leum
pet-ti-ness
petty
pet-u-lance
pet-u-lant
pe-tu-nia
pew
pew-ter
pha-lanx
phan-tasm
phan-tom
pha-raoh
phar-i-see
phar-ma-ceu-ti-cal
phar-ma-cist
phar-ma-col-ogy
phar-ma-co-poeia
phar-macy
phase (aspect)
  cf. faze (disturb)
phe-no-bar-bi-tal
phe-nom-e-nal
Phi Beta Kappa *(n.)*
phi-lan-der
phi-lan-derer
phil-an-thropic

phi-lan-thro-pist
phi-lan-thropy
phi-lat-e-list
Phil-har-monic
Phi-lip-pi-ans
phi-lis-tine
philo-den-dron
phi-lol-o-gist
phi-lol-ogy
phi-los-o-pher
philo-sophic
phi-los-o-phize
phi-los-o-phizer
phi-los-o-phy
phle-bi-tis
phlegm
phleg-matic
phlox
pho-bia
Phoe-ni-cian
pho-netic
pho-nics
pho-no-graph
pho-nog-ra-phy
pho-nol-o-gist
pho-nol-ogy
phony
  or pho-ney
phos-gene
phos-phate
phos-pho-resce
phos-pho-res-cence
phos-pho-res-cent
phos-pho-rus
pho-to-bi-ol-ogy
pho-to-cath-ode

Plural, past tense, adverbial, and noun derivatives formed by adding
s, d or *ed, ly, ness, ment, ful, less,* or *ing* to an unchanged root word are
not listed, nor are words formed by dropping the final *e* and adding *ing*.

pho-to-cell
pho-to-chem-i-cal
pho-to-chem-is-try
pho-to-com-po-si-tion
pho-to-copy
pho-to-elec-tric
pho-to-en-grave
pho-to-flash
pho-to-ge-nic
pho-to-ge-ol-ogy
pho-to-graph
pho-to-graphic
pho-tog-ra-phy
pho-to-gra-vure
pho-to-jour-nal-ism
pho-to—off-set
pho-to-sen-si-ti-za-tion
pho-to-sphere
pho-to-stat *(v.)*
pho-to-static
pho-to-syn-the-sis
pho-to-tube
pho-to-type-set-ting
pho-to-ty-pog-ra-phy
phrasal
phrase
phrase-ol-o-gist
phrase-ol-ogy
phre-nol-o-gist
phre-nol-ogy
phys-iat-rics
phys-iat-rist
physic (medicine)
  cf. **phy-sique** (bodily
  structure)
phys-i-cal

phy-si-cian
phys-i-cist
phys-i-co-chem-i-cal
phys-ics
phys-i-og-nomy
phys-i-og-ra-phy
phys-i-o-log-i-cal
phys-i-ol-o-gist
phys-i-ol-ogy
phys-io-ther-a-pist
phy-sique (bodily structure)
  cf. **physic** (medicine)
pi (ratio)
  cf. **pie** (dessert)
pi-a-nis-simo
pi-a-nist
pi-ano
pi-as-ter
  or pi-as-tre
pi-azza
pica (type size)
  cf. **piker** (cheap person)
pic-a-dor
pic-a-yune
pic-ca-lilli
pic-colo
pick
pickax
pick-erel
picket
picket line
pickle
pick-pocket
pic-nic
pi-co-sec-ond
pic-to-gram

pic-to-graph
pic-tog-ra-phy
pic-to-rial
pic-to-ri-al-ize
pic-ture
pic-tur-esque
picture tube
picture window
picture writing
pic-tur-ize
pid-dle
pie (dessert)
  cf. **pi** (ratio)
piece (fragment)
  cf. **peace** (order)
piece-meal
pie chart
pie-crust
pied-mont
pie in the sky
pier (dock)
  cf. **peer** (look)
pierce
pi-etism
pi-etis-tic
pi-ety
pif-fle
pig
pig-boat
pi-geon
pi-geon-hole
pigeon—toed
pig-gish
pig-gy-back
pig-headed
pig in a poke

Do not divide one-syllable words. Divide words by syllables, but leave
at least two letters of the word on the first line and three letters on the
following line. For additional guidelines, see page ix.

144

pig iron
pig latin
pig-let
pig-men-ta-tion
pig-pen
pig-skin
pig-sty
pike
piker (cheap person)
 cf. pica (type size)
pi-las-ter
pile
pile driver (n.)
pileup
pil-fer
pil-fer-age
pil-grim
pil-grim-age
pill
pil-lage
pil-lar
pill-box
pil-lory
pil-low
pil-low-case
pi-lot
pi-lot-house
pilot light (n.)
pil-sner
or pil-sener
pi-miento
pim-ple
pin
pin-afore
pi-ñata
or pi-nata

pin-ball ma-chine
pince—nez
pin-cer
pinch
pinch—hit (v.)
pinch hitter (n.)
pin curl (n.)
pin-cush-ion
pine
pine-ap-ple
pine-cone
ping
pin-hole
pin-ion
pink
pin money (n.)
pin-na-cle
pi-nochle
pin-point
pin-prick
pins and needles (n. pl.)
pin-set-ter
pin-spot-ter
pin-stripe
pint
pin-tle
pinto
pint—size
or pint—sized
pinup
pin-wheel
pi-o-neer
pi-ous
pip
pipe
pipe cleaner

pipe dream
pipe fit-ter
pipe-line
pipe or-gan
piper
pipe wrench
pip-pin
pip—squeak
pi-quancy
pi-quant
pique (anger)
 cf. peak (summit)
 cf. peek (look)
pi-racy
pi-ra-nha
pi-rate
pi-rat-i-cal
pir-ou-ette
pis-mire
pis-ta-chio
pis-til (flower)
 cf. pes-tle (tool)
 cf. pis-tol (weapon)
pis-tol (weapon)
 cf. pes-tle (tool)
 cf. pis-til (flower)
pis-ton
piston ring (n.)
piston rod (n.)
pit
pit—a—pat (n.)
pitch
pitch—black (adj.)
pitch—dark (adj.)
pitcher
pitch-fork

Plural, past tense, adverbial, and noun derivatives formed by adding
s, d or ed, ly, ness, ment, ful, less, or ing to an unchanged root word are
not listed, nor are words formed by dropping the final e and adding ing.

145

pitch pipe	pla-gia-rism	plas-ter-board
pit-e-ous	pla-gia-rist	plas-ter cast *(n.)*
pit-fall	pla-gia-ris-tic	plas-ter of paris
pithy	pla-gia-rize	plas-ter-work
piti-able	pla-gia-rizer	plas-tic
piti-ably	pla-giary	plas-tic-ity
piti-ful	plague	plas-ti-cize
piti-less	plaid	plate (dish)
pit-tance	**plain** (ordinary)	*cf.* **plait** (fold)
pit-ter—pat-ter *(n.)*	*cf.* **plane** (flat surface)	pla-teau
pi-tu-itary	plain-clothes-man	pla-teaus *(n. pl.)*
pit viper *(n.)*	**plain-tiff** (person in lawsuit)	*or* pla-teaux
pity	**plain-tive** (mournful)	plate-ful
pivot	**plait** (fold)	plate-glass
piv-otal	*cf.* **plate** (dish)	plat-form
pixie	plan	plat-i-num
or **pixy**	**plane** (flat surface)	plat-i-num blonde
pizza	*cf.* **plain** (ordinary)	plat-i-tude
piz-zazz	plane-load	plat-i-tu-di-nal
or **pi-zazz**	planet	plat-i-tu-di-nar-ian
pla-ca-bil-ity	plan-e-tar-ium	plat-i-tu-di-nize
pla-ca-ble	plan-e-tary	plat-i-tu-di-nous
pla-ca-bly	plan-e-toid	pla-tonic
plac-ard	plan-e-tol-o-gist	pla-toon
pla-cate	plan-e-tol-ogy	plat-ter
pla-ca-tion	plank	plau-dit
pla-ca-tive	plank-ton	plau-si-bil-ity
pla-ca-tory	planned	plau-si-ble
place	plan-ning	plau-si-bly
place-holder	plant	play
place-kick	plan-tain	play-back
place mat *(n.)*	plan-ta-tion	play-boy
pla-centa	planter	play—by—play *(adj.)*
pla-centas	plaque	player
or **pla-cen-tae**	plasma	play-ground
placid	plas-ter	play-house

Do not divide one-syllable words. Divide words by syllables, but leave at least two letters of the word on the first line and three letters on the following line. For additional guidelines, see page ix.

146

play-land
play-mate
play-pen
play-room
play-suit
play-wright
plaza
plea
plead
pleas-ant
please
plea-sur-able
plea-sur-ably
plea-sure
pleat
ple-be-ian
pleb-i-scite
pledge
ple-nip-o-tent
pleni-po-ten-tiary
plen-i-tude
plen-ti-ful
plenty
pleth-ora
pleu-risy
Plex-i-glas
plexus
pli-abil-ity
pli-able
pli-ably
pli-ancy
pli-ant
pli-cate
pli-ca-tion
pli-ers
plight

plink
plod
plop
plopped
plot
plow
plow-share
ploy
pluck
pluck-ier
pluck-i-est
plug
plugged
plum (fruit)
  cf. plumb (weight)
plum-age
plumber
plun-der
plun-der-able
plun-der-age
plun-der-ous
plunge
plunger
plunk
plu-ral
plu-ral-ism
plu-ral-ist
plu-ral-is-tic
plu-ral-ity
plu-ral-ize
plus
plush
plush-ier
plush-i-est
plu-toc-racy
plu-to-crat

plu-ton
plu-tonic
plu-to-nium
ply
ply-wood
pneu-matic
pneu-mo-nia
pneu-monic
pneu-mo-tho-rax
poach
poacher
pocket
pock-et-book
pock-et-knife
pocket—size
or pocket—sized
pock-mark
pod
po-di-a-trist
po-di-a-try
po-dium
po-etic
po-et-i-cal
po-et-i-cism
poet laureate
po-etry
pogo stick
po-grom
poi
poi-gnancy
poi-gnant
poin-ci-ana
poin-set-tia
point
point—blank
poise

Plural, past tense, adverbial, and noun derivatives formed by adding
s, d or *ed, ly, ness, ment, ful, less,* or *ing* to an unchanged root word are
not listed, nor are words formed by dropping the final *e* and adding *ing*.

poi-son
poi-son-ous
poison—pen *(adj.)*
poke
po-ker
poky
or pokey
po-lar
Po-laris
po-lar-ity
po-lar-iz-abil-ity
po-lar-iz-able
po-lar-iza-tion
po-lar-ize
Po-lar-oid
pole (stick)
  cf. poll (vote)
po-lemic
po-lem-i-cize
po-le-mist
pole—vault *(v.)*
pole-ward
po-lice
po-lice-man
po-lice-woman
pol-i-cies
pol-icy
pol-icy-holder
pol-i-cy-mak-ing
po-lio
po-lio-my-eli-tis
po-lio-vi-rus
pol-ish
po-lit-buro
po-lite
pol-i-tic

po-lit-i-cal
pol-i-ti-cian
po-lit-i-ci-za-tion
po-lit-i-cize
po-lit-ico
po-lit-i-cos *(n. pl.)*
  or po-lit-i-coes
polka
polka dot
poll (vote)
  cf. pole (stick)
pol-len
pol-lin-ate
pol-li-na-tion
pol-li-wog
  or pol-ly-wog
poll-ster
pol-lut-ant
pol-lute
pol-lu-tion
Pol-ly-anna
Pol-ly-an-na-ish
  or Pol-ly-an-nish
polo
po-lo-naise
poly-chrome
poly-clinic
poly-es-ter
poly-es-trous
poly-eth-yl-ene
poly-gamic
po-lyg-a-mous
po-lyg-a-mist
po-lyg-amy
poly-gon
poly-graph

poly-mer
Poly-ne-sian
poly-nu-clear
poly-pro-pyl-ene
poly-sty-rene
poly-syl-labic
poly-syl-la-ble
poly-tech-nic
poly-the-ism
poly-the-is-tic
poly-un-sat-u-rated
poly-ure-thane
po-made
pome-gran-ate
pom-mel
po-mol-ogy
pomp
pom-pa-dour
pom-pos-ity
pomp-ous
pon-cho
pon-der
pon-der-able
pon-der-ous
pon-tiff
pon-tif-i-cal
pon-tif-i-cate
pon-tif-i-ca-tion
pon-toon
pony
po-ny-tail
poo-dle
pooh—pooh
  or pooh *(v.)*
pool
poor box

Do not divide one-syllable words. Divide words by syllables, but leave at least two letters of the word on the first line and three letters on the following line. For additional guidelines, see page ix.

poor-house
poor—mouth *(v.)*
pop
pop art *(n.)*
pop-corn
pope
pop-lar (tree)
  cf. pop-u-lar (liked)
popped
pop-ping
poppy
pop-py-cock
pop-u-lace *(n.)*
pop-u-lar (liked)
  cf. pop-lar (tree)
pop-u-lar-ity
pop-u-lar-ize
pop-u-late
pop-u-la-tion
pop-u-lous *(adj.)*
por-ce-lain
porch
por-cu-pine
pore (opening)
  cf. pour (flow)
por-nog-ra-pher
por-no-graphic
por-nog-ra-phy
po-rose
po-ros-ity
po-rous
por-poise
por-ridge
por-ringer
port
por-ta-bil-ity

por-ta-ble
por-ta-bly
por-tage
por-tal
por-tend *(v.)*
por-tent *(n.)*
por-ten-tous
por-ter
port-fo-lio
port-hole
por-tico
por-tion
por-trait
por-trai-ture
por-tray
por-trayal
por-trayer
pose
po-si-tion
pos-i-tive
pos-i-tiv-ism
posse
pos-sess
pos-ses-sion
pos-ses-sive
pos-si-bil-i-ties
pos-si-bil-ity
pos-si-ble
pos-si-bly
post
post-age
postal
postal card
post-card
poster
pos-te-rior

pos-ter-ity
post-grad-u-ate
post-hu-mous
post-hyp-notic
post-man
post-mark
post-mas-ter
post-mis-tress
post-mor-tem
post-na-sal
post-na-tal
post-nup-tial
post office
post-op-er-a-tive
post-pone
post-script
pos-tu-lant
pos-tu-late
pos-tu-la-tor
pos-ture
post-war
pot
po-ta-ble
po-tage
pot-ash
po-tas-sic
po-tas-sium
po-tato
po-tent
po-ten-tate
po-ten-tial
po-ten-ti-al-ity
pot-head
pot-hole
po-tion
pot-luck

Plural, past tense, adverbial, and noun derivatives formed by adding
s, d or *ed, ly, ness, ment, ful, less,* or *ing* to an unchanged root word are
not listed, nor are words formed by dropping the final *e* and adding *ing*.

149

pot-pourri
pot roast *(n.)*
pot-shot
pot-ted
pot-ter
pot-tery
pouch
poul-try
pounce
pound
pour (flow)
  cf. **pore** (opening)
pout
pov-erty
pow-der
power
pow-er-boat
pow-er-house
power play *(n.)*
pow-wow
pox
pox *(n, pl.)*
or poxes
prac-ti-ca-bil-ity
prac-ti-ca-ble
prac-tice
or prac-tise
prac-tice—teach *(v.)*
prac-ti-cum
prac-ti-tio-ner
prag-matic
prag-mat-i-cism
prag-mat-i-cist
prag-ma-tism
prag-ma-tist
prai-rie

praise
praise-wor-thy
pram
prance
prank
prank-ster
pray (worship)
  cf. **prey** (victim)
prayer
prayer book *(n.)*
pray-ing man-tis *(n.)*
preach
pre-am-ble
pre-ar-range
pre-atomic
Pre-cam-brian
pre-car-i-ous
pre-cast
pre-cau-tion
pre-cau-tion-ary
pre-cede (go before)
  cf. **pro-ceed** (move forward)
pre-ce-dence
prec-e-dent
pre-cept
pre-cep-tive
pre-cep-tor
pre-ces-sion (going first)
  cf. **pro-ces-sion** (parade)
pre—Christian *(adj.)*
pre-cious
prec-i-pice
pre-cip-i-tate
pre-cip-i-ta-tion
pre-cip-i-ta-tive
pre-cip-i-tous

pré-cis
pre-cise
pre-ci-sion
pre-clude
pre-co-cious
pre-con-ceive
pre-con-cep-tion
pred-a-tor
pred-a-to-rial
pred-a-tory
pre-de-cease
pre-de-ces-sor
pre-des-ti-na-tion
pre-des-tine
pre-de-ter-mine
pre-dic-a-ment
pred-i-cate
pred-i-ca-tion
pred-i-ca-tory
pre-dict
pre-dict-able
pre-dict-ably
pre-dic-tion
pre-dic-tive
pre-di-lec-tion
pre-dis-pose
pre-dom-i-nance
pre-dom-i-nant
pre-dom-i-nate
pre-emer-gence
pre-em-i-nence
pre-em-i-nent
pre-empt
preen
pre-fab
pre-fab-ri-cate

Do not divide one-syllable words. Divide words by syllables, but leave at least two letters of the word on the first line and three letters on the following line. For additional guidelines, see page ix.

150

pref-ace
pre-fer
pref-er-a-ble
pref-er-a-bly
pref-er-ence
pref-er-en-tial
pre-ferred
pre-fer-ring
pre-flight
preg-nancy
preg-nant
pre-heat
pre-his-toric
pre-judge
prej-u-dice
prej-u-di-cial
prej-u-di-cious
prel-ate
pre-lim-i-nary
pre-lude
pre-mar-i-tal
pre-ma-ture
pre-med-i-cal
pre-med-i-tate
pre-med-i-ta-tion
pre-mier (principal)
  cf. **pre-miere** (first
  public performance)
prem-ise
pre-mium
pre-mo-ni-tion
pre-na-tal
pre-oc-cu-pa-tion
pre-oc-cu-pied
pre-or-dain
prep-a-ra-tion

pre-pa-ra-tory
pre-pare
pre-pared-ness
pre-pay
pre-pon-der-ance
prep-o-si-tion (word)
  cf. **prop-o-si-tion** (proposal)
pre-pos-ter-ous
pre—reg-is-tra-tion
pre-req-ui-site
pre-rog-a-tive
pres-age
Pres-by-te-rian
pres-by-tery
pre-school
pre-scribe (order)
  cf. **pro-scribe** (prohibit)
pre-scrip-tion
pre-scrip-tive
pres-ence (being there)
  cf. **pres-ents** (gifts)
pre-sent *(v.)*
pre-sent-able
pre-sen-ta-tion
pre-sen-ti-ment (foreboding)
  cf. **pre-sent-ment**
  (presentation)
pres-er-va-tion-ist
pre-ser-va-tive
pre-serve
pres-er-va-tion
pre-set
pre-shrunk
pre-side
pres-i-dency
pres-i-dent

pre-si-dio
pre-soak
press
pres-sure
pres-sur-iza-tion
pres-sur-ize
pres-ti-dig-i-ta-tion
pres-ti-dig-i-ta-tor
pres-tige
pres-ti-gious
pre-sum-able
pre-sum-ably
pre-sume
pre-sump-tion
pre-sump-tive
pre-sump-tu-ous
pre-sup-pose
pre-tend
pre-tender
pre-tense
  or **pre-tence**
pre-ten-sion
pre-ten-tious
pre-test
pre-text
pretty
pre-vail
prev-a-lence
prev-a-lent
pre-var-i-cate
pre-var-i-ca-tion
pre-var-i-ca-tor
pre-vent
pre-vent-able
  or **pre-vent-ible**
pre-ven-tion

Plural, past tense, adverbial, and noun derivatives formed by adding
s, d or *ed, ly, ness, ment, ful, less,* or *ing* to an unchanged root word are
not listed, nor are words formed by dropping the final *e* and adding *ing*.

pre-ven-tive
pre-ver-bal
pre-view
pre-vi-ous
prey (victim)
 cf. pray (worship)
price
prickly
pride
priest
priest-hood
prig
prig-gish
prim
prima donna
prima fa-cie
pri-mal
pri-mar-ily
pri-mary
pri-mate
prime
primer (book)
 cf. prim-mer
 (more prim)
pri-me-val
prim-i-tive
primp
prince
prin-cess
prin-ci-pal (person)
 cf. prin-ci-ple (rule)
prin-ci-pal-ity
prin-ci-ple (rule)
 cf. prin-cip-al (person)
print
print-able
printer

print-out
prior
pri-or-ess
pri-or-ity
prism
pris-matic
prison
prissy
pris-tine
pri-vacy
pri-vate
pri-va-teer
pri-va-tion
priv-i-lege
prize
prize-fight
prize-win-ner
prob-a-bi-lis-tic
prob-a-bil-ity
prob-a-ble
prob-a-bly
pro-bate
pro-ba-tion
pro-ba-tional
pro-ba-tion-ary
pro-ba-tioner
probe
prob-lem
prob-lem-atic
 or prob-lem-at-i-cal
pro-bos-cis
pro-ce-dural
pro-ce-dure
pro-ceed
 (more forward)
 cf. pre-cede (go before)
pro-cess

pro-cess-ible
 or pro-cess-able
pro-ces-sion (parade)
 cf. pre-ces-sion
 (going first)
pro-ces-sional
pro-ces-sor
pro-claim
proc-la-ma-tion
pro-cliv-ity
pro-cras-ti-nate
pro-cras-ti-na-tion
pro-cras-ti-na-tor
pro-cre-ate
pro-cre-ation
proc-tor
pro-cure
prod
prod-i-gal
pro-di-gious
prod-igy
pro-duce
pro-duc-ible
pro-duce
pro-ducer
prod-uct
pro-duc-tion
pro-duc-tive
pro-duc-tiv-ity
pro-fane
pro-fan-ity
pro-fess
pro-fes-sion
pro-fes-sional
pro-fes-sion-al-ism
pro-fes-sion-al-iza-tion
pro-fes-sion-al-ize

Do not divide one-syllable words. Divide words by syllables, but leave
at least two letters of the word on the first line and three letters on the
following line. For additional guidelines, see page ix.

152

pro-fes-sor
pro-fes-so-rial
pro-fes-so-riat
or pro-fes-so-ri-ate
pro-fes-sor-ship
prof-fer
pro-fi-ciency
pro-fi-cient
pro-file
profit (gain)
 cf. prophet (person)
prof-it-able
prof-i-teer
 (unfair gainer)
pro-flu-ent
pro forma
pro-found
pro-fun-dity
pro-fuse
pro-fu-sion
pro-gen-i-tor
prog-eny
prog-no-sis
prog-nos-tic
prog-nos-ti-cate
prog-nos-ti-ca-tion
pro-gram
or pro-gramme
pro-gram-matic
pro-grammed
or pro-gramed
pro-gram-mer
or pro-gramer
prog-ress *(n.)*
pro-gress *(v.)*
pro-gres-sion
pro-gres-sional

pro-gres-sion-ist
pro-gres-sive
pro-hibit
pro-hi-bi-tion
pro-hi-bi-tion-ist
pro-hib-i-tive
pro-ject (throw)
 cf. proj-ect
 (design)
pro-ject-able
pro-jec-tile
pro-jec-tion
pro-le-tar-ian
pro-le-tar-i-an-iza-tion
pro-le-tar-i-an-ize
pro-le-tar-iat
pro-lif-er-ate
pro-lif-er-a-tion
pro-lif-er-ous
pro-lific
pro-loc-u-tor
pro-logue
or pro-log
pro-long
prom-e-nade
prom-i-nence
prom-i-nent
pro-mis-cu-ity
pro-mis-cu-ous
prom-ise
prom-i-sor
or prom-iser
prom-is-sory
prom-on-tory
pro-mot-able
pro-mote
pro-moter

pro-mo-tion
pro-mo-tional
prompt
pro-mul-gate
pro-nate
prone
prong
pro-noun
pro-nounce
pro-nounce-able
pro-nun-ci-a-tion
proof
proof-read
prop
pro-pa-ganda
pro-pa-gan-dism
pro-pa-gan-dist
pro-pa-gan-dis-tic
pro-pa-gan-dize
prop-a-gate
prop-a-ga-tor
prop-a-ga-tion
pro-pane
pro-pel
pro-pel-lant
or pro-pel-lent
pro-pelled
pro-pel-ler
or pro-pel-lor
pro-pen-sity
proper
prop-erty
proph-ecy (prediction)
or proph-esy
 cf. proph-esy
 (to predict)
prophet (person)

Plural, past tense, adverbial, and noun derivatives formed by adding
s, d or *ed, ly, ness, ment, ful, less,* or *ing* to an unchanged root word are
not listed, nor are words formed by dropping the final *e* and adding *ing*.

cf. **profit** (gain)
pro-phetic
pro-phy-laxis
pro-pin-quity
pro-pi-tious
prop-jet engine *(n.)*
pro-po-nent
pro-por-tion
pro-por-tional
pro-por-tion-ate
pro-posal
pro-pose
prop-o-si-tion (proposal)
cf. **prep-o-si-tion** (word)
pro-pound
propped
pro-pri-etar-ies
pro-pri-etary
pro-pri-etor
pro-pri-etor-ship
pro-pri-etress
pro-pri-ety
pro-pul-sion
pro-pul-sive
pro-pyl-ene
pro rata
pro-rate
pro-saic
pro-sa-ist
pro-scribe (prohibit)
cf. **pre-scribe** (order)
pro-scriber
pro-scrip-tion
pros-e-cute (bring into court) *or* **pros-tes-tor**
cf. **per-se-cute** (annoy)
pros-e-cu-tion

pros-e-cu-tor
pros-e-lyte
pros-e-ly-tism
pros-e-ly-tize
pro-sem-i-nar
pros-pect
pros-pec-tive (expected)
cf. **per-spec-tive** (visual)
pros-pec-tor
pros-pec-tus
pros-per
pros-per-ity
pros-per-ous
pros-tate
pros-thetic
prosth-odon-tics
pros-ti-tute
pros-ti-tu-tion
pros-trate
pros-tra-tion
pro-tag-o-nist
pro-tect
pro-tec-tion
pro-tec-tor
pro-tec-tor-ate
pro-tégé (male)
pro-té-gée (female)
pro-tein
pro tem
pro tem-pore
Pro-tero-zoic
pro-test
pro-tester
or **pro-tes-tor**
prot-es-tant
pro-tes-ta-tion

pro-to-col
pro-to-lithic
pro-ton
pro-to-plasm
pro-to-type
pro-to-zoan
pro-tract
pro-trac-tile
pro-trac-tion
pro-trac-tor
pro-trude
pro-tru-sion
pro-tu-ber-ance
proud
prov-able
prove
prov-erb
pro-ver-bial
Prov-erbs
pro-vide
prov-i-dence
prov-i-dent
prov-i-den-tial
pro-vider
prov-ince
pro-vin-cial
pro-vin-cial-ism
pro-vi-sion
pro-vi-sional
pro-viso
prov-o-ca-tion
pro-voc-a-tive
pro-voke
pro-vost
prow
prow-ess

Do not divide one-syllable words. Divide words by syllables, but leave at least two letters of the word on the first line and three letters on the following line. For additional guidelines, see page ix.

154

prowl
prox-i-mate
prox-im-i-ty
prox-ies
proxy
prude
pru-dence
pru-dent
pru-den-tial
prud-ish
prune
pru-ri-ence
pru-ri-ent
pry
psalm
psalm-book
p's and q's *(n. pl.)*
pseudo
pseud-onym
pseud-onym-ity
pshaw
psi
pso-ri-a-sis
psych
or psyche
psy-che-delic
psy-chi-a-try
psy-chi-at-ric
psy-chi-a-trist
psy-chic
psy-cho
psy-cho-anal-y-sis
psy-cho-an-a-lyze
psy-cho-drama
psy-cho-dy-nam-ics
psy-cho-gen-e-sis

psy-cho-log-i-cal
psy-chol-o-gize
psy-chol-ogy
psy-cho-met-ric
psy-cho-neu-ro-sis
psy-cho-path
psy-cho-pathic
psy-cho-pa-thol-o-gy
psy-chop-a-thy
psy-cho-sex-ual
psy-cho-sis
psy-cho-so-matic
psy-cho-ther-a-peu-tic
psy-cho-ther-apy
ptar-mi-gan
pto-maine
pub
pu-berty
pu-bes-cence
pu-bes-cent
pub-lic
pub-li-ca-tion
pub-li-cist
pub-lic-ity
pub-li-cize
public—spirited *(adj.)*
pub-lish
pub-lisher
pud-ding
pud-dle
pudgy
pueblo
pu-er-ile
puff
pu-gi-lism
pu-gi-list

pug-na-cious
puis-sance
pul-chri-tude
pull
pul-let
pul-ley
pull-over
pul-mo-nary
pul-mo-tor
pulp
pul-pit
pul-sate
pul-sa-tion
pulse
pulse—jet en-gine *(n.)*
pul-ver-ize
pum-ice
pum-mel
pump
pum-per-nickel
pun
punch
punch-ball
punch bowl
punch card *(n.)*
or punched card
punc-til-i-ous
punc-tual
punc-tu-al-i-ty
punc-tu-ate
punc-tu-a-tion
punc-ture
pun-dit
pun-gent
pun-ish
pu-ni-tive

Plural, past tense, adverbial, and noun derivatives formed by adding
s, d or *ed, ly, ness, ment, ful, less,* or *ing* to an unchanged root word are
not listed, nor are words formed by dropping the final *e* and adding *ing*.

155

punk
pun-ster
punt
pupa
pu-pae *(n. pl.)*
pu-pil
pup-pet
pup-pe-teer
pup-petry
puppy
pur-chase
pure
pure-blood
pure-bred
purer
pur-est
pur-ga-tory
purge
pu-ri-fi-ca-tion
pu-rify
pur-ism
pur-ist
pu-ri-tan
pu-ri-tan-i-cal
pu-rity
purl (knit)
  cf. **pearl** (gem)
pur-loin
pur-ple
pur-plish
pur-port
pur-pose
purr
purse
purser
pur-su-ant

pur-sue
pur-suit
pur-vey
pur-veyor
pur-view
pus
push
push-cart
pusher
push-over
pu-sil-lan-i-mous
put
pu-tre-fac-tion
pu-trefy
pu-trid
putt
put-ter
putty
puz-zle
Pyg-ma-lion
pygmy
py-lon
py-or-rhea
pyr-a-mid
py-ra-mi-dal
pyre
py-rene
Py-rex
py-rite
py-ro-chem-i-cal
py-ro-genic
py-ro-ma-nia
py-ro-ma-niac
py-ro-tech-nic
Pyth-ias
py-thon

quack
quack-ery
quad-ran-gle
quad-rant
qua-dra-tic
qua-drille
quad-ru-ped
qua-dru-ple
qua-dru-pli-cate
quag-mire
quail
quaint
quake
Quak-er-ism
qual-i-fi-able
qual-i-fi-ca-tion
qual-i-fied
qual-i-fier
qual-ify
qual-i-ta-tive
qual-ity
qualm
quan-da-ries
quan-dary
quan-ti-fi-ca-tion
quan-ti-fier
quan-tify
quan-ti-tate
quan-ti-ta-tive
quan-tity
quar-an-tin-able
quar-an-tine
quar-rel

Do not divide one-syllable words. Divide words by syllables, but leave at least two letters of the word on the first line and three letters on the following line. For additional guidelines, see page ix.

quar-rel-some
quarry
quar-ter
quar-ter-deck
quar-ter horse *(n.)*
quar-ter-mas-ter
quar-tet
or quar-tette
quar-tile
quartz (mineral)
  cf. quarts (part of a gallon)
quash
quasi
qua-ver
queasy
or queazy
queen
queer
quell
quench
query
quest
ques-tion
ques-tion-able
ques-tion-naire
queue (braid; line)
  cf. cue (hint)
quib-ble
quick
quicken
quick—freeze *(v.)*
quid-nunc
quid pro quo
qui-es-cence
qui-es-cent

quiet
qui-etude
quill
quilt
quince
qui-nine
quin-tes-sence
quin-tet
or quin-tette
quin-tu-ple
quin-tu-plet
quin-tu-pli-cate
quip
quire (measure)
  cf. choir (singers)
quirk
quis-ling
quit
quit-claim
quite
quit-ter
quiver
qui-xote
quix-otic
quiz
quiz-mas-ter
quiz show *(n.)*
quizzed
quiz-zi-cal
quoit
Quon-set (trademark)
quota
quot-able
quo-ta-tion
quote
quo-tient

R

rab-bet (reduce)
  cf. rab-bit (animal)
rabbi
rab-bin-ate
rab-binic
rab-bit (animal)
  cf. rab-bet (reduce)
rab-bit ears *(n.)*
rab-bit punch
rab-ble
rabble—rouser
ra-bid
ra-bies
rac-coon
race
race-course
race-horse
ra-ceme
racer
race riot
rachet
ra-cial
ra-cial-ism
rac-ism
rack (shelf)
  cf. wrack (wreckage)
racket
or rac-quet
rack-e-teer
ra-con-teur
racy
ra-dar
ra-dar-scope

Plural, past tense, adverbial, and noun derivatives formed by adding *s, d* or *ed, ly, ness, ment, ful, less,* or *ing* to an unchanged root word are not listed, nor are words formed by dropping the final *e* and adding *ing.*

157

ra-dial	raid	ranch house
ra-di-ance	raider	ran-cid
ra-di-ant	rail	ran-cor
ra-di-ate	rail-road	ran-dom
ra-di-a-tion	rain (water)	random—access *(adj.)*
ra-di-a-tor	*cf.* reign (rule)	ran-dom-iza-tion
rad-i-cal	*cf.* rein (strap)	rang
rad-i-cal-ism	rain-bow	range
rad-i-cal-ize	rain check	ranger
rad-i-cle	rain-coat	rangy
ra-dio	raise (lift)	rani
ra-dio-ac-tiv-ity	*cf.* raze (destroy)	*or* ra-nee
ra-dio-broad-cast	rai-sin	rank
ra-dio-gram	rai-son d'être	rank and file
ra-dio-iso-tope	raja	ran-kle
ra-di-ol-o-gist	*or* ra-jah	ran-sack
ra-di-ol-ogy	rake	ran-som
ra-dio-man	rak-ish	rant
ra-di-om-e-ter	rally	rap (knock)
ra-dio-phone	ram	*cf.* wrap (cover)
ra-dio-ther-a-pist	ram-ble	ra-pa-cious
ra-dio-ther-apy	ram-bunc-tious	rape
radio wave	ram-i-fi-ca-tion	rapid
ra-dius	ram-ify	ra-pier
raf-fle	ram-jet engine *(n.)*	rap-ine
raft	rammed	rapped
raf-ter	ram-ming	rap-per
rag	ramp	rap-port
rag-a-muf-fin	ram-page	rapt (engrossed)
rage	ram-pant	*cf.* wrapped (covered)
rag-ged	ram-part	rap-ture
ra-gout	ram-rod	rare
rag-tag	ram-shackle	rar-efied
rag-time	ran	*or* rar-i-fied
rag-weed	ranch	rar-ity
rah—rah *(adj.)*	rancher	ras-cal

Do not divide one-syllable words. Divide words by syllables, but leave
at least two letters of the word on the first line and three letters on the
following line. For additional guidelines, see page ix.

ras-cal-ity
rash
rasp
rasp-berry
rat
ratchet
rate
rater
rather
raths-kel-ler
rat-ify
ra-tio
ra-tion
ra-tio-nal
ra-tio-nale
ra-tio-nal-ism
ra-tio-nal-ity
ra-tio-nal-ize
rat-tan
rat-tle
rat-tler
rat-tle-snake
rat-trap
ratty
rau-cous
raun-chy
rav-age
rave
ravel
ra-ven
rav-en-ous
ra-vine
rav-i-oli
rav-ish
raw
raw deal

raw-hide
raw score
ray
rayon
raze (destroy)
  cf. raise (lift)
ra-zor
raz-zle—daz-zle (n.)
razz-ma-tazz
reach
reach-able
re-act
re-ac-tion
re-ac-tion-ary
re-ac-ti-vate
re-ac-tor
read (understand print)
  cf. reed (tall grass)
read-able
reader
readily
read-out (n.)
ready
ready—made (adj.) (n.)
ready—to—wear (adj.)
real (actual)
  cf. reel (spool)
re-align
re-al-ism
re-al-ity
re-al-iza-tion
re-al-ize
re-ally
realm
real time (n.)
re-alty

ream
reap
rear
re-arm
re-ar-ma-ment
rea-son
rea-son-able
re-as-sur-ance
re-as-sure
re-bate
rebel
re-bel-lion
re-bel-lious
re-birth
re-bound
re-buff
re-build
re-buke
re-but
re-but-tal
re-cal-ci-trance
re-cal-ci-trant
re-call
re-cant
re-cap
re-ca-pit-u-late
re-cap-ture
re-cede
re-ceipt
re-ceiv-able
re-ceive
re-ceiver
re-cent
re-cep-ta-cle
re-cep-tion
re-cep-tion-ist

Plural, past tense, adverbial, and noun derivatives formed by adding
s, d or *ed, ly, ness, ment, ful, less,* or *ing* to an unchanged root word are
not listed, nor are words formed by dropping the final *e* and adding *ing*.

re-cep-tive
re-cess
re-ces-sion
re-ces-sional
re-charge
re-cid-i-vism
re-cid-i-vist
rec-ipe
re-cip-i-ent
re-cip-ro-cal
re-cip-ro-cate
re-cip-ro-ca-tive
rec-i-proc-ity
re-cital
rec-i-ta-tion
re-cite
reck-less
reckon
re-claim
rec-la-ma-tion
re-cline
re-cluse
re-clu-sion
rec-og-ni-tion
re-cog-ni-zance
rec-og-nize
rec-og-niz-able
re-coil
rec-ol-lect
rec-ol-lec-tion
rec-om-mend
rec-om-men-da-tion
re-com-mit
rec-om-pense
rec-on-cil-able
rec-on-cile

rec-on-cil-i-a-tion
rec-on-dite
re-con-nais-sance
re-con-noi-ter
re-con-sider
re-con-sti-tute
re-con-struct
re-con-struc-tion
re-cord
re-count
re-coup
re-course
re-cover
re-cov-ery
re-cre-ation (create again)
rec-re-ation (diversion)
re-crim-i-nate
re-cruit
rect-an-gle
rect-an-gu-lar
rec-ti-fi-able
rec-ti-fier
rec-tify
rec-ti-tude
rec-tor
rec-tory
re-cu-per-ate
re-cu-per-a-tion
re-cu-per-a-tive
re-cur
re-cur-rent
re-cy-cla-ble
re-cy-cle
re-dact
re-dec-o-rate
re-deem

re-deem-able
re-deemer
re-demp-tion
re-dis-trict
red—letter *(adj.)*
re-doubt
re-dress
re-duce
re-duc-tion
re-dun-dancy
re-dun-dant
reed (tall grass)
   cf. read (understand print)
re-ed-u-cate
re-ed-u-ca-tive
reef
reel (spool)
   cf. real (actual)
re-elect
reel—to—reel *(adj.)*
re-en-act
re-en-ter
re-en-try
re-fer
ref-er-ee
ref-er-ence
ref-er-en-dum
re-fer-ral
re-ferred
re-fine
re-fin-ery
re-fin-ish
re-flect
re-flec-tion
re-flec-tive
re-flec-tor

Do not divide one-syllable words. Divide words by syllables, but leave at least two letters of the word on the first line and three letters on the following line. For additional guidelines, see page ix.

re-flex
re-for-est
re-for-es-ta-tion
re-form
ref-or-ma-tion
re-for-ma-tory
re-former
re-frac-tion
re-frac-tive
re-frac-tor
re-frain
re-fresh
re-frig-er-ant
re-frig-er-ate
re-frig-er-a-tor
re-fuel
ref-uge
ref-u-gee
re-fund
re-fur-bish
re-fusal
re-fuse
re-fute
re-fut-able
re-fut-ably
re-gain
re-gal
re-gale
re-ga-lia
re-gard
re-gatta
re-gency
re-gen-er-acy
re-gen-er-ate
re-gen-er-a-tion
re-gen-er-a-tive

re-gen-er-a-tor
re-gent
reg-i-cide
re-gime
or ré-gime
reg-i-ment
reg-i-men-ta-tion
re-gion
re-gional
re-gion-al-ism
re-gion-al-ize
reg-is-ter
reg-is-tra-ble
reg-is-trant
reg-is-trar
reg-is-tra-tion
reg-is-try
re-gress
re-gres-sion
re-gret
re-gret-ta-ble
re-gret-ta-bly
re-group
reg-u-lar
reg-u-lar-ity
reg-u-lar-ize
reg-u-late
reg-u-la-tion
reg-u-la-tive
reg-u-la-tor
reg-u-la-tory
re-gur-gi-tate
re-gur-gi-ta-tion
re-ha-bil-i-tate
re-ha-bil-i-ta-tion
re-ha-bil-i-ta-tor

re-hash
re-hearsal
re-hearse
re-house
reichs-mark
reign (rule)
cf. **rain** (water)
cf. **rein** (strap)
re-im-burs-able
re-im-burse
rein (strap)
cf. **rain** (water)
cf. **reign** (rule)
rein-deer
re-in-force
re-in-state
re-is-sue
re-it-er-ate
re-it-er-a-tion
re-ject
re-jecter
or re-jec-tor
re-jec-tion
re-joice
re-join
re-ju-ve-nate
re-kin-dle
re-lapse
re-late
re-la-tion
re-la-tion-ship
rel-a-tive
rel-a-tiv-ism
rel-a-tiv-ity
re-lax
re-lax-ant

Plural, past tense, adverbial, and noun derivatives formed by adding
s, d or *ed, ly, ness, ment, ful, less,* or *ing* to an unchanged root word are
not listed, nor are words formed by dropping the final *e* and adding *ing*.   161

re-lax-a-tion
re-lay
re-lease
rel-e-gate
rel-e-ga-tion
re-lent
rel-e-vance
rel-e-vant
re-li-abil-ity
re-li-able
re-li-ably
re-li-ance
relic
re-lief
re-lieve
re-li-gion
re-li-gious
re-lin-quish
rel-ish
re-lo-cate
re-luc-tance
re-luc-tant
rely
re-main
re-main-der
re-mand
re-mark
re-mark-able
re-me-dial
rem-edy
re-mem-ber
re-mem-brance
re-mind
rem-i-nisce
rem-i-nis-cence
rem-i-nis-cent

re-mise
re-miss
re-mis-si-ble
re-mis-sion
re-mit
re-mit-tance
re-mit-ted
re-mit-ting
rem-nant
re-model
re-mon-strate
re-morse
re-mote
re-mov-able
re-moval
re-move
re-mu-ner-ate
re-mu-ner-a-tion
re-mu-ner-a-tive
re-nais-sance
rend
ren-der
ren-dez-vous
ren-di-tion
ren-e-gade
re-nege
re-new
re-new-able
re-newal
re-nounce
ren-o-vate
re-nown
rent
rent—a—car *(n.)*
rental
re-num-ber

re-nun-ci-a-tion
re-open
re-or-ga-ni-za-tion
re-or-ga-nize
re-pair
rep-a-ra-ble
rep-a-ra-tion
rep-ar-tee
re-past
re-pa-tri-ate
re-pa-tri-a-tion
re-pay
re-peal
re-peal-able
re-peat
re-pel
re-pelled
re-pel-lent
or re-pel-lant
re-pel-ling
re-pent
re-pen-tance
re-pen-tant
re-per-cus-sion
rep-er-toire
rep-er-tory
rep-e-ti-tion
rep-e-ti-tious
re-pet-i-tive
re-place
re-play
re-plen-ish
rep-lica
rep-li-cate
rep-li-ca-tion
re-ply

Do not divide one-syllable words. Divide words by syllables, but leave
at least two letters of the word on the first line and three letters on the
following line. For additional guidelines, see page ix.

re-port
re-port-able
re-porter
re-pose
re-pos-i-tory
re-pos-sess
rep-re-hen-si-ble
rep-re-sent
rep-re-sent-able
rep-re-sen-ta-tion
rep-re-sen-ta-tive
re-press
re-pres-sion
re-prieve
rep-ri-mand
re-pri-sal
re-proach
rep-ro-bate
re-pro-duce
re-pro-duc-tion
re-prove
rep-tile
rep-til-ian
re-pub-lic
re-pub-li-can
re-pu-di-ate
re-pu-di-a-tion
re-pugn
re-pug-nance
re-pug-nant
re-pulse
re-pul-sion
re-pul-sive
rep-u-ta-ble
rep-u-ta-tion
re-pute

re-quest
re-quiem
re-quire
req-ui-site
req-ui-si-tion
re-quital
re-quite
re-sal-able
re-sale
re-scind
res-cue
re-search
re-search-able
re-sem-blance
re-sem-ble
re-sent
res-er-va-tion
re-serve
re-serv-ist
res-er-voir
re-set
re-set-table
re-set-ting
re-shape
re-shuf-fle
re-side
res-i-dence
res-i-den-cies
res-i-dency
res-i-dent
res-i-den-tial
re-sid-ual
res-i-due
re-sign
res-ig-na-tion
re-sil-ience

re-sil-iency
re-sil-ient
resin
res-in-ous
re-sist
re-sis-tance
re-sis-tant
re-sister
re-sist-ible
or re-sist-able
re-sis-tor
re-sole
re-sol-u-ble
res-o-lute
res-o-lu-tion
re-solv-able
re-solve
res-o-nance
res-o-nant
res-o-nate
res-o-na-tor
re-sorp-tion
re-sort
re-sound
re-source
re-spect
re-spect-abil-ity
re-spect-able
re-spect-ably
re-spec-tive
re-spi-ra-ble
res-pi-ra-tion
re-spi-ra-tory
res-pi-ra-tor
re-spite
re-splen-dence

re-splen-dent
re-spond
re-spon-dent
re-sponse
re-spon-si-bil-ity
re-spon-si-ble
re-spon-si-bly
re-spon-sive
rest (relax)
  cf. wrest (wrench)
res-tau-rant
res-tau-ra-teur
rest home (n.)
res-ti-tute
res-ti-tu-tion
res-tive
re-stor-able
re-sto-ra-tion
re-stor-ative
re-strain
re-straint
re-strict
re-stric-tion
re-stric-tive
re-struc-ture
re-sult
re-sume (begin again)
  cf. ré-su-mé (summary)
re-sumé
or re-sume
re-sump-tion
re-sur-face
re-sur-gence
re-sur-gent
res-ur-rect
res-ur-rec-tion

re-sus-ci-tate
re-sus-ci-ta-tion
re-sus-ci-ta-tive
re-sus-ci-ta-tor
re-tail
re-tain
re-tainer
re-tal-i-ate
re-tal-i-a-tion
re-tal-ia-tory
re-tard
re-tar-dant
re-tar-da-tion
retch (to vomit)
  cf. wretch (villain)
re-ten-tion
re-ten-tive
re-test
re-think
ret-i-cence
ret-i-cent
ret-ina
ret-i-nue
re-tire
re-tiree
re-tort
re-tract
re-tract-able
re-trac-tion
re-trac-tor
re-tread
ret-ri-bu-tion
re-trieval
ret-ro-ac-tive
ret-ro-grade
ret-ro-gres-sion

retro—rocket (n.)
ret-ro-spect
ret-ro-spec-tion
ret-ro-spec-tive
ret-sina
re-turn
re-turn-able
re-union
re-unite
re—up (v.)
re-us-able
re-vamp
re-veal
rev-eille
revel
rev-e-la-tion
re-ve-la-tory
re-venge
rev-e-nue
re-ver-ber-ant
re-ver-ber-ate
re-ver-ber-a-tion
re-ver-ber-a-tive
re-vere
rev-er-ence
rev-er-end
rev-er-ent
re-ver-sal
re-verse
re-vers-ible
re-vers-ibly
re-ver-sion
re-vert
re-vet
re-view (study)
  cf. re-vue (entertainment)

Do not divide one-syllable words. Divide words by syllables, but leave
at least two letters of the word on the first line and three letters on the
following line. For additional guidelines, see page ix.

re-viewer
re-vile
re-vise
re-vi-sion
re-vi-tal-iza-tion
re-vi-tal-ize
re-vival
re-vive
re-vo-ca-ble
re-vo-ca-tion
re-voke
re-volt
rev-o-lu-tion
rev-o-lu-tion-ist
rev-o-lu-tion-ize
re-volve
re-vue (entertainment)
  cf. re-view (study)
re-vulsed
re-vul-sion
re-ward
rhap-sodic
rhap-so-dize
rhap-sody
rhet-o-ric
rhe-tor-i-cal
rheu-matic
rheu-ma-tism
rheu-ma-toid
Rh factor (n.)
rhine-stone
rhi-noc-eros
rhi-noc-er-oses (n. pl.)
or rhi-noc-eros
or rhi-noc-eri
Rh—negative (adj.)

rho-do-den-dron
Rh—positive (adj.)
rhu-barb
rhyme
rhythm
rhyth-mic
rib
rib-ald
ribbed
rib-bon
ri-bo-fla-vin
rice
rich
rick-ety
rick-sha
or rick-shaw
ric-o-chet
rid
ridded
rid-den
rid-dle
ride
ridge
rid-i-cule
ri-dic-u-lous
riff
riff-raff
ri-fle
ri-fle-man
ri-flery
ri-fling
rift
rig
rig-a-ma-role
rigged
rig-ging

right (correct)
  cf. rite (solemn ceremony)
  cf. write (make letters)
righ-teous
right—of—way
rigid
ri-gid-ity
rigor
rigor mor-tis
rig-or-ous
rim
rimmed
rind
ring (circle; sound)
  cf. wring (twist)
rink
rinse
riot
ri-ot-ous
rip cord (n.)
ripe
ripen
rip off (v.)
rip—off (n.)
ri-poste
ripped
rip-ple
rise
risk
ris-qué
rite (solemn ceremony)
  cf. right (correct)
  cf. write (make letters)
rit-ual
rit-u-al-ism
rit-u-al-is-tic

Plural, past tense, adverbial, and noun derivatives formed by adding
s, d or *ed, ly, ness, ment, ful, less,* or *ing* to an unchanged root word are
not listed, nor are words formed by dropping the final *e* and adding *ing*.

rit-u-al-ize	ro-deo	ro-ta-tor
ri-val	roe *(fish eggs)*	rote *(mechanical way)*
ri-valry	*cf.* row *(move with oars)*	*cf.* wrote *(made letters)*
river	roent-gen	ro-tis-serie
riv-er-bed	rogue	ro-to-gra-vure
rivet	role *(a part)*	ro-tor
ri-vi-era	*cf.* roll *(move)*	rot-ten
riv-u-let	roller derby *(n.)*	ro-tund
roach	roly—poly *(adj.)*	ro-tunda
road *(highway)*	ro-mance	roué
cf. rode *(driven)*	ro-man-tic	rouge
road-a-bil-ity	ro-man-ti-cism	rough *(not smooth)*
road-bed	ro-man-ti-cize	*cf.* ruff *(collar)*
road hog *(n.)*	rondo	rough-age
road-ster	roof	rough—and—ready *(adj.)*
road test	rookie	rough-neck
roam	room	rou-lette
roar	roomer *(lodger)*	round
roast	*cf.* ru-mor *(gossip)*	rouse
roaster	room-mate	roust
rob	roost	rout
robbed	rooster	route *(way to go)*
rob-bery	root *(part of plant)*	*cf.* root *(part of plant)*
rob-bing	*cf.* route *(way to go)*	rou-tine
robe	rope	rou-tin-ize
ro-bot	Ror-schach test *(n.)*	rover
ro-bust	ro-sary	row *(move with oars)*
rock	rose	*cf.* roe *(fish eggs)*
rock—bottom *(adj.)*	ro-sette	row-boat
rocket	Rosh Ha-sha-nah	rowdy
rock-etry	ros-ter	royal
rocket ship	rosy	roy-alty
rod	rot	rub
rode *(driven)*	ro-tary	rubbed
cf. road *(highway)*	ro-tate	rub-ber
ro-dent	ro-ta-tion	rub-bish

Do not divide one-syllable words. Divide words by syllables, but leave
at least two letters of the word on the first line and three letters on the
following line. For additional guidelines, see page ix.

rub-ble
rub-down
ru-bella
ru-be-ola
ruby
rud-der
ruddy
rude
ru-di-ment
ru-di-men-tary
rue
ruff (collar)
cf. **rough** (not smooth)
ruf-fle
rug
rug-ged
ruin
ru-in-ate
ru-in-ation
ru-in-ous
rule
ruler
rumba
rum-ble
ru-mi-nant
ru-mi-nate
rum-mage
ru-mor (gossip)
cf. **roomer** (lodger)
rump
rum-ple
run
rung (did ring)
cf. **wrung** (twisted)
run-ner
run-ning

run—of—the—mill *(adj.)*
ru-pee
ru-ral
ruse
rust
rus-tle
rusty
rut
rye (grain)
cf. **wry** (twist)

S

Sab-bath
sab-bat-i-cal
sa-ber
or **sa-bre**
sa-ble
sab-o-tage
sab-o-teur
sac (pouch in animal)
cf. **sack** (bag; loot)
sac-cha-rin (calorie-free
sweetener)
cf. **sac-cha-rine** (sickishly
sweet)
sack (bag)
cf. **sac** (pouch in animal)
sac-ra-ment
sac-ra-men-tal
sa-cred
sac-ri-fice

sac-ri-fi-cial
sac-ri-lege
sac-ro-sanct
sad
sad-der
sad-dle
sa-dism
sa-dist
sa-dis-tic
sa-fari
safe
safe-guard
safety
safety belt
sag
saga
sa-ga-cious
sa-gac-i-ty
sage
sagged
Sag-it-tar-ius
sail (cloth)
cf. **sale** (exchange)
sailor
saint
sake (purpose)
sake
or **saki** (alcoholic beverage)
sal-able
or **sale-able**
salad
sa-lami
sal-ary
sale (exchange)
cf. **sail** (cloth)
sales check *(n.)*

Plural, past tense, adverbial, and noun derivatives formed by adding
s, d or *ed, ly, ness, ment, ful, less,* or *ing* to an unchanged root word are
not listed, nor are words formed by dropping the final *e* and adding *ing.*

sales-clerk
sales-room
sales slip
sales tax
sa-lient
sa-line
sa-li-ni-za-tion
sa-li-nize
sa-liva
sal-i-vary
sal-i-vate
sal-low
salmon
sal-mo-nella
sa-lon (room)
  cf. sa-loon (tavern)
salt
salt-cel-lar
sa-lu-bri-ous
sal-u-tary
sal-u-ta-tion
sa-lute
sal-vage (rescue)
  cf. sel-vage
  or sel-vedge (edge)
sal-va-tion
salve
salvo
Sa-mar-i-tan
same
sam-o-var
sam-ple
sam-pler
sam-u-rai
san-a-tar-ium
  or san-a-to-rium

sanc-ti-fi-ca-tion
sanc-tify
sanc-ti-mo-nious
sanc-tion
sanc-tity
sanc-tu-ary
sand
san-dal
sand-bag
sand-pa-per
sand-wich
sane (rational)
  cf. seine (net)
sang
san-gui-nary
san-guine
san-guin-e-ous
san-i-tary
san-i-ta-tion
san-ity
sank
sap
sa-pi-ens
sap-phire
sar-casm
sar-cas-tic
sar-coma
sar-coph-a-gous (carnivorous)
  cf. sar-coph-a-gus (coffin)
sar-dine
sar-donic
sari
  or sa-ree
sa-rong
sar-sa-pa-rilla
sash

sassy
Sa-tan
sa-tanic
satchel
sate
sat-el-lite
sa-tia-ble
sa-tiate
satin
sat-ire
sa-tiric
sat-i-rist
sat-is-fac-tion
sat-is-fac-to-rily
sat-is-fac-tory
sat-isfy
sat-u-rate
sat-u-ra-tion
sa-tyr
sauce
sau-cer
sau-er-kraut
sauna
saun-ter
sau-sage
sauté
sau-téed
sau-terne
sav-age
sav-agery
sa-vanna
  or sa-van-nah
sav-ior
  or sav-iour (saver)
  cf. savor (taste)
  or sa-vour

Do not divide one-syllable words. Divide words by syllables, but leave
at least two letters of the word on the first line and three letters on the
following line. For additional guidelines, see page ix.

saw	scat-ter	sci-en-tific
sax-o-phone	scat-ter-brain	sci-en-tist
say	scat-ter rug	scim-i-tar
say—so *(n.)*	scav-en-ger	scin-tilla
scab	sce-nario	scin-til-late
scab-bard	sce-nar-ist	scin-til-la-tor
scaf-fold	scene	scin-til-la-tion
scald	scen-ery	scion
scale	sce-nic	scis-sors
scal-lion	scent (odor)	scle-ro-sis
scal-lop	*cf.* **cent** (one penny)	scoff
scalp	*cf.* **sent** (did send)	scoff-law
scal-pel	sched-ule	scold
scamp	Sche-her-a-zade	scone
scan	sche-matic	scoop
scan-dal	scheme	scope
scan-dal-ize	schism	scorch
scan-dal-ous	schis-matic	score-board
scanned	schiz-oid	score-keeper
scan-ner	schizo-phre-nia	scorn
scant	scholar	Scor-pio
scape-goat	scho-las-tic	scor-pion
scap-ula (bone)	scho-las-ti-cism	scoun-drel
cf. **scap-u-lar** (cloth)	school	scour
scar	school age *(n.)*	scourge
scarab	school board *(n.)*	scout
scarce	school-book	scout-mas-ter
scar-city	school bus *(n.)*	scow
scare-crow	school dis-trict *(n.)*	scowl
scarf	school-house	scram-ble
scar-ify	school-teacher	scrap
scar-let	school-work	scrap-book
scary	schoo-ner	scrape
scarred	schot-tische	scratch
scarves *(n. pl.)*	sci-at-ica	scrawl
scathe	sci-ence	scraw-nier

Plural, past tense, adverbial, and noun derivatives formed by adding
s, d or *ed, ly, ness, ment, ful, less,* or *ing* to an unchanged root word are
not listed, nor are words formed by dropping the final *e* and adding *ing*.

scraw-ni-est	sculp-tor	sea-sonal
scrawny	sculp-tress	sea-son-ing
scream	sculp-ture	seat
screech	sculp-tur-esque	sea-weed
screen	scum	sea-wor-thy
screen-play	scur-ril-ity	se-cede
screen test *(n.)*	scur-ri-lous	se-ces-sion
screw	scur-ried	se-ces-sion-ist
screw-driver	scurry	se-clude
screw-worm	scurvy	se-clu-sion
scrib-ble	scut-tle	sec-ond
scribe	scut-tle-butt	sec-ond-arily
scrim-mage	scythe	sec-ond-ary
scrimp	sea (ocean)	sec-ond—rate *(adj.)*
scrim-shaw	*cf.* see (look)	se-cre-cies
scrip (writing)	sea-coast	se-crecy
cf. script (manuscript)	sea-farer	se-cret
scrip-ture	sea horse	sec-re-tar-iat
script-writer	seal	sec-re-tary
scroll	seam (joint)	secretary—general
scrounge	*cf.* seem (appear)	secretaries–general *(n. pl.)*
scrub	sea-man	se-crete
scrubby	seam-stress	se-cre-tion
scruff	seamy	se-cre-tive
scrunch	sé-ance	sect
scru-ple	sea-plane	sec-tar-ian
scru-pu-lous	sea power	sec-tion
scru-ta-ble	sear (burn)	sec-tional
scru-ti-nize	*cf.* seer (prophet)	sec-tor
scru-tiny	search	sec-u-lar
scuba	search-light	sec-u-lar-ism
scuff	search war-rant	sec-u-lar-ize
scuf-fle	sea-shell	se-cure
scull (move with oar)	sea-shore	se-cu-rity
cf. skull (head)	sea-sick	se-dan
scul-lery	sea-son	se-date

Do not divide one-syllable words. Divide words by syllables, but leave
at least two letters of the word on the first line and three letters on the
170   following line. For additional guidelines, see page ix.

se-da-tion
sed-a-tive
sed-en-tary
sed-i-ment
sed-i-men-tary
sed-i-men-ta-tion
se-di-tion
se-di-tious
se-duce
se-duc-tion
se-duc-tive
sed-u-lous
see (look)
  cf. **sea** (ocean)
seed (germ)
  cf. **cede** (yield)
seek
seem (appear)
  cf. **seam** (joint)
seep
seep-age
seer (prophet)
  cf. **sear** (burn)
seer-sucker
see-saw
seethe
seg-ment
seg-re-gate
seg-re-ga-tion
seg-re-ga-tion-ist
seine (net)
  cf. **sane** (rational)
seis-mic
seis-mo-graph
seize (grab)
  cf. **sees** (looks)

sei-zure
sel-dom
se-lect
se-lec-tion
se-lec-tive
se-lect-man
se-lec-tor
self
self—addressed *(adj.)*
self—assured *(adj.)*
self—centered *(adj.)*
self—complacent *(adj.)*
self—composed *(adj.)*
self—conceit *(n.)*
self—confidence *(n.)*
self—conscious *(adj.)*
self—contained *(adj.)*
self—defense *(n.)*
self—denial *(n.)*
self—destruct *(v.)*
self—discipline *(n.)*
self—educated *(adj.)*
self—employed *(adj.)*
self—esteem *(n.)*
self—evident *(adj.)*
self—immolation *(n.)*
self—imposed *(adj.)*
self—incrimination *(n.)*
self—indulgence *(n.)*
self-ish
self—made *(adj.)*
self—mastery *(n.)*
self—pity *(n.)*
self—poised *(adj.)*
self—possessed *(adj.)*
self—preservation *(n.)*

self—regulating *(adj.)*
self—reliance *(n.)*
self—respect *(n.)*
self—righteous *(adj.)*
self—sacrifice *(n.)*
self—satisfaction *(n.)*
self—sufficient *(adj.)*
self—support *(n.)*
self—taught *(adj.)*
sell (exchange)
  cf. **cell** (small room)
seller (offers for sale)
  cf. **cel-lar** (basement)
sell-out *(n.)*
sell out *(v.)*
selt-zer
sel-vage
or sel-vedge (edge)
  cf. **sal-vage** (rescue)
se-man-tic
or se-man-ti-cal
se-man-ti-cist
sema-phore
sem-blance
se-mes-ter
se-mes-tral
se-mes-trial
se-mes-ter hour *(n.)*
semi
semi-an-nual
semi-arid
semi-au-to-matic
semi-cir-cle
semi-clas-si-cal
semi-co-lon
semi-con-scious

Plural, past tense, adverbial, and noun derivatives formed by adding
s, d or *ed, ly, ness, ment, ful, less,* or *ing* to an unchanged root word are
not listed, nor are words formed by dropping the final *e* and adding *ing*.

semi-dark-ness
semi-des-ert
semi-di-ur-nal
semi-for-mal
sem-i-nal
sem-i-nar
sem-i-nar-ian
sem-i-nar-ies
sem-i-nary
Sem-i-nole
semi-pre-cious
semi-pri-vate
semi-pro-fes-sional
semi-re-tired
Sem-ite
semi-ter-res-trial
Se-mitic
Sem-i-tism
semi-trailer
semi-trop-i-cal
sen-ate
sen-a-tor
sen-a-to-rial
send
send—off *(n.)*
se-nile
se-nil-ity
se-nior
se-nior-ity
se-nor
or se-ñor
se-nora
or se-ñora
se-no-rita
or se-ño-rita
sen-sa-tion

sen-sa-tional
sen-sa-tion-al-ism
sen-sa-tion-al-ist
sense
sen-si-bil-ity
sen-si-ble
sen-si-bly
sen-si-tive
sen-si-tiv-i-ties
sen-si-tiv-ity
sen-si-ti-za-tion
sen-si-tize
sen-sory
sen-sual
sen-su-al-ism
sen-su-al-ist
sen-su-al-is-tic
sen-su-al-ize
sen-su-ous
sent (did send)
cf. cent (one penny)
cf. scent (odor)
sen-tence
sen-ten-tious
sen-tient
sen-ti-ment
sen-ti-men-tal
sen-ti-men-tal-ism
sen-ti-men-tal-ist
sen-ti-men-tal-ity
sen-ti-men-tal-ize
sen-ti-nel
sen-try
sen-try box
sep-a-ra-bil-ity
sep-a-ra-ble

sep-a-ra-bly
sep-a-rate
sep-a-ra-tion
sep-a-ra-tion-ist
sep-a-ra-tism
sep-a-ra-tist
sep-a-ra-tor
se-pia
sep-sis
sep-ten-nial
sep-tet
sep-tic
sep-ti-ci-dal
sep-ul-cher
or sep-ul-chre
se-quence
se-quen-tial
se-ques-ter
se-ques-trate
se-ques-tra-tion
se-ques-trum
se-quin
se-ra-glio
ser-aph
ser-a-phim
se-rene
serf (slave)
cf. surf (waves)
serge (cloth)
cf. surge (rise and fall)
ser-geant
se-rial (sequence)
cf. ce-real (food)
se-ri-al-ist
se-ri-al-iza-tion

Do not divide one-syllable words. Divide words by syllables, but leave at least two letters of the word on the first line and three letters on the following line. For additional guidelines, see page ix.

se-ri-al-ize
se-ri-ate
se-ries
se-ri-ous
ser-mon
ser-mon-ize
se-rol-ogy
ser-pent
ser-pen-tine
ser-rate
ser-ra-tion
se-rum
serve
ser-vice
ser-vice-abil-ity
ser-vice-able
ser-vice-ably
service charge
ser-vice-man
service station
ser-vile
ser-vi-tude
ses-ame
ses-qui-cen-te-nary
ses-qui-cen-ten-nial
ses-sion (meeting)
  cf. ces-sion
  (surrender)
ses-tet
set
se-ta-ceous
set—aside (n.)
set-back (n.)
set back (v.)
set—in (adj.)
set-off (n.)

set off (v.)
set-screw
set-ter
set-ting
set-tler
set-up (n.)
set up (v.)
seven
sev-en-fold
seven seas (n. pl.)
sev-en-teen
sev-en-teenth
sev-enth
sev-en-ti-eth
sev-enty
sever
sev-er-abil-ity
sev-er-able
sev-eral
sev-er-al-fold
sev-er-ance
se-vere
se-ver-ity
sew (stitch)
  cf. so (this way)
  cf. sow (plant)
sew-age
sewer
sew-er-age
sex
sex-a-ge-nar-ian
sex-a-ges-i-mal
sex-ism
sex-ol-ogy
sex-tant
sex-tet

sex-til-lion
sex-ton
sex-tu-ple
sex-tu-pli-cate
sex-ual
sex-u-al-ity
sexy
Shab-bat
shab-bier
shab-bi-est
shabby
shade
shadow
shad-ow-box (v.)
shadow box (n.)
shady
shaft
shag
shagged
shag-gier
shag-gi-est
shaggy
shah
shah-dom
shak-able
  or shake-able
shake
shake-down (n.)
shake down (v.)
shaken
shaker
Shake-spear-ean
  or Shake-spear-ian
  or Shak-sper-ean
shake—up (n.)
shake up (v.)

shako	shay	shib-bo-leth
shaky	she	shield
shale	sheaf	shift
shall	shear (cut)	shift-ier
shal-lop	*cf.* **sheer** (thin)	shift-i-est
shal-low	sheath (blade case)	shil-le-lagh
sha-lom	*cf.* **sheathe** (cover)	*or* shil-la-lah
sha-lom alei-chem *(interj.)*	sheath knife *(n.)*	shilly—shally
sham	she-bang	shim-mer
sha-man	shed	shin
sham-ble	sheen	shin-dig
shammy	sheep	shine
sham-poo	sheep-herder	shin-gle
sham-rock	sheepish	Shinto
shang-hai	sheep-skin	Shin-to-ism
Shangri—la	sheer (thin)	Shin-to-ist
shank	*cf.* **shear** (cut)	shiny
shanty	sheet	ship
shap-able	sheikh	ship-board
or shape-able	*or* sheik	ship-builder
shape	sheikh-dom	ship-per
shapen	*or* sheik-dom	ship-shape
shard	shelf *(n.)*	ship-wreck
share	shelf life	ship-yard
share-crop-per	shel-lac	shirk
share-holder	shell-fire	shirt
shark	shel-ter	shirt—sleeve
shark-skin	shelve *(v.)*	*or* shirt—sleeves
sharp	she-nan-i-gan	*or* shirt—sleeved *(adj.)*
sharpen	shep-herd	shirt-tail
shat-ter	shep-herd-ess	shish ke-bab
shat-ter-proof	sher-bet	shiv-a-ree
shave	*or* sher-bert	shiver
shaver	sher-iff	shoal
shave-tail	sher-lock	shock
shawl	sherry	shock-proof

Do not divide one-syllable words. Divide words by syllables, but leave
at least two letters of the word on the first line and three letters on the
following line. For additional guidelines, see page ix.

174

shock therapy	shot	shud-der
shock wave	shot-gun	shuf-fle
shoddy	should	shuf-fle-board
shoe	shoul-der	shunt
shoe-horn	shoul-der bag *(n.)*	shush
shoe-lace	shoul-der strap *(n.)*	shut
shoe-string	shove	shut-down *(n.)*
sho-far	shovel	shut down *(v.)*
sho-froth *(n. pl.)*	show	shut—in *(adj.) (n.)*
sho-gun	show-boat	shut in *(v.)*
shone (radiated)	show-case	shut-ter
cf. **shown** (displayed)	show-down	shut-ter-bug
shoo—in *(n.)*	shower	shut-tle
shook	shower bath	shy
shook—up *(adj.)*	shown (displayed)	shy-ster
shoot (fire at)	*cf.* **shone** (radiated)	Si-a-mese
cf. **chute** (inclined trough)	show—off *(n.)*	sib-i-lant
shop	show off *(v.)*	sib-i-late
or shoppe	show-piece	sib-i-la-tion
shop-keeper	show-place	sib-ling
shop-lift	show-room	sick
shop-per	shrap-nel	sick and tired *(adj.)*
shop-talk	shred	sick bay
shore	shred-ded	sick-bed
shore leave *(n.)*	shrewd	sick call
shorn	shriek	sicken
short	shrill	sicker
short-age	shrimp	sick-ish
short-change	shrine	sickle
short—circuit *(v.)*	shrink	sick leave
short cir-cuit *(n.)*	shrink-age	sickle—cell ane-mia
short-com-ing	shrivel	sick pay
short-cut	shroud	sick-room
shorten	shrub	sic pas-sim
short-hand	shrub-bery	side
short-sighted	shuck	side-arm

Plural, past tense, adverbial, and noun derivatives formed by adding
s, d or *ed, ly, ness, ment, ful, less,* or *ing* to an unchanged root word are
not listed, nor are words formed by dropping the final *e* and adding *ing*.   175

side ef-fect
side-kick
side-light
side-line
side-show
side-swipe
side-walk
si-dle
siege
si-erra
sieve
sift
sigh
sight (vision)
  cf. cite (quote)
  cf. site (place)
sight—seeing *(adj.)*
sigma
sign (gesture)
  cf. sine (trigonometry)
sig-nal
sig-naled
or sig-nalled
sig-nal-man
sig-na-ture
sign-board
sig-ni-fi-able
sig-nif-i-cance
sig-nif-i-cancy
sig-nif-i-cant
sig-ni-fi-ca-tion
sig-nify
sign-post
Sikh
si-lage
si-lence

si-lent
sil-hou-ette
sil-ica
silica gel
sil-i-cate
si-li-ceous
or si-li-cious
sil-i-con
sil-i-cone
sil-i-co-sis
silk
silken
silk screen *(n.)*
silk—screen *(v.)*
silk-worm
sill
sil-lier
sil-li-est
silly
silo
silt
sil-ver
sil-ver plate *(n.)*
sil-ver-smith
sil-ver spoon *(n.)*
sil-ver-ware
sim-ian
sim-i-lar
sim-i-lar-ity
sim-ile
sim-mer
si-mo-nize
sim-pa-tico
sim-per
sim-ple
sim-pler

sim-plest
sim-ple-ton
sim-plic-ity
sim-pli-fi-ca-tion
sim-plify
sim-plis-tic
sim-ply
sim-u-late
sim-u-la-tion
sim-u-la-tor
si-mul-cast
si-mul-ta-ne-ity
si-mul-ta-ne-ous
sin
since
sin-cere
sin-cer-ity
sine (trigonometry)
  cf. sign (gesture)
si-ne-cure
si-ne qua non
sinew
sin-ful
singe
sin-gle
sin-gle-ton
single—track *(adj.)*
sin-gu-lar
sin-gu-lar-ity
sin-is-ter
sink
sink-age
sink-hole
sinned
si-nol-ogy
sin-u-ous

Do not divide one-syllable words. Divide words by syllables, but leave
at least two letters of the word on the first line and three letters on the
176   following line. For additional guidelines, see page ix.

si-nus	size	skinned
si-nus-itis	siz-zle	skin-nier
si-nu-soid	skat	skin-ni-est
si-phon	skate	skinny
sire	ske-dad-dle	skin-tight *(adj.)*
si-ren	skeet	skip
sir-loin	skein	ski pole
si-sal	skel-e-tal	skipped
sissy	skel-ter	skip-per
sis-ter	skep-tic	skir-mish
sis-ter-hood	skep-ti-cal	skirt
sister—in—law	skep-ti-cism	ski run
sisters—in—law *(n. pl.)*	sketch	skit
si-tar	skewer	ski tow
sit—down *(n.)*	ski	skit-tish
site (place)	ski-able	ski-wear
cf. sight (vision)	ski-bob	skul-dug-gery
cf. cite (quote)	ski boot	*or* skull-dug-gery
sit—in *(n.)*	skid	skulk
sit in *(v.)*	skid-doo	skull (head)
sit-ter	*or* ski-doo	*cf.* scull (move with oar)
sit-u-ate	skiff	skull-cap
sit-u-a-tion	ski jump	skunk
sit-u-a-tional	ski lift	sky
sit—up *(n.)*	skill	sky-borne
sit up *(v.)*	skil-let	sky-cap
sitz bath *(n.)*	skim	sky-jacker
sitz-mark	ski mask	sky-lark
six-fold	skimmed	sky-line
six—pack *(n.)*	skim-mer	sky-rocket
six-teen	skim milk	sky-scraper
sixth	skim-ming	slab
six-ti-eth	skimp	slack
sixth	skin	slacken
siz-able	skin—dive *(v.)*	slacker
or size-able	skin-flint	slag

Plural, past tense, adverbial, and noun derivatives formed by adding
s, *d* or *ed*, *ly*, *ness*, *ment*, *ful*, *less*, or *ing* to an unchanged root word are
not listed, nor are words formed by dropping the final *e* and adding *ing*.   177

sla-lom
slam
slam—bang *(adj.)*
slammed
slam-ming
slan-der
slang
slant
slap
slapped
slap-ping
slap-stick
slash
slat
slate
slat-tern
slaugh-ter
slaugh-ter-house
slaugh-ter-ous
slave
slav-ery
slay (kill)
   cf. **sleigh** (sled)
sleazy
sled
sled dog
sledge
sledge-ham-mer
sleek
sleep
sleeper
sleep-ier
sleep-i-est
sleepy
slept
sleeve

sleigh (sled)
   cf. **slay** (kill)
sleight (skill)
   cf. **slight** (small)
slen-der
slen-der-ize
sleuth
slew
slick
slide
slide rule *(n.)*
slight (small)
   cf. **sleight** (skill)
slim
slime
slim-mer
slim-mest
slimsy
   or slimpsy
sling
sling-shot
slink
slip
slip-cover
slip-page
slipped
slip-per
slip-pery
slit
slither
sliver
slob
slo-gan
slope
sloppy
slouch

slough
sloven
slow
sludge
slug
slug-fest
slugged
slug-gish
sluice
slum
slum-ber
slump
slunk
slur
slush
sly
small
small-pox
smart
smart al-eck *(n.)*
smash
smear
smell
smile
smirch
smite
smock
smog
smoke
smol-der
smooch
smooth
smor-gas-bord
smother
smudge
smug

Do not divide one-syllable words. Divide words by syllables, but leave
at least two letters of the word on the first line and three letters on the
following line. For additional guidelines, see page ix.

smug-gle	snow-bound *(adj.)*	so-ci-etal
smut	snow-drift	so-ci-ety
snack	snow-fall	so-cio-eco-nomic
snack bar	snow fence	so-cio-log-i-cal
snag	snow-flake	so-ci-ol-o-gist
snail	snow-mo-bile	so-ci-ol-o-gy
snake	snow-plow	sock
snake-skin	snow-suit	socket
snap	snow—white *(adj.)*	soda
snap-pier	snub	so-dal-ity
snap-pi-est	snubbed	sod-bust-er
snappy	snuff	sod-den
snare	snug	so-dium
snarl	snug-gle	sofa
snatch	**so** (this way)	soft
sneak	*cf.* **sew** (stitch)	soft-ball
sneaker	*cf.* **sow** (plant)	soft—boiled *(adj.)*
sneer	soak	soft—cover *(adj.)*
sneeze	soap	soft drink *(n.)*
snide	soap-box	soften
sniff	**soar** (fly)	soft-ware
snif-fle	*cf.* **sore** (painful)	soggy
snip	sob	soil
snipe	sobbed	soil-age
snitch	so-ber	soil bank *(n.)*
snob	so-bri-ety	soi-ree
snook	soc-cer	*or* soi-rée
snoopy	so-cia-bil-ity	so-journ
snooze	so-cia-ble	so-lace
snore	so-cia-bly	so-lar
snout	so-cial	so-lar-ium
snow	so-cial-ism	so-lar-iza-tion
snow-ball	so-cial-ist	so-lar-ize
snow-bank	so-cial-is-tic	solar plexus *(n.)*
snow—blind *(adj.)*	so-cial-ite	sol-der
or snow—blinded	so-cial-ize	sol-dier

Plural, past tense, adverbial, and noun derivatives formed by adding
s, d or *ed, ly, ness, ment, ful, less,* or *ing* to an unchanged root word are
not listed, nor are words formed by dropping the final *e* and adding *ing*.   179

sole (only)
cf. soul (spiritual)
sol-emn
so-lem-nify
so-lem-nity
sol-em-nize
so-le-noid
so-licit
so-lic-i-ta-tion
so-lic-i-tor
so-lic-i-tous
so-lic-i-tude
solid
sol-i-dar-ity
so-lid-ify
so-lid-ity
solid—state *(adj.)*
so-lil-o-quy
sol-i-taire
sol-i-tary
sol-i-tude
sol-mi-za-tion
solo
so-lo-ist
so-lon
sol-stice
sol-u-bil-ity
sol-u-bi-lize
sol-u-ble
so-lu-tion
solv-able
solve
sol-vency
sol-vent
som-ber
or som-bre

som-brero
some (not all)
cf. sum (total)
son (male offspring)
cf. sun (celestial body)
sore (painful)
cf. soar (fly)
sor-ghum
so-ror-ity
sor-row
sorry
sort
sor-tie
souf-flé
soul (spiritual)
cf. sole (only; fish)
soul brother *(n.)*
soul food *(n.)*
soul—searching *(n.)*
sound
soup
soup du jour
sour
source
sour-dough
south
south-east
south-east-ern
south-ern
South-erner
south pole *(n.)*
south-wester
south-west-ern
sou-ve-nir
sov-er-eign
or sov-ran

sov-er-eignty
or sov-ranty
so-viet
sow
cf. sew (stitch)
cf. so (this way)
soy-bean
spa
space
space-craft
space-flight
space heater *(n.)*
space-ship
space suit *(n.)*
space walk *(n.)*
spa-cious (much space)
cf. spe-cious (false)
spade
spa-ghetti
span
span-iel
span-ner
spare
spare-ribs
spark
spar-kle
spark plug *(n.)*
spar-row
sparse
spasm
spas-modic
spas-mod-i-cal
spas-tic
spas-tic-ity
spat
spat-ter

Do not divide one-syllable words. Divide words by syllables, but leave at least two letters of the word on the first line and three letters on the following line. For additional guidelines, see page ix.

spat-ula	speed-om-e-ter	spi-ral
spawn	speed-trap *(n.)*	spire
speak	speed-way	spirit
speak-er-phone	spell	spir-it-ism
spear	spell-bound	spir-i-tual
spear-head	spe-lunker	spir-i-tu-al-ism
spe-cial	spe-lunk-ing	spir-i-tu-al-ist
spe-cial-ism	spend	spit
spe-cial-ist	spend-thrift	spite
spe-ci-al-ity	spent	splash
spe-cial-ize	sperm	splash-board
spe-cialty	sper-ma-to-zoan	splash-down
spe-cie (money)	sperm oil	splat-ter
cf. spe-cies (kind)	sperm whale	splen-dent
spe-cific	spew	splen-did
spec-i-fi-ca-tion	spheral	splen-dif-er-ous
spec-i-fic-ity	sphere	splen-dor
spec-ify	spher-i-cal	splice
spe-cious (false)	spher-oid	split
cf. spa-cious (much space)	sphinx	split—level *(adj.)*
speck	sphinxes	splurge
spec-ta-cle	*or* sphin-ges *(n. pl.)*	spoil
spec-tac-u-lar	spice	spoil-age
spec-ta-tor	spic-ier	spoke
spec-ter	spic-i-est	spo-ken
or spec-tre	spicy	spokes-man
spec-tral	spigot	spokes-woman
spec-tro-graph	spike	sponge
spec-trum	spill	sponge cake
spec-u-late	spin	spongy
spec-u-la-tor	spin-ach	spon-sor
spec-u-la-tion	spin-dle	spon-ta-ne-ous
spec-u-la-tive	spine	spoof
speech	spin-ster	spool
speed	spinned	spo-radic
speed-boat	spin-ning	spore

Plural, past tense, adverbial, and noun derivatives formed by adding
s, d or *ed, ly, ness, ment, ful, less,* or *ing* to an unchanged root word are
not listed, nor are words formed by dropping the final *e* and adding *ing*.

sport	spurge	stabbed
sport-fish-ing	spu-ri-ous	sta-bil-ity
sports car	spurn	sta-bil-ize
or sport car	spur–of–the–moment (adj.)	sta-bi-lizer
sports-cast	spurred	sta-ble
sports-man	spurt	stac-cato
sports-wear	sput-nik	stack
sports-writer	sput-ter	sta-dium
sporty	spu-tum	staff
spot	spy	stag
spot—check(v.)	squab	stage
spot-light	squab-ble	stage-coach
spot-ter	squad	stage-struck
spouse	squad-ron	stag-ger
spout	squalid	stag-nant
sprain	squall	stag-nate
sprawl	squa-lor	staid (quiet)
spray	squan-der	cf. stayed (remain)
spray gun (n.)	square	stain
spread	squash	stair (step)
spread-able	squat	cf. stare (look)
spreader	squat-ter	stair-way
spree	squaw	stake (stick)
sprig	squawk	cf. steak (meat)
sprightly	squeak	stake-out
spring	squea-mish	sta-lac-tite
spring-time	squee-gee	sta-lag-mite
springy	squeeze	stale
sprin-kle	squelch	stale-mate
sprite	squid	Sta-lin-ism
sprocket	squint	stalk
sprout	squire	stall
spruce	squirm	stal-lion
spry	squir-rel	stal-wart
spun	squirt	stam-ina
spur	stab	stam-mer

Do not divide one-syllable words. Divide words by syllables, but leave at least two letters of the word on the first line and three letters on the following line. For additional guidelines, see page ix.

stam-pede
stance
stan-chion
stan-dard
stan-dard-iza-tion
stan-dard-ize
standby
stand—in *(n.)*
stand-ing room
stand-off *(adj.) (n.)*
stand off *(v.)*
stanza
stare (look)
  cf. **stair** (step)
star-fish
star-gazer
stark
star-let
star-light
star-ling
starry
starry—eyed *(adj.)*
start
starter
star-tle
star-va-tion
starve
stash
state
state-hood
state-house
state-room
state-side
states-man
static
sta-tion

sta-tion-ary (not moving)
  cf. **sta-tion-ery** (paper)
sta-tion-mas-ter
station wagon
stat-ism
sta-tis-tic
sta-tis-ti-cal
stat-is-ti-cian
stat-u-ary
statue (image)
  cf. **stat-ure** (height)
  cf. **stat-ute** (law)
stat-u-esque
sta-tus
sta-tus quo
stat-ute (law)
  cf. **statue** (image)
  cf. **stat-ure** (height)
stat-u-tory
staunch
stay
stayed
or **staid** (remain)
  cf. **staid** (quiet)
stead-fast
stead-ier
stead-i-est
steady
steak (meat)
  cf. **stake** (stick)
steal (rob)
  cf. **steel** (metal)
stealth
steam
steam-boat
steam iron *(n.)*

steam-ship
steed
steel (metal)
  cf. **steal** (rob)
steel-yard
steep
stee-ple
steer-age
stein
stel-lar
stem
stemmed
stem-ware
stench
sten-cil
steno-graph
ste-nog-ra-pher
ste-nog-ra-phy
ste-no-sis
steno-type
step (stair)
  cf. **steppe** (treeless tract)
step-brother
step—by—step *(adj.)*
step-lad-der
steppe (treeless tract)
  cf. **step** (stair)
step-son
ste-reo
ste-reo-scope
ste-reo-scopic
ste-reo-type
ster-ile
ster-il-iza-tion
ster-il-ize
ster-ling

Plural, past tense, adverbial, and noun derivatives formed by adding
s, d or *ed, ly, ness, ment, ful, less,* or *ing* to an unchanged root word are
not listed, nor are words formed by dropping the final *e* and adding *ing*.

stern
ster-num
stetho-scope
stet-son
ste-ve-dore
stew
stew-ard
stew-ard-ess
sticks (branches)
cf. Styx (river)
sti-fle
stigma
stig-ma-tism
stig-ma-tize
stile (turnstile)
cf. style (fashion)
still
still-born
still life (n.)
stilt
stim-u-lant
stim-u-late
stim-u-lus
sting
sting-ray
stingy
stint
sti-pend
stip-u-late
stip-u-la-tion
stir
stirred
stir-rup
stitch
stock
stock-ade

stock-broker
stock-car (cattle car)
cf. stock car (racer)
stock mar-ket
stock-pile
stock-room
stock-yard
stoic
sto-icism
stoke
stom-ach
stom-ach-ache
stone
stooge
stool
stoop
stop
stop-light
stop-page
stopped
stop-per
stop-watch
stor-age
store
sto-ried
stork
storm
stout
stout-hearted
stove
stove-pipe
stow
stow-age
strad-dle
Strad-i-var-ius
strafe

strag-gle
straight (direct)
cf. strait (channel)
straight-edge
straighten
straight face
strain
strait (channel)
cf. straight (direct)
strand
strange
stranger
stran-gle
stran-gu-late
strap
stra-te-gic
stra-te-gi-cal
stra-te-gies
strat-egy
strat-i-fi-ca-tion
strat-ify
strato-sphere
stra-tus
straw
straw-berry
streak
stream
street
street-car
street-light
strength
strengthen
stren-u-ous
strep-to-ba-cil-lus
strep-to-coc-cal
strep-to-coc-cus

184

Do not divide one-syllable words. Divide words by syllables, but leave
at least two letters of the word on the first line and three letters on the
following line. For additional guidelines, see page ix.

strep-to-my-cin	stru-del	stur-dier
stress	strug-gle	stur-di-est
stretch	strum	sturdy
stretch-able	strummed	stur-geon
stretcher	strum-ming	stut-ter
stretcher bearer *(n.)*	strut	stut-terer
strew	strych-nine	sty
stri-a-tion	stub	style *(fashion)*
stricken	stubbed	*cf.* stile *(turnstile)*
strict	stub-ble	style-book
stric-ture	stub-born	styl-ish
stride	stubby	styl-ist
stri-dency	stucco	sty-lus
stri-dent	stud	sty-mie
strife	stu-dent	sty-rene
strike	stu-dio	Sty-ro-foam
strike-out *(n.)*	stu-di-ous	Styx *(river)*
strike out *(v.)*	study	*cf.* sticks *(branches)*
strike-over	stuff	su-able
string	stuff-ier	suave
strin-gent	stuffy	sub-con-scious
strip	stul-ti-fi-ca-tion	sub-con-trac-tor
strip chart *(n.)*	stul-ti-fied	sub-cul-ture
strip—cropping *(n.)*	stul-tify	sub-dea-con
stripe	stum-ble	sub-di-vid-able
strip mine *(n.)*	stump	sub-di-vide
strip—mine *(v.)*	stun	sub-di-vi-sion
strive	stun-ning	sub-due
strode	stunt	sub-hu-man
stroke	stu-pe-fac-tion	sub-ject
stroll	stu-pe-fied	sub-jec-tion
strong	stu-pefy	sub-jec-tive
strong-box	stu-pen-dous	sub-jec-tiv-ism
struck	stu-pid	sub-join
struc-tural	stu-pid-ity	sub-ju-ga-tion
struc-ture	stu-por	sub-ju-gate

Plural, past tense, adverbial, and noun derivatives formed by adding
s, d or *ed, ly, ness, ment, ful, less,* or *ing* to an unchanged root word are
not listed, nor are words formed by dropping the final *e* and adding *ing*.

sub-junc-tion
sub-junc-tive
sub-king-dom
sub-let
sub-li-ma-tion
sub-li-mate
sub-lime
sub-lim-i-nal
sub-lim-ity
sub-ma-chine gun
sub-mar-ginal
sub-ma-rine
sub-merge
sub-mer-gence
sub-merg-ible
sub-merse
sub-mers-ible
sub-mer-sion
sub-mi-cro-scopic
sub-mis-sion
sub-mis-sive
sub-mit
sub-mit-ted
sub-mit-ting
sub-nor-mal
sub-nor-mal-ity
sub-or-bital
sub-or-di-nate
sub-pilot
sub-poena
sub-po-lar
sub-ro-ga-tion
sub-ro-gate
sub-rosa *(adj.)*
sub rosa *(adv.)*
sub-sat-el-lite

sub-scribe
sub-script
sub-scrip-tion
sub-sec-tion
sub-se-quent
sub-ser-vi-ence
sub-side
sub-sid-iary
sub-si-di-za-tion
sub-si-dize
sub-si-dies
sub-sidy
sub-sist
sub-sis-tence
sub-soil
sub-space
sub-spe-cies
sub-stance
sub-stan-dard
sub-stan-tial
sub-stan-ti-ate
sub-stan-ti-a-tion
sub-stan-tive
sub-sta-tion
sub-sti-tute
sub-sti-tu-tion
sub-strato-sphere
sub-stra-tum
sub-sur-face
sub-sys-tem
sub-ter-fuge
sub-ter-ra-nean
sub-ti-tle
sub-tle
sub-tler
sub-to-tal

sub-tract
sub-trac-tion
sub-trac-tive
sub-tra-hend
sub-trop-i-cal
sub-urb
sub-ur-ban
sub-ur-ban-ite
sub-ur-ban-iza-tion
sub-ur-ban-ize
sub-ur-bia
sub-ven-tion
sub-ver-sion
sub-vert
sub-way
suc-ce-dent
suc-ceed
suc-cess
suc-ces-sion
suc-ces-sive
suc-ces-sor
suc-cinct
suc-cor (help)
    cf. **sucker** (drink)
suc-co-tash
suc-cu-lence
suc-cu-lent
suc-cumb
such
suck
sucker (drink)
    cf. **suc-cor** (help)
suckle
su-crose
suc-tion
sud-den

Do not divide one-syllable words. Divide words by syllables, but leave at least two letters of the word on the first line and three letters on the following line. For additional guidelines, see page ix.

sudsy
sue
suede
or suède
suet
suf-fer
suf-fer-able
suf-fer-ably
suf-fer-ance
suf-fice
suf-fi-ciency
suf-fi-cient
suf-fix
suf-fo-cate
suf-fo-ca-tion
suf-frage
suf-frag-ette
suf-frag-ist
suf-fuse
suf-fu-sive
sugar
sug-ar-cane
sug-ary
sug-gest
sug-gest-ible
sug-ges-tion
sug-ges-tive
sui-cidal
sui-cide
suit
suit-abil-ity
suit-able
suit-ably
suit-case
suite (rooms)
  cf. **sweet** (taste)

sui ge-neris
suitor
su-ki-ya-ki
Suk-koth
sulfa
sul-fa-di-a-zine
sulfa drug
sul-fa-nil-amide
sul-fide
sulf-ox-ide
sul-fur
or sul-phur
sul-fu-ric
sul-fu-rous
sulk
sul-len
sul-tan
sul-try
sum (total)
  cf. **some** (not all)
su-mac
or su-mach
summa cum laude *(adv.)(adj.)*
sum-ma-ri-za-tion
sum-ma-rize
sum-ma-ries
sum-marily
sum-mary
sum-ma-tion
sum-mer
summer stock
sum-mer-time
sum-mery
sum-mit
sum-mon
sump

sump pump *(n.)*
sump-tu-ous
sun (celestial body)
  cf. **son** (male offspring)
sun-baked
sun-bath
sun-burn
sun-dae (ice cream)
  cf. **Sun-day** (day)
sun-dial
sun-dries
sun-dry
sunk
sunken
sun-lamp
sun-light
sunny
sun-rise
sun-roof
sun-set
sun-shine
sun-stroke
sun-suit
sun-tan
sup
su-per
su-per-an-nu-ate
su-per-an-nu-a-tion
su-perb
su-per-charge
su-per-cil-ious
su-per-ego
su-per-fi-cial
su-per-fi-ci-al-ity
su-per-flu-ous
su-per-high-way

Plural, past tense, adverbial, and noun derivatives formed by adding
s, d or *ed, ly, ness, ment, ful, less,* or *ing* to an unchanged root word are
not listed, nor are words formed by dropping the final *e* and adding *ing*.

187

su-per-im-pose	sup-pli-cate	sur-mount
su-per-in-ten-dence	sup-pli-ca-tion	sur-name
su-per-in-ten-dency	sup-pli-ca-tory	sur-pass
su-per-in-ten-dent	sup-plied	sur-plice (gown)
su-pe-rior	sup-ply	*cf.* sur-plus (excess)
su-pe-ri-or-ity	sup-port	sur-prise
su-per-jet	sup-port-able	sur-real
su-per-la-tive	sup-port-ive	sur-re-al-ism
su-per-man	sup-pose	sur-re-al-ist
su-per-mar-ket	sup-po-si-tion	sur-re-al-is-tic
su-per-nat-u-ral	sup-pos-i-tory	sur-ren-der
su-per-nat-u-ral-ism	sup-press	sur-rep-ti-tious
su-per-pa-triot	sup-pres-sant	sur-ro-gate
su-per-power	sup-pres-sion	sur-ro-ga-tion
su-per-scribe	sup-pres-sive	sur-round
su-per-script	sup-pres-sor	sur-tax
su-per-scrip-tion	su-pra-na-tional	sur-veil-lance
su-per-sede	su-prem-a-cist	sur-vey
su-per-sen-si-tive	su-prem-acy	sur-veyor
su-per-sonic	su-preme	sur-vival
su-per-star	sur-charge	sur-vive
su-per-sti-tion	sure	sus-cep-ti-bil-ity
su-per-stra-tum	surety	sus-cep-ti-ble
su-per-struc-ture	surf (waves)	sus-cep-tive
su-per-tanker	*cf.* serf (slave)	sus-pect
su-per-vise	sur-face	sus-pend
su-per-vi-sion	surface–to–air mis-sile *(n.)*	sus-pender
su-per-vi-sor	surf-board	sus-pense
su-pi-na-tion	sur-feit	sus-pen-sion
su-pi-na-tor	surge (rise and fall)	sus-pi-cion
su-pine	*cf.* serge (cloth)	sus-pi-cious
sup-per	sur-geon	sus-tain
sup-plant	sur-gery	sus-tain-able
sup-ple	sur-gi-cal	sus-te-nance
sup-ple-men-tal	surly	su-ture
sup-ple-men-tary	sur-mise	svelte

Do not divide one-syllable words. Divide words by syllables, but leave at least two letters of the word on the first line and three letters on the following line. For additional guidelines, see page ix.

swab	swipe	syn-a-gogue
swab-ber	swirl	*or* syn-a-gog
swag-ger	switch	syn-chro-mesh
Swa-hili	swivel	syn-chro-nism
swain	swoon	syn-chro-nis-tic
swal-low	swoop	syn-chro-ni-za-tion
swami	sword	syn-chro-nize
swamp	syc-a-more	syn-chro-nous
swamp-land	sy-co-phant	syn-co-pate
swan	syl-labic	syn-co-pa-tion
swan dive *(n.)*	syl-lab-i-cate	syn-di-cate
swank	syl-lab-i-ca-tion	syn-di-ca-tion
swan song *(n.)*	syl-lab-i-fi-ca-tion	syn-drome
swarm	syl-lab-ify	syn-er-gism
swash-buckle	syl-la-ble	syn-er-gist
swas-tika	syl-lo-gism	syn-er-gis-tic
swat	syl-lo-gis-tic	syn-e-sis
swath	**sym-bol** (image)	syn-ge-neic
sway	*cf.* **cym-bal** (percussion	synod
swear	instrument)	syn-onym
sweat	sym-bolic	syn-on-y-mous
sweep	sym-bol-ism	syn-on-ymy
sweep—second	sym-bol-ize	syn-op-sis
sweet (taste)	sym-met-ri-cal	syn-op-tic
cf. **suite** (rooms)	*or* sym-met-ric	syn-tax
sweet-heart	sym-me-try	syn-the-sis
swell	sym-pa-thetic	syn-the-size
swept	sym-pa-thize	syn-thetic
swerve	sym-pa-thy	*or* syn-thet-i-cal
swift	sym-phonic	syph-i-lis
swim	sym-pho-ni-ous	syph-i-litic
swim-suit	sym-pho-nist	sy-ringe
swin-dle	sym-phony	syrup
swine	sym-po-sium	system
swing	symp-tom	sys-tem-atic
swing shift *(n.)*	symp-tom-atic	sys-tem-atize

Plural, past tense, adverbial, and noun derivatives formed by adding
s, d or *ed, ly, ness, ment, ful, less,* or *ing* to an unchanged root word are
not listed, nor are words formed by dropping the final *e* and adding *ing*.

189

sys-tem-iza-tion
sys-tem-ize
systems analysis
systems analyst

T

tab
tabbed
tab-er-na-cle
ta-ble
tab-leau
tab-leaux *(n. pl.)*
or tab-leaus
ta-ble-cloth
ta-ble d'hôte
table—hop *(v.)*
ta-ble-spoon
tab-let
ta-ble-top
tab-loid
ta-boo
or tabu
tab-u-lar
tab-u-late
tab-u-la-tion
tach
ta-chis-to-scope
ta-chom-e-ter
tachy-car-dia
ta-chym-e-ter
tac-i-turn

tack
tackle
taco
tac-o-nite
tact
tac-tics
tac-ti-cal
tac-ti-cian
tac-tile
tad-pole
taf-feta
taffy
tag
tag-board
tagged
tag-ging
tail (end)
  cf. tale (story)
tail-gate
tail-light
tai-lor
tailor—made *(adj.) (n.)*
tail pipe *(n.)*
tail-spin
taint
take
take-down *(adj.) (n.)*
take down *(v.)*
taken
talc
tal-cum powder *(n.)*
tale (story)
  cf. tail (end)
tal-ent
talent scout
talent show

tales-man (juryman)
  cf. tal-is-man (sign)
talk
talk-athon
talk-ative
talk show *(n.)*
tall
tal-low
tally
tal-lyho
Tal-mud
talon
ta-male
tam-bou-rine
tame
Tam-many
Tam o' Shan-ter
or tam—o'—shanter
tamp
tam-per
tan
tan-dem
tang
tan-gent
tan-ger-ine
tan-gi-ble
tan-gle
tango
tank
tan-kard
tanker
tanned
tan-nery
tan-nic
tan-ning
tan-ta-lize

Do not divide one-syllable words. Divide words by syllables, but leave at least two letters of the word on the first line and three letters on the following line. For additional guidelines, see page ix.

tan-ta-mount
tan-trum
Tao
Tao-ism
tap
tap dance *(n.)*
tap—dance *(v.)*
tape
tape deck *(n.)*
tape mea-sure
tape player
ta-per (pointed)
  cf. **ta-pir** (animal)
tape—record *(v.)*
tape re-cord-er *(n.)*
tap-es-tried
tap-es-try
tap-i-oca
ta-pir (animal)
  cf. **ta-per** (pointed)
tap-root
tar
ta-ran-tula
tar-dily
tardy
tare (weight)
  cf. **tear** (rip)
  cf. **tier** (row)
tar-get
tar-iff
tar-nish
tarp
tar paper *(n.)*
tar-pon
tart
tar-tan

tar-tar
task
task force
task-mas-ter
task-mis-tress
tas-sel
tas-seled
or **tas-selled**
taste
taste bud
tast-ier
tast-i-est
tasty
tat-ter
tat-ter-sall
tat-tle
tat-tle-tale
tat-too
taught (did teach)
  cf. **taut** (tight)
taunt
Tau-rus
taut (tight)
  cf. **taught** (did teach)
tav-ern
taw-dry
tawny
tax
tax-able
tax-a-tion
tax—exempt *(adj.)*
taxi
tax-ied
taxi-ing
or **taxy-ing**
taxi-der-mist

taxi-der-my
taxi stand
tax-payer
tax shelter
tax stamp
T—bar lift
T—bone
tea (beverage)
  cf. **tee** (golf mound)
tea bag
tea ball
tea cake
tea cart
teach
teach-able
teacher
teach—in *(n.)*
teach-ing ma-chine *(n.)*
tea-cup
teak
tea-ket-tle
team (group)
  cf. **teem** (swarm)
team-mate
team-ster
team-work
tea-pot
tear (rip)
  cf. **tare** (weight)
  cf. **tier** (row)
tear-drop
tear-jerker
tea-room
tear sheet
tease
tea service

Plural, past tense, adverbial, and noun derivatives formed by adding
s, d or *ed, ly, ness, ment, ful, less,* or *ing* to an unchanged root word are
not listed, nor are words formed by dropping the final *e* and adding *ing*.

191

tea-spoon
tech-ne-tronic
tech-ni-cal
tech-ni-cal-i-ties
tech-ni-cal-ity
tech-ni-cian
tech-nique
tech-noc-racy
tech-no-crat
tech-no-log-i-cal
tech-nol-o-gist
tech-nol-ogy
te-dious
te-dium
tee (golf mound)
 cf. tea (beverage)
teem (swarm)
 cf. team (group)
teen
teen-age
teen-ager
teensy
or teentsy
tee shirt
tee-ter
tee-ter-board
teeth
teethe
tee-to-taler
or tee-to-tal-ler
Tef-lon
tele-cam-era
tele-cast
tele-com-mu-ni-ca-tion
tele-gram
tele-graph

tele-graphic
te-leg-ra-phy
tele-ki-ne-sis
tele-me-ter
te-lep-a-thy
tele-pathic
tele-phone
te-le-pho-nist
te-le-phony
tele-photo
tele-pho-tog-ra-phy
tele-play
tele-printer
Tele-Prompt-Ter
tele-scope
tele-scopic
tele-thon
Tele-type
tele-type-writer
tele-typ-ist
tele-view
tele-vise
tele-vi-sion
tele-vi-sor
telex
tell
teller
tell-tale
tem-er-ar-i-ous
te-mer-ity
tem-per
tem-pera
tem-per-a-ment
tem-per-a-men-tal
tem-per-ance
tem-per-ate

tem-per-a-ture
tem-pest
tem-pes-tu-ous
tem-plate
or tem-plet
tem-ple
tempo
tem-po-ral
tem-po-rar-ily
tem-po-rary
tem-po-rize
tempt
tempter
temp-tress
tem-pura
ten
ten-a-ble
te-na-cious
te-nac-ity
ten-ancy
ten-ant
tend
ten-den-cies
ten-dency
ten-den-tious
or ten-den-cious
ten-der (easily broken)
tender (ship)
ten-der-foot
ten-der-hearted
ten-der-ize
ten-der-izer
ten-der-loin
ten-don
ten-e-brous
ten-e-ment

Do not divide one-syllable words. Divide words by syllables, but leave
at least two letters of the word on the first line and three letters on the
following line. For additional guidelines, see page ix.

te-net
ten-fold
ten-nis
tenon
tenor (trend)
  cf. ten-ure (possessing)
ten-pin
tense (strain)
  cf. tents (dwellings)
ten-sile
ten-sion
ten-sity
ten-sor
tent
ten-ta-cle
ten-tac-u-lar
ten-ta-tive
tents (dwellings)
  cf. tense (strain)
te-nu-ity
ten-ure (possessing)
  cf. tenor (trend)
te-pee
tepid
te-quila
ter-cen-ten-nial
ter-i-yaki
term
ter-ma-gant
ter-mi-na-ble
ter-mi-nal
ter-mi-nate
ter-mi-na-tion
ter-mi-na-tor
ter-mi-nol-ogy
ter-mi-nus

ter-mite
term paper
tern (sea gull)
  cf. turn (move)
ter-nary
terp-si-cho-rean
ter-race
ter-ra—cotta
terra firma
ter-rain
ter-ra-pin
ter-razzo
ter-res-trial
ter-ri-ble
ter-ri-bly
ter-rier
ter-rific
ter-ri-fied
ter-rify
ter-ri-to-rial
ter-ri-to-ri-al-ism
ter-ri-to-ri-al-ize
ter-ri-tory
ter-ror
ter-ror-ism
ter-ror-ist
ter-ror-ize
terse
ter-tian
ter-tiary
test
tes-ta-ceous
tes-tacy
tes-ta-ment
tes-ta-men-tary
tes-tate

tes-ta-tor
test ban
test case
test—drive *(v.)*
test—fire *(v.)*
test—fly *(v.)*
tes-ti-fier
tes-tify
tes-ti-mo-nial
tes-ti-mony
tes-tos-ter-one
test pattern
test pilot
test—tube *(adj.)*
test tube *(n.)*
tet-a-nus
tête-à-tête *(adj.) (adv.) (n.)*
tether
tet-ra-chlo-ride
tet-ra-hy-drate
tet-ra-pod
te-trar-chy
text
text-book
tex-tile
tex-tual
tex-ture
Thai
Thai-land
thal-a-mus
tha-lid-o-mide
than (compared with)
  cf. then (at that time)
thank
thanker
thanks-giv-ing

Plural, past tense, adverbial, and noun derivatives formed by adding
s, d or *ed, ly, ness, ment, ful, less,* or *ing* to an unchanged root word are
not listed, nor are words formed by dropping the final *e* and adding *ing.*

that	the-ory	thi-a-mine
thatch	the-os-o-phy	thi-a-zide
thaw	ther-a-peu-tic	thi-a-zine
the-ater	ther-a-pist	thick
or the-atre	ther-a-py	thick-headed *(adj.)*
the-ater-goer	there (that place)	thicken
theater–in–the–round *(n.)*	*cf.* their (possessive)	thicket
the-at-ri-cal	*cf.* they're (they are)	thief
the-at-rics	there-abouts	thieves *(n. pl.)*
theft	*or* there-about	thigh
their (possessive)	there-af-ter	thim-ble
cf. there (that place)	thereat	thin
cf. they're (they are)	thereby	thing
the-ism	there-for (in exchange for)	thing-am-a-jig
the-ist	*cf.* there-fore (consequently)	*or* thing-um-a-jig
the-is-ti-cal	therein	think
them	there-upon	think-able
the-matic	ther-mal	think tank
theme	ther-mo-dy-nam-ics	thin-ner
them-selves	ther-mo-elec-tric	third
then (at that time)	ther-mog-ra-phy	thirst
cf. than (compared with)	ther-mom-e-ter	thirst-ily
thence	ther-mo-nu-clear	thir-teen
thence-for-ward	ther-mo-plas-tic	thirty
the-oc-racy	ther-mos	this
theo-crat	ther-mo-sphere	this-tle
theo-lo-gian	ther-mo-stat	thither
theo-log-i-cal	the-sau-rus	thong
the-ol-o-gize	the-sauri *(n. pl.)*	tho-racic
the-ol-ogy	*or* the-sau-ruses	tho-rax
the-on-o-mous	the-sis	thorn
the-o-rem	thes-pian	thor-ough
the-o-ret-i-cal	they	thor-ough-bred
the-o-rist	they're (they are)	thor-ough-fare
the-o-rize	*cf.* their (possessive)	thor-ough-go-ing
the-o-ries	*cf.* there (that place)	thou

Do not divide one-syllable words. Divide words by syllables, but leave
at least two letters of the word on the first line and three letters on the
following line. For additional guidelines, see page ix.

194

though
thought
thou-sand
thrall
thrash
thread
thread-bare
threat
threaten
three
three-fold
three—ring circus
three-some
thresh
thresher
thresh-old
threw (did throw)
  cf. through (beyond)
thrice
thrift
thrift shop
thrill
thril-ler
thrive
throat
throb
throbbed
throe (spasm)
  cf. throw (hurl)
throm-bo-sis
throne (chair)
  cf. thrown (hurled)
throng
throt-tle
through (beyond)
  cf. threw (did throw)

through-out
through-put
through street
throw (hurl)
  cf. throe (spasm)
throw-away (n.) (adj.)
throw away (v.)
thrown (hurled)
  cf. throne (chair)
thrush
thrust
thru-way
thud
thug
thumb
thumb-nail
thumb-print
thumb-tack
thump
thun-der
thun-der-bolt
thun-der-clap
thun-der-cloud
thun-der-head
thun-der-ous
thun-der-shower
thun-der-storm
thus
thwart
thyme
thy-mus
thy-roid
ti-ara
tibia
tic (twitching)
  cf. tick (sound)

ticker tape (n.)
ticket
tickle
tick-lish
tick-tack
  or tic-tac
tidal
tidal wave
tid-bit
tide (water)
  cf. tied (fastened)
tide-land
tide-wa-ter
tidy
tie
tied (fastened)
  cf. tide (water)
tier (row)
  cf. tare (weight)
  cf. tear (rip)
ti-ger
tight
tighten
tile
till
till-age
til-ler
tilt
tim-ber (wood)
  cf. tim-bre (sound)
tim-bre
  or tim-ber (sound)
  cf. tim-ber (wood)
time
time-keeper
time—lapse (adj.)

Plural, past tense, adverbial, and noun derivatives formed by adding
s, d or *ed, ly, ness, ment, ful, less,* or *ing* to an unchanged root word are
not listed, nor are words formed by dropping the final *e* and adding *ing*.

195

time lock *(n.)*	title page	tol-er-a-tor
timer	tit-u-lar	toll
time—saver *(n.)*	**to** (toward)	toll-booth
time—sharing *(n.)*	*cf.* **too** (also)	toll bridge
time-ta-ble	*cf.* **two** (number)	toll call
tim-o-rous	toad	toll-gate
tin	toad-stool	tom-a-hawk
tin can *(n.)*	toast	to-mato
tinc-ture	toaster	tomb
tin-der	toast-mas-ter	tom-boy
tine	to-bacco	tomb-stone
tin-foil	to-bog-gan	tome
tinge	toc-sin (warning signal)	to-mor-row
tinge-ing	*cf.* **toxin** (poison)	tom—tom
or ting-ing	to-day	tonal
tin-gle	tod-dle	tone
tin-ker	tod-dler	tong
tin-kle	**toe** (part of foot)	tongue
tin-sel	*cf.* **tow** (pull)	tonic
tint	toe-hold	ton-nage
tip	toe-nail	ton-sil
tipped	toga	ton-sil-lec-tomy
tip-ping	to-gether	ton-sil-li-tis
tip-toe	tog-gle	ton-so-rial
ti-rade	toil	**too** (also)
tire	toi-let	*cf.* **to** (toward)
tis-sue	toi-letry	*cf.* **two** (number)
ti-tan	to-ken	tool
ti-tanic	to-ken-ism	tool-box
ti-tan-ism	tol-er-a-bil-ity	tooth
ti-ta-nium	tol-er-a-ble	tooth-paste
tithe	tol-er-a-bly	top
tit-il-late	tol-er-ance	to-paz
tit-il-la-tion	tol-er-ant	topic
ti-tle	tol-er-ate	top-i-cal
ti-tle-holder	tol-er-a-tion	to-pog-ra-pher

Do not divide one-syllable words. Divide words by syllables, but leave
at least two letters of the word on the first line and three letters on the
following line. For additional guidelines, see page ix.

to-po-graphic
to-po-graph-i-cal
to-pog-ra-phy
to-po-log-i-cal
to-pol-ogy
top-onymic
to-pon-ymy
top-ping
top-ple
top-side
topsy—turvy
To-rah
to-re-ador
to-rero
tor-ment
tor-men-tor
or **tor-menter**
tor-nado
tor-pedo
torque
tor-rent
tor-ren-tial
tor-rid
tor-sion
tor-sion bar *(n.)*
torso
tort
tor-ti-lla
tor-toise
tor-tu-ous
tor-ture
tor-tur-ous
toss
to-tal
to-tal-ism
to-tal-i-tar-ian

to-tal-i-tar-ian-ism
to-tal-ity
to-tal-ize
tote
to-tem
tot-ter
touch
touch-able
touch-down *(n.)*
touch down *(v.)*
touché
tough
toughen
tou-pee
tour
tour-ism
tour-ist
tour-na-ment
tour-ni-quet
tou-sle
tout
tow (pull)
cf. **toe** (part of foot)
to-ward
or **to-wards**
towel
tower
town
town house
town-ship
tow rope
tow truck
toxic
tox-i-cant
tox-i-co-log-i-cal
tox-i-col-ogy

toxin (poison)
cf. **toc-sin** (warning signal)
toy
trace
trace-able
tracer
tra-chea
tra-che-itis
tra-cheo-bron-chial
tra-che-ot-omy
track
tract
trac-ta-ble
trac-tion
trac-tor
trade
trade-mark
trading stamp
tra-di-tion
tra-di-tional
tra-di-tion-al-ism
tra-di-tion-al-ist
tra-duce
traf-fic
traf-fic-able
trag-edy
tragic
or **trag-i-cal**
trail
trailer
trailer park
train
trainee
traipse
trait
trai-tor

trai-tor-ous
tra-ject
tra-jec-tion
tra-jec-tory
tram
tramp
tram-ple
tram-po-line
tran-quil
tran-quil-ize
tran-quil-izer
tran-quil-lity
or tran-quil-ity
trans-act
trans-ac-tion
trans-at-lan-tic
trans-re-ceiver
tran-scend
tran-scen-dence
tran-scen-dency
tran-scen-dent
tran-scen-den-tal
tran-scen-den-tal-ism
trans-con-ti-nen-tal
tran-scribe
tran-scriber
tran-script
tran-scrip-tion
trans-duce
trans-duc-tion
tran-sept
trans-fer
trans-fer-abil-ity
trans-fer-able
trans-feral
trans-fer-ence

transferred
trans-fig-u-ra-tion
trans-fig-ure
trans-fix
trans-form
trans-for-ma-tion
trans-former
trans-fuse
trans-fus-ible
or trans-fus-able
trans-fu-sion
trans-gress
trans-gres-sion
trans-gres-sor
tran-sience
tran-sient
tran-sis-tor
tran-sis-tor-ize
tran-sit
tran-si-tion
tran-si-tive
tran-si-tiv-ity
tran-si-tory
trans-late
trans-la-tion
trans-la-tive
trans-lu-cence
trans-lu-cent
trans-mi-gra-tion
trans-mis-si-ble
trans-mis-sion
trans-mit
trans-mit-tance
trans-mit-ter
trans-mu-ta-tion
trans-oce-anic

tran-som
tran-sonic
or trans-sonic
trans-par-ence
trans-par-ency
trans-par-ent
tran-spire
trans-plant
trans-port
trans-port-able
trans-por-ta-tion
trans-pose
trans-pos-able
trans-po-si-tion
trans-sex-ual
trans-ship
tran-sub-stan-ti-ate
trans-verse
trans-ves-tism
trans-ves-tite
trap
trap-door
tra-peze
trap-e-zoid
trape-zoi-dal
trapped
trap-ping
trash
trauma
trau-matic
trau-ma-tism
trau-ma-tize
tra-vail
travel
trav-eled
or trav-elled

Do not divide one-syllable words. Divide words by syllables, but leave
at least two letters of the word on the first line and three letters on the
following line. For additional guidelines, see page ix.

trav-el-ogue
or trav-elog
tra-verse
trav-es-ties
trav-esty
trawl
tray (carrier)
cf. trey (three)
treach-er-ous
treach-ery
trea-cle
tread
trea-dle
tread-mill
trea-son
trea-son-able
trea-son-ous
trea-sur-able
trea-sure
trea-surer
trea-sury
treat
treat-able
trea-tise
treaty
tre-ble
tree
tree-top
trek
trekked
trel-lis
trem-ble
tre-men-dous
tremor
trem-u-lous
trench

tren-chancy
tren-chant
trend
tre-pan
tre-phine
trep-i-da-tion
tres-pass
tress
trey (three)
cf. tray (carrier)
triad
tri-alogue
tri-an-gle
tri-an-gu-lar
tri-an-gu-late
tri-an-gu-la-tion
tri-ar-chy
tribal
trib-al-ism
tribe
trib-u-late
trib-u-la-tion
tri-bu-nal
tri-bune
trib-u-tary
trib-ute
tri-ceps
trich-i-no-sis
tri-chot-o-mous
trick
trick-ery
trickle
trick-ster
tri-cus-pid
tri-dent
tried

tri-en-nial
tri-fle
tri-fo-cal
tri-fo-li-o-late
tri-fur-cate
trig-ger
trig-o-no-met-ric
trig-o-nom-e-try
tri-lat-eral
tri-lin-gual
trill
tril-ogy
trim
tri-mes-ter
trim-mer
tri-monthly
Trin-ity
trin-ket
trin-oc-u-lar
tri-no-mial
trio
trip
tri-par-tite
tri-par-ti-tion
tri-ple
trip-let
trip-li-cate
trip-lic-ity
tri-pod
trite
tri-umph
tri-um-phant
tri-um-vi-rate
trivia
triv-ial
triv-i-al-ity

Plural, past tense, adverbial, and noun derivatives formed by adding
s, d or *ed, ly, ness, ment, ful, less,* or *ing* to an unchanged root word are
not listed, nor are words formed by dropping the final *e* and adding *ing*.

troika
troll
trol-ley
trom-bone
tromp
troop (march)
cf. troupe (performers)
troop-ship
tro-phy
tropic
trop-i-cal
tro-po-sphere
trot
Trots-ky-ism
trot-ter
trou-ba-dour
trou-ble
trough
trounce
troupe (performers)
cf. troop (march)
trou-ser
trous-seau
trout
trowel
tru-ancy
tru-ant
truce
truck
truck-load
tru-cu-lent
trudge
true
tru-ism
truly
trump

trum-pet
trum-peter
trun-cate
trun-cheon
trun-dle
trunk
truss
trust
trustee
trustee-ship
trust-i-ness
trust-wor-thy
truth
try-out
tryst
tsetse
T—shirt (n.)
T square (n.)
tuba
tube
tu-ber
tu-ber-cu-lar
tu-ber-cu-lin
tu-ber-cu-loid
tu-ber-cu-lo-sis
tu-ber-cu-lous
tu-ber-ous
tu-bu-lar
tuck
tuft
tug
tug-boat
tu-ition
tu-lip
tum-ble
tu-me-fac-tion

tu-mes-cent
tu-mor
tu-mor-ous
tu-mult
tu-mul-tu-ous
tuna
tun-dra
tune
tung-sten
tu-nic
tun-nel
tur-ban
tur-bine
turbo
tur-bo-fan
tur-bo-jet
tur-bo-prop
turbo—propeller engine
turboprop—jet engine
turbo-ram-jet engine
tur-bu-lence
tur-bu-lent
turf
tur-gid
tur-key
tur-meric
tur-moil
turn (move)
cf. tern (sea gull)
turn-about
turn-around
turn-coat
tur-nip
turn-over (n.)
turn over (v.)
turn-pike

Do not divide one-syllable words. Divide words by syllables, but leave at least two letters of the word on the first line and three letters on the following line. For additional guidelines, see page ix.

turn-stile
turn-ta-ble
turn-up *(n.) (adj.)*
turn up *(v.)*
tur-pen-tine
tur-pi-tude
tur-quoise
or tur-quois
tur-ret
tur-tle
tusk
tus-sle
tu-te-lage
tu-te-lary
tu-tor
tu-tor-age
tu-to-rial
tu-tor-ship
tux-edo
twad-dle
twang
tweak
twee-zer
twelfth
twelve
twid-dle
twig
twi-light
twill
twin
twine
twinge
twin-kle
twin—size *(adj.)*
twin-ning
twirl

twist
twitch
twit-ter
twixt
two (number)
cf. to (toward)
cf. too (also)
two—by—four *(n.)*
two-some
tym-panic
type
type-case
type-face
type-script
type-set-ter
type-write
type-writer
ty-phoid
ty-phus
typ-i-cal
typ-i-fied
typ-ify
typ-ist
typo
ty-pog-ra-pher
ty-po-graphic
ty-po-graph-i-cal
ty-pog-ra-phy
ty-po-log-i-cal
ty-ran-ni-cal
ty-ran-ni-cide
tyr-an-nize
ty-ran-no-saur
tyr-anny
ty-rant
tzar

ubiq-ui-tous
ubiq-uity
ud-der
ugh
ug-lier
ug-li-est
ug-li-ness
ugly
uh—huh
uku-lele
ul-cer
ul-cer-ate
ul-cer-ous
ulna
ul-te-rior
ul-ti-macy
ul-tima ra-tio
ul-ti-mate
ul-ti-ma-tum
ul-tra
ul-tra-con-ser-va-tive
ul-tra-fiche
ul-tra-high
ul-tra-mi-cro-scopic
ul-tra-mod-ern
ul-tra-sonic
ul-tra-so-phis-ti-cated
ul-tra-vi-o-let
Ulys-ses
um-bil-i-cal
um-bi-li-cus
um-brage
um-brella

Plural, past tense, adverbial, and noun derivatives formed by adding
s, d or *ed, ly, ness, ment, ful, less,* or *ing* to an unchanged root word are
not listed, nor are words formed by dropping the final *e* and adding *ing*.

um-pire
ump-teen
un-abated
un-abridged
un-ac-cept-able
un-ac-com-mo-dated
un-ac-com-pa-nied
un-ac-cus-tomed
un-adorned
un-adul-ter-ated
un-af-fected
un-alien-able
un-al-ter-able
un-Amer-i-can
una-nim-ity
unan-i-mous
un-an-swer-able
un-an-tic-i-pated
un-ap-peal-able
un-ap-peas-able
un-ap-pe-tiz-ing
un-ap-proach-able
un-armed
un-ashamed
un-as-sail-able
un-as-sisted
un-as-suage-able
un-at-tached
un-at-trac-tive
un-avail-able
un-avoid-able
un-aware
un-bal-anced
un-bear-able
un-beat-able
un-be-com-ing

un-be-known
un-be-liev-able
un-be-liever
un-bend
un-bi-ased
un-born
un-bound
un-bri-dle
un-bro-ken
un-buckle
un-budge-able
un-bur-den
un-but-toned
uncalled—for *(adj.)*
un-cer-e-mo-ni-ous
un-cer-tain
un-cer-tainty
un-chal-lenge-able
un-change-able
un-char-ac-ter-is-tic
un-char-i-ta-ble
un-charted
un-chaste
un-chiv-al-rous
un-chris-tian
un-civ-i-lized
un-clas-si-fied
un-cle
un-clean
un-clench
Un-cle Sam
un-climb-able
un-cloak
un-clut-ter
un-com-fort-able
un-com-mit-ted

un-com-mon
un-com-mu-ni-ca-ble
un-com-mu-ni-ca-tive
un-com-plain-ing
un-com-pli-cated
un-com-pli-men-tary
un-con-ceiv-able
un-con-cerned
un-con-di-tional
un-con-for-mity
un-con-ge-nial
un-con-scio-na-ble
un-con-scious
un-con-sol-i-dated
un-con-sti-tu-tional
un-con-trol-la-ble
un-con-ven-tional
un-cou-ple
un-couth
un-cover
unc-tion
unc-tu-ous
un-curl
un-de-bat-able
un-de-ni-able
un-der
un-der-achiever
un-der-act
un-der-class-man
un-der-coat
un-der-de-vel-oped
un-der-dog
un-der-ed-u-cated
un-der-em-pha-size
un-der-em-ployed
un-der-es-ti-mate

Do not divide one-syllable words. Divide words by syllables, but leave
at least two letters of the word on the first line and three letters on the
following line. For additional guidelines, see page ix.

un-der-ex-pose
un-der-grad-u-ate
un-der-growth
un-der-hand
un-der-in-sured
un-der-lie
un-der-mine
un-der-neath
un-der-nour-ished
un-der-paid
un-der-pass
un-der-pin-ning
un-der-play
un-der-priv-i-leged
un-der-pro-duc-tive
un-der-score
un-der-sell
un-der-signed
un-der-sized
un-der-stand
un-der-stand-able
un-der-state
un-der-stood
un-der-strength
un-der-take
under–the–counter *(adj.)*
un-der-way *(adj.)*
un-der way *(adv.)*
un-de-sir-able
un-dis-guised
undo (loosen)
cf. un-due (not due)
un-dressed
un-due (not due)
cf. undo (loosen)
un-du-late

un-duly
un-earned
un-earthly
un-eas-ily
un-em-ployed
un-en-cum-bered
un-en-dur-able
un-en-thu-si-as-tic
un-equal
un-equiv-o-cably
un-even
un-ex-cep-tional
un-ex-ploited
un-faith-ful
un-fa-mil-iar
un-fash-ion-able
un-fas-ten
un-fath-om-able
un-fa-vor-able
un-fin-ished
un-fit-ting
un-flinch-ing
un-fold
un-for-get-ta-ble
un-for-giv-ing
un-for-tu-nate
un-gainly
un-gram-mat-i-cal
un-grate-ful
un-gu-late
un-hap-pily
un-healthy
unheard—of *(adj.)*
un-hinge
un-holy
uni-corn

uni-cy-cle
uni-fi-ca-tion
uni-fo-li-o-late
uni-form
uni-for-mity
unify
uni-lat-eral
uni-lin-ear
uni-lin-gual
un-imag-in-able
un-im-peach-able
un-in-hib-ited
un-in-tel-li-gi-ble
un-in-ten-tional
union
union-ism
union-iza-tion
union shop *(n.)*
uni-po-lar
unique
uni-sex
uni-son
unit
uni-tar-ian
uni-tary
unite
unit-ize
unity
uni-ver-sal
uni-ver-sal-ity
uni-verse
uni-ver-si-ties
uni-ver-sity
univ-o-cal
un-kempt
un-let-tered

Plural, past tense, adverbial, and noun derivatives formed by adding
s, d or *ed, ly, ness, ment, ful, less,* or *ing* to an unchanged root word are
not listed, nor are words formed by dropping the final *e* and adding *ing.*

un-like-li-hood
un-lim-ited
un-listed
un-load
un-loosen
un-mask
un-men-tion-able
un-mis-tak-able
un-mit-i-gated
un-nat-u-ral
un-nec-es-sar-ily
un-ob-tru-sive
un-oc-cu-pied
un-of-fi-cial
un-or-ga-nized
un-or-tho-dox
un-pal-at-able
un-prec-e-dented
un-pre-dict-able
un-pre-ten-tious
un-prin-ci-pled
un-print-able
un-prof-it-able
un-qual-i-fied
un-ques-tion-able
un-quote
un-real (artificial)
 cf. un-reel (unwind)
un-re-al-is-tic
un-rea-son-able
un-reel (unwind)
 cf. un-real (artificial)
un-re-strained
un-ri-valed
or un-ri-valled
un-ruf-fled

un-sat-u-rated
un-sci-en-tific
un-scru-pu-lous
un-sea-son-able
un-set-tled
un-sheathe
un-sightly
un-so-cia-ble
un-so-phis-ti-cated
un-speak-able
un-sta-ble
un-stop-pa-ble
un-struc-tured
un-suc-cess-ful
un-sym-met-ri-cal
un-ti-dily
un-til
un-touch-able
un-tu-tored
un-usual
un-wary
un-wa-ver-ing
un-wor-thi-ness
un-wor-thy
up
up-braid
up-bring-ing
up-heaval
up-hill
up-hol-ster
up-per
up-per-class-man
up-per-most
up-right
up-roar
up-set

up–to–the–minute *(adj.)*
up-ward
or up-wards
ura-nium
ur-ban (city)
 cf. ur-bane (polite)
ur-ban-ism
ur-ban-ite
ur-ban-iza-tion
ur-ban-ize
ur-ban re-newal *(n.)*
ure-mia
ure-thra
urge
ur-gency
ur-gent
uri-nal-y-sis
uri-nary
urine
urn (vase)
 cf. earn (be paid)
urol-o-gist
urol-ogy
us-able
or use-able
us-age
use
usher
usual
usu-ri-ous
usurp
usury
uten-sil
uter-ine
uter-us
util-i-tar-ian

Do not divide one-syllable words. Divide words by syllables, but leave at least two letters of the word on the first line and three letters on the following line. For additional guidelines, see page ix.

util-ity
uti-li-za-tion
uti-lize
ut-most
uto-pia
uto-pi-an-ism
ut-ter
ut-ter-ance
ux-o-ri-ous

V

va-cancy
va-cant
va-cate
va-ca-tion
va-ca-tion-ist
va-ca-tion-land
vac-ci-nate
vac-ci-na-tion
vac-cine
vac-il-late
vac-il-la-tion
va-cu-ity
vac-u-ous
vac-uum
vac-uums *(n. pl.)*
or vacua
vacuum—packed *(adj.)*
vag-a-bond
va-gar-i-ous
va-gary

va-grancy
va-grant
vague
vain (worthless)
  cf. **vane** (wind signal)
  cf. **vein** (blood vessel)
va-lance (drapery)
  cf. **va-lence** (chemical term)
vale (valley)
  cf. **veil** (covering)
vale-dic-to-rian
vale-dic-tory
va-lence (chemical term)
  cf. **va-lance** (drapery)
val-en-tine
va-let
Val-halla
val-iant
valid
va-lid-ity
val-i-date
val-i-da-tion
va-lise
val-ley
valor
valu-able
val-u-ate
val-u-a-tion
value
valve
vamp
vam-pire
van
van-dal
van-dal-ism
van-dal-ize

vane (wind signal)
  cf. **vain** (worthless)
  cf. **vein** (blood vessel)
van-guard
va-nilla
van-ish
van-ity
van-quish
van-tage
va-por
va-por-ize
va-por-ous
vari-able
vari-ance
vari-ant
vari-a-tion
var-i-cose
var-ie-gate
va-ri-et-ies
va-ri-ety
var-i-ous
var-mint
var-nish
var-sity
vary (change slightly)
  cf. **very** (exceedingly)
vas-cu-lar
vase
vas-sal
vast
vaude-ville
vault
vaunt
veal
vec-tor
veer

Plural, past tense, adverbial, and noun derivatives formed by adding
s, d or *ed, ly, ness, ment, ful, less,* or *ing* to an unchanged root word are
not listed, nor are words formed by dropping the final *e* and adding *ing*.

veg-e-ta-ble
veg-e-tate
veg-e-ta-tion
ve-he-mence
ve-he-ment
ve-hi-cle
veil (covering)
  cf. **vale** (valley)
vein (blood vessel)
  cf. **vain** (worthless)
  cf. **vane** (wind signal)
veld
or veldt
vel-lum
ve-loc-i-ties
ve-loc-ity
vel-vet
vel-ve-teen
vel-vety
ve-nal (open to bribes)
  cf. **ve-nial** (pardonable)
vend
vendee
vender
or vendor
ven-detta
vend-ible
or vend-able
ve-neer
ven-er-able
ven-er-ate
ven-er-a-tion
ve-ne-tian blind
ven-geance
ve-nial (pardonable)
  cf. **ve-nal** (open to bribes)

ve-nire
ven-i-son
venom
ven-om-ous
vent
ven-ti-late
ven-ti-la-tion
ven-tri-cle
ven-tric-u-lar
ven-tril-o-quism
ven-tril-o-quist
ven-ture
ven-turer
ven-ture-some
ven-tur-ous
venue
ve-ra-cious (truthful)
  cf. **vo-ra-cious** (greedy)
ve-randa
verb
ver-bal
ver-ba-tim
ver-biage
ver-bose
ver-bo-ten
ver-dant
ver-dict
verge
ver-gence
ver-i-fi-able
ver-i-fi-ca-tion
ver-i-fied
ver-ify
ver-ily
veri-sim-i-lar
ver-i-ta-ble

ver-i-ta-bly
ver-mic-u-lite
ver-min
ver-min-ous
ver-mouth
ver-nac-u-lar
ver-nac-u-lar-ism
ver-nal
ver-sa-tile
ver-sa-til-ity
verse
ver-sion
ver-sus
ver-te-bra
ver-tex (highest point)
  cf. **vor-tex** (whirl)
ver-ti-cal
ver-ti-cil-late
ver-tigo
very (exceedingly)
  cf. **vary** (change slightly)
ves-i-cant
ves-pers
ves-pi-ary
ves-pid
ves-sel
vest
ves-tal
ves-ti-bule
ves-tige
vest-ment
ves-try
vetch
vet-eran
vet-er-i-nar-ian
vet-er-i-nary

Do not divide one-syllable words. Divide words by syllables, but leave at least two letters of the word on the first line and three letters on the following line. For additional guidelines, see page ix.

veto
vetoes *(n. pl.)*
vex
vexed
or vext
vex-a-tion
vex-a-tious
via
vi-a-ble
via-duct
vial (bottle)
  cf. vile (bad)
  cf. viol (string)
vibes
vi-brant
vi-bra-phone
vi-brate
vi-bra-tion
vi-bra-tor
vi-bra-tory
vicar
vi-car-i-ous
vice (evil)
  cf. vise (tool)
vice—chancellor
vice—consul
vice—presidency
vice—president
vice-roy
vice squad
vi-chys-soise
Vi-chy water
vi-cin-ity
vi-cious
vi-cis-si-tude
vi-cis-si-tu-di-nous

vic-tim
vic-tim-ize
vic-tor
Vic-to-rian
vic-to-ri-ous
vic-tory
vict-ual-ler
vi-cuña
video
vid-eo-phone
vid-eo-tape
Viet-cong
Viet-minh
Viet-nam-ese
view
vigil
vig-i-lance
vig-i-lant
vig-i-lante
vi-gnette
vigor
vig-o-rish
vile (bad)
  cf. vial (bottle)
  cf. viol (string)
vil-i-fi-ca-tion
vil-ify
villa
vil-lage
vil-lain
vil-lain-ous
vim
vin-ci-ble
vin-di-cate
vin-di-ca-tion
vin-dic-a-tive

vin-di-ca-tory
vin-dic-tive
vine
vin-e-gar
vine-yard
vin-tage
vi-nyl
vint-ner
viol (string)
  cf. vial (bottle)
  cf. vile (bad)
vi-ola
vi-o-la-bil-ity
vi-o-la-bly
vi-o-la-ble
vi-o-late
vi-o-la-tion
vi-o-lent
vi-o-let
vi-o-lin
vi-per
vi-per-ous
vi-rago
vi-ral
vir-gin
vir-ginal
vir-gin-ity
Virgo
vir-gule
vir-ile
vi-ril-ity
vi-rol-ogy
vir-tual
vir-tu-al-ity
vir-tue
vir-tu-os-ity

Plural, past tense, adverbial, and noun derivatives formed by adding
s, d or *ed, ly, ness, ment, ful, less,* or *ing* to an unchanged root word are
not listed, nor are words formed by dropping the final *e* and adding *ing*.

vir-tu-oso
vir-tu-ous
vir-u-lent
vi-rus
visa
vis-age
vis—à—vis
vis-ceral
vis-cid
vis-cose
vis-cos-ity
vis-count
vis-cous
vise (tool)
 cf. vice (evil)
vise-like
Vishnu
vis-i-bil-ity
vis-i-ble
vis-i-bly
vi-sion
vi-sion-ary
visit
vis-i-ta-tion
vis-i-tor
vi-sor
vista
vi-sual
visual aid *(n.)*
vi-su-al-iza-tion
vi-su-al-ize
vita
vi-tal
vi-tal-ity
vi-tal-ize
vi-ta-min

vi-ti-cul-ture
vit-riol
vi-tu-per-ate
vi-tu-per-a-tion
vi-tu-per-a-tive
vi-va-cious
vi-vac-ity
viva voce
vivid
viv-i-fi-ca-tion
viv-ify
vivi-sec-tion
vixen
vo-cab-u-lary
vo-cal
vo-cal-ist
vo-cal-ize
vo-ca-tion
vo-ca-tional
vo-ca-tion-al-ism
vo-cif-er-ous
vodka
vogue
voice
voice-over
voice-print
void
void-able
void-ance
vol-a-tile
vol-ca-nic
vol-cano
vo-li-tion
vol-i-tive
vol-ley
volt

volt-age
volt-a-me-ter
volt-me-ter
vol-u-ble
vol-ume
vo-lu-mi-nous
vol-un-tarily
vol-un-tary
vol-un-teer
vo-lup-tu-ary
vo-lup-tuous
vomit
voo-doo
voo-doo-ism
vo-ra-cious (greedy)
 cf. ve-ra-cious (truthful)
vo-rac-ity
vor-tex (whirl)
 cf. ver-tex (highest point)
vote
vouch
voucher
vouch-safe
vow
vowel
vox po-puli
voy-age
voya-geur
vul-ca-ni-za-tion
vul-ca-nize
vul-gar
vul-gar-ism
vul-gar-ity
vul-gar-ize
vul-ner-abil-ity
vul-ner-a-ble

Do not divide one-syllable words. Divide words by syllables, but leave at least two letters of the word on the first line and three letters on the following line. For additional guidelines, see page ix.

208

W

vul-ture
vul-tur-ous

wad
wad-ding
wade (step in water)
 cf. weighed (measured)
wa-fer
waf-fle
waft
wag
wage
wa-ger
wagon
waif
wail (cry)
 cf. whale (mammal)
waist (midline)
 cf. waste (misuse)
waist-line
wait (stay)
 cf. weight (heaviness)
waiter
wait-ress
waive (give up)
 cf. wave (movement)
waiver (relinquishing)
 cf. waver (vacillate)
wake
waken

walk
walkie—talkie
wal-let
wall-flower
wal-lop
wall-pa-per
wall plug
Wall Street
wal-nut
wal-rus
waltz
wam-pum
wan-der
wan-derer
wan-der-lust
wane
wan-gle
Wan-kel engine
want
wan-ton
war
war-ble
war-bler
war bride
war crime
ward
war-den
ward-robe
ware (article)
 cf. wear (clothes)
 cf. where (place)
ware-house
ware-house-man
war-fare
war hawk
warm

war-mon-ger
warmth
warm—up (n.)
warm up (v.)
warn
warp
war-path
war-rant
war-ran-tee
war-ran-tor
 or war-ranter
war-rior
war-ship
wart
wary
war zone
wash
wash-able
wash and wear (adj.)
washer
wash-room
wasp
waste (misuse)
 cf. waist (midline)
waste-bas-ket
waste-land
waster
wast-rel
watch
watch-band
watch-dog
watch-word
wa-ter
wa-ter-color
wa-ter-cress
wa-ter-fall

Plural, past tense, adverbial, and noun derivatives formed by adding
s, d or ed, ly, ness, ment, ful, less, or ing to an unchanged root word are
not listed, nor are words formed by dropping the final e and adding ing.

209

wa-ter-line
wa-ter-log
wa-ter-mark
wa-ter-proof
water—repellent *(adj.)*
water ski *(n.)*
water—ski *(v.)*
watt
watt-age
wave (movement)
  cf. waive (give up)
wave-length
wa-ver (vacillate)
  cf. waiver (relinquishing)
wavy
wax
waxen
way (method)
  cf. weigh (measure)
ways and means *(n. pl.)*
way-side
way-ward
we (pronoun)
  cf. wee (tiny)
weak (not strong)
  cf. week (time)
weaken
weak—kneed *(adj.)*
wealth
weapon
wear (clothes)
  cf. ware (article)
  cf. where (place)
wear and tear *(n.)*
wea-ri-some
weary

wea-sel
weather (climate)
  cf. whether (choice)
weath-er-man
weather strip *(n.)*
weather vane
weather—wise *(adj.)*
weave (make cloth)
  cf. we've (we have)
web
web-bing
wed
wed-ding
wedge
wed-lock
wee (tiny)
  cf. we (pronoun)
weed
week (time)
  cf. weak (not strong)
week-day
weep
wee-vil
weigh (measure)
  cf. way (method)
weighed (measured)
  cf. wade (step in water)
weight (heaviness)
  cf. wait (stay)
weird
wel-come
weld
welder
wel-fare
welt
wel-ter-weight

wept
were-wolf
west
west-ern
West-erner
west-ward
wet (moist)
  cf. whet (sharpen)
wet-back
wet suit *(n.)*
we've (we have)
  cf. weave (make cloth)
whack
whale
  cf. wail (cry)
whale-boat
wham
wharf
what-ever
what-not
what-so-ever
wheat
whee-dle
wheel
wheel-bar-row
wheel-chair
wheel-er-dealer
wheeze
whelp
when
whence
where (place)
  cf. ware (article)
  cf. wear (clothes)
where-abouts
  or where-about

Do not divide one-syllable words. Divide words by syllables, but leave
at least two letters of the word on the first line and three letters on the
following line. For additional guidelines, see page ix.

210

whereas	whit (small bit)	wife
where-at	*cf.* wit (sense)	wig
whereby	white	wig-gle
where-fore	White House	wig-wag
wherein	whiten	wig-wam
whereof	whither (where)	wild
where-upon	*cf.* wither (dry up)	wil-der-ness
where-withal	whit-tle	wild-life
whet (sharpen)	whiz	wile (trick)
cf. wet (moist)	*or* whizz	*cf.* while (time)
whether (choice)	whiz-zer	will
cf. weather (climate)	who-ever	will—o'—the—wisp (*n.*)
which	whole (entire)	wil-low
whiff	*cf.* hole (opening)	wilt
while (time)	whole-sale	wily
cf. wile (trick)	whole-some	wince
whim	wholly	wind
whim-per	whom-ever	wind-age
whim-si-cal	whom-so-ever	wind-bag
whine (cry)	whoop	wind-blown
cf. wine (liquid)	whoop—de—do	wind-chill
whinny	*or* whoop—de—doo	wind-fall
whip	whop-per	wind-lass
whip-lash	whose	wind-mill
whir	why	win-dow
or whirr	wick	win-dow box
whirl	wicked	wind-shield
whirl-pool	wicket	wind-storm
whisk	wick-iup	wine (liquid)
whis-ker	wide	*cf.* whine (cry)
whis-key	wide—screen (*adj.*)	wine-glass
or whisky	wid-get	win-ery
whis-per	widow	wing
whis-pery	wid-ow-hood	wink
whist	width	win-ner
whis-tle	wield	win-ning

Plural, past tense, adverbial, and noun derivatives formed by adding *s*, *d* or *ed*, *ly*, *ness*, *ment*, *ful*, *less*, or *ing* to an unchanged root word are not listed, nor are words formed by dropping the final *e* and adding *ing*.

win-now	wives	word
win-some	wiz-ard	word-age
win-ter	wiz-ardry	word-book
win-ter-ize	wizen	word—for—word *(adj.)*
win-ter-green	wob-ble	word—of—mouth *(adj.)*
win-ter-time	woe	wore
win-try	woe-be-gone	work
wipe	wolf	work-able
wiper	wolf-ish	work-a-day
wire	woman	work-bench
wire—puller *(n.)*	wom-an-hood	work-book
wire-tap	wom-an-ish	work-day
wis-dom	wom-an-power	worker
wise	womb	work farm *(n.)*
wish	won (victorious)	work-horse
wish-bone	*cf.* one (number)	work load *(n.)*
wishy—washy *(adj.)*	won-der	work-man
wisp	won-der-land	work-man-ship
wit (sense)	won-drous	work-shop
cf. whit (small bit)	wont (custom)	world
witch	*cf.* won't (will not)	worm
witch-craft	woo	wor-ri-ment
witch—hunt *(n.)*	wood (lumber)	worry
with	*cf.* would (will)	worse
with-draw	wood-chop-per	wor-ship
with-drawal	wood-craft	worst
with-drawn	wooden	worth
wither (dry up)	wood-land	worth-while
cf. whither (where)	wood pulp	worth-ier
with-hold	wood-shed	worth-i-est
within	wood-wind	wor-thy
with-out	wood-work	would (will)
with-stand	wool	*cf.* wood (lumber)
wit-ness	woolen	wound
wit-ness box	*or* wool-len	wrack (wreckage)
witty	woozy	*cf.* rack (shelf)

Do not divide one-syllable words. Divide words by syllables, but leave
at least two letters of the word on the first line and three letters on the
following line. For additional guidelines, see page ix.

wran-gle
wrap (cover)
 cf. **rap** (knock)
wrapped (covered)
 cf. **rapt** (engrossed)
wrap-around
wrap-per
wrath
wreath (entwined)
 cf. **wreathe** (twisted)
wreck
wreck-age
wrecker
wrench
wrest (wrench)
 cf. **rest** (relax)
wres-tle
wretch (villian)
 cf. **retch** (to vomit)
wrig-gle
wring (twist)
 cf. **ring** (circle)
wrin-kle
wrist
wrist-band
wrist-lock
wrist-watch
writ
write (make letters)
 cf. **right** (correct)
 cf. **rite** (solemn ceremony)
writer
writhe
wrong
wrong-doer
wrote (made letters)

cf. **rote** (mechanical way)
wrought
wry (twist)
 cf. **rye** (grain)

X

xe-no-phile
xe-no-phobe
xe-no-pho-bia
xe-rog-ra-phy
xe-rox *(v.)*
x—ray *(v.)*
X—ray *(n.)*
X—ray therapy
X—ray tube
xy-log-ra-phy
xy-loph-a-gous
xy-lo-phone
xy-lo-phon-ist

Y

yacht
yachts-man
yak
yam
Yan-kee
Yan-kee—Doo-dle

yap
yard
yard-age
yard-stick
yaw
yawl
yawn
yea
year
year-book
year-ling
year-long
yearly
yearn
year—round *(adj.)*
yeast
yell
yel-low
yelp
yen
yeo-man
yerba maté *(n.)*
yes
yes—man *(n.)*
yes-ter-day
yes-ter-year
yet
yew (shrub)
 cf. **ewe** (female sheep)
 cf. **you** (pronoun)
Yid-dish
yield
yip
yo-del
yoga
yogi

Plural, past tense, adverbial, and noun derivatives formed by adding
s, d or *ed, ly, ness, ment, ful, less,* or *ing* to an unchanged root word are
not listed, nor are words formed by dropping the final *e* and adding *ing*.

yo-gurt
_or_ yo-ghurt
yoke (wooden frame)
  _cf._ yolk (egg part)
yo-kel
yolk (egg part)
  _cf._ yoke (wooden frame)
Yom Kip-pur
yon-der
yoo—hoo _(interj.)_
yore (time past)
  _cf._ your (pronoun)
  _cf._ you're (you are)
you (pronoun)
  _cf._ ewe (female sheep)
  _cf._ yew (shrub)
you'd
you'll (you will)
  _cf._ yule (nativity)
young
young-ster
your (pronoun)
  _cf._ yore (time past)
  _cf._ you're (you are)
your-self
your-selves

youth
yowl
yo—yo _(n.)_
yule (nativity)
  _cf._ you'll (you will)
Yule log _(n.)_
yule-tide

Z

zag
zany
zap
zeal
zealot
ze-bra
Zen
ze-nith
zephyr
zep-pe-lin
zero
zest
Zeus
zig-zag

zil-lion
zin-nia
Zion
Zi-on-ism
Zi-on-ist
zip
zip—code _(v.)_
zip code _(n.)_
  _or_ ZIP code
zip-per
zir-con
zither
zo-diac
zo-di-a-cal
zom-bie
  _or_ zombi
zonal
zone
zoo
zoo-log-i-cal
zo-ol-o-gist
zo-ol-ogy
zoom
zoom lens _(n.)_
zuc-chini
zwie-back

Plural, past tense, adverbial, and noun derivatives formed by adding
_s_, _d_ or _ed_, _ly_, _ness_, _ment_, _ful_, _less_, or _ing_ to an unchanged root word are
not listed, nor are words formed by dropping the final _e_ and adding _ing_.

REFERENCE SECTION

Punctuation Review

1. APOSTROPHE

1.1 Indicates possession in nouns and indefinite pronouns.

John's car is in the garage.

Charles' car is in the garage.

The boy's car is in the garage.

The boys' cars are in the garage.

The women's cars are in the garage.

My brother-in-law's car is in the garage.

My brothers-in-law's cars are in the garage.

Someone's car is in the garage.

1.2 Indicates omissions in contractions and in dates.

She can't go to the meeting.

Today's my lucky day.

Mr. Lopez can see you at five o'clock.

Do you remember the hurricane of '38?

1.3 Forms plurals of letters, numbers, and words when they are used as words.

You were told to mind your p's and q's.

Many Europeans cross their 7's.

Marsha consistently confuses her *which's* and *that's*.

2. BRACKETS

2.1 Indicate an explanation, a correction, or a comment within a direct quote.

"Mrs. Cardozo then pointed out that he [meaning the defendant] had an excellent record."

2.2 Set off parenthetical words or phrases appearing within parentheses.

Many long-established organizations (for example, the International Labor Organization [I.L.O.]) became affiliates of the United Nations.

3. COLON

3.1 Introduces a series of explanatory words, phrases, or clauses.

These series may or may not be preceded by such anticipatory words as *the following, as follows, thus,* and *these.*

The following students have been elected to the student governing council:

> George Brown
> Arthur Caruso
> Martha Daniels
> Audrey Feingold
> Ross Nelson

Our secretarial department has the latest equipment: electric typewriters, audiovisual aids, dictating and transcribing machines, and individualized-instruction carrels.

3.2 Introduces a second independent clause that clarifies or amplifies a preceding independent clause.

Petroleum is vital to our national economy: without fuel, many of our industries would have to shut down.

3.3 Directs attention to appositives:

Mr. Pierce possesses the most desired attribute of an effective politician: integrity.

3.4 Separates figures in ratios and expressions of time.

The student-teacher ratio in our school is 20:1.
His plane will leave at 2:15 p.m.

3.5 Follows the salutation in most business letter styles.

Dear Mr. Bradlee:
Gentlemen:

4. COMMA

4.1 Separates words, phrases, and clauses in a series.

Her favorite hobbies are rug-making, swimming, and golfing.

The relief pitcher loaded the bases, allowed the tying run to score on a wild pitch, and walked the next batter for the game-winning run.

Marie ordered the stuffed shrimp, Jeanne ordered the watercress and beanshoot salad, and I ordered the beef Wellington.

4.2 Separates coordinate adjectives (adjectives of equal importance). If you can change the order of the adjectives and insert the word *and* between them without sacrificing clarity, the adjectives are coordinate.

Carson is a sullen, impertinent employee.

4.3 Separates two main clauses (clauses that could stand alone as separate sentences) in a compound sentence. Usually the comma is preceded by a coordinating conjunction: *and, but, nor, or, yet,* and *for.*

Frank is going to the opera, and I am going to the ballpark.

4.4 Separates nonrestrictive words, phrases, or clauses that follow a noun. Nonrestrictive clauses are not essential to the meaning of the sentence and are often introduced by *who, which, that,* and *where.*

Robert Merrill, baritone, will sing tonight.

Mrs. Watkins, spry for her age, competed in the tournament.

Mildred's uncle, who lives in Chicago, is arriving tomorrow.

4.5 Sets off long introductory phrases.

After weighing all the pros and cons of the issue, he agreed to accept the committee's decision.

4.6 Sets off words, phrases, or clauses that interrupt a sentence.

This is, indeed, a fine example of his work.

The wine is, in my opinion, completely characterless.

Her grandchildren were, she discovered, even less interesting than she had anticipated.

4.7 Sets off words, phrases, and clauses that are appositives.

Mr. Janeway, her uncle, is active in civic affairs.

My original idea, to reorganize the group, was not accepted.

Howard O'Neill, the man who was hired to complete the project, proved incompetent.

4.8 Sets off the elements in dates and place names.

On June 6, 1944, Allied forces landed on Omaha beach.

The drive from Barstow, California, to Las Vegas, Nevada, is short but boring.

4.9 Indicates the omission of words.

Brian has a sports car; Jay, a racing car; and Cliff, an antique car.

4.10 Separates words or numbers that would otherwise be confusing.

For Carol, Ann was a great help.

In 1973, 125,000 people died from unknown causes.

As I said, nothing she does is correct.

5. DASH

5.1 Indicates a sudden change in thought.

The early Romans did not live much beyond 25 years—but remember that such sciences as medicine and nutrition were still in their earliest stages of infancy.

5.2 Sets off a clause or phrase that summarizes a series of preceding words or phrases.

Germany, Italy, and Japan—our enemies during World War II—are friendlier than many of our then-allies.

5.3 Indicates a forceful summation.

Students, parents, and teachers—everyone must be present.

5.4 Indicates an afterthought.

All members of the board voted in favor of the program—even Mr. Winslow.

6. ELLIPSIS

6.1 Indicates the omission of parts of a quotation. When the omitted portion appears in the middle of the quoted sentence, use a series of three spaced dots. When the omitted portion appears at the end of the quoted sentence or when one or more sentences are omitted, use three spaced dots plus a terminal punctuation mark (period, question mark, or exclamation point).

"Friends ... lend me your ear."

"To every thing there is a season, and a time to every purpose under the heaven. A time to be born, and a time to die...."

7. EXCLAMATION POINT

7.1 Indicates excitement, emotion, or a command.

Help!

Bravo!

Leave!

7.2 Emphasizes irony.

He was caught at the scene of the crime with a gun in his hand, and he says he's innocent!

8. HYPHEN

8.1 Divides the last word in a line where necessary. (See *Word Division Guidelines*, page ix.)

8.2 Is used for clarity.

The six foot-soldiers were placed in the last rank.

The six-foot soldiers were placed in the last rank.

8.3 Is used in joining certain prefixes and suffixes to base words: prefixes ending in *a* or *i* when joined to base words beginning with the same vowel; *self*, when used as a prefix; prefixes added to words beginning with a capital; the prefixes *ex* and *all*; suffixes beginning with *l* when joined with base words ending in *l*, and to avoid ambiguity with some *re* prefixes.

His writings are anti-intellectual.

These tapes are self-destructing.

The growth of suburban shopping centers is a post-World War II phenomenon.

This is an all-purpose cleaner.

She sang in bell-like tones.

Frankenstein performed some experiments just for recreation, but he built his monster for re-creation.

8.4 Is used with compound adjectives which immediately *precede* a noun. Compound adjectives that *follow* a noun generally are not hyphenated.

Ethel is wearing an old-fashioned dress.

Ethel's dress is old fashioned.

8.5 Is used when writing out numbers 21 to 99 and fractions that are used as modifiers.

Ralph celebrated his twenty-ninth birthday again.

The resolution was adopted by a two-thirds majority of the eligible voters.

9. PARENTHESES

9.1 Set off non-essential explanatory material. The parentheses create a stronger break than does the comma but not as strong as the dash. Parenthetical material may fall within a sentence, at the end of a sentence, or outside of a sentence.

He wanted the coin (it would complete his collection) and paid a high price to obtain it.

Please itemize your expenses (lines 10–17).

Mr. Martin was an extremely aggressive sales manager. (Some of his salesmen secretly called him Mr. Martinet.)

9.2 Set off dates and references.

Luther Burbank (1849–1926) was an American horticulturist.

Review the use of the tabulator mechanism (Lesson 8).

9.3 Set off enumerated lists or parts of a sentence.

There are three items on the agenda:
(a) Sales forecasts for the next quarter
(b) Submission of departmental budget requests
(c) Revision of promotion procedures

Each applicant is required to submit a resume detailing (1) previous work experience, (2) salary demands, and (3) local references.

10. PERIOD

10.1 Terminates a sentence, an indirect question, or a courteous request.

He always marches to a different drummer.

They asked me if we could join them later.

May we count on your cooperation.

10.2 Is used in decimals and in some abbreviations.

She was given a 9.5 percent salary increase.

Mrs. Robinson is an extremely friendly neighbor.

11. QUESTION MARK

11.1 Terminates a direct question.

Where are you going?

11.2 Indicates doubt or uncertainty.

The gifted(?) soprano constantly sang off-key.

His first published article (June, 1953?) received little attention.

12. QUOTATION MARKS

12.1 Enclose all direct quotations. Periods and commas go inside the quotation marks; colons, dashes, and semicolons go outside the quotation marks; and exclamation points and question marks go inside the quotation marks if they are part of the quoted material and outside if they are not.

She said, "I can't remain here."

She said, "I can't remain here, can you?"

Did she say, "I can't remain here"?

12.2 Indicate titles that are only part of a larger published work: essays in an anthology, chapters in a book, articles in a magazine.

I found Chapter 3, "101 Ways to Economize," especially helpful.

Flannery O'Conner's short story, "The Comforts of Home," is reprinted in her book, *Everything That Rises Must Converge.*

12.3 Set off slang or words that are intended to convey a meaning different from their usual meaning.

She told me to "buzz off."

She says she had had seven "happy" marriages.

13. SEMICOLON

13.1 Joins two main clauses not separated by a coordinating conjunction (*and, but, or,* or *nor*).

His business is expanding rapidly; it now has six branches.

13.2 Joins two main clauses connected by a conjunctive adverb (*however, nevertheless, consequently, therefore, furthermore, hence, moreover*).

We know we couldn't win; nevertheless, we continued the struggle.

13.3 Clarifies series of words and phrases that requires internal comma punctuation.

Our last five presidents have been Dwight D. Eisenhower, Republican; John F. Kennedy, Democrat; Lyndon B. Johnson, Democrat; Richard M. Nixon, Republican; and Gerald R. Ford, Republican.

14. UNDERSCORE

14.1 Indicates words or phrases in typewritten material that are to be italicized when set in type—for example, books, magazines, plays, and foreign phrases.

The Mousetrap, by Agatha Christie, is London's longest-running play.

14.2 Sets off a word when it is referred to as a word.

Marie still does not know when to use the word <u>take</u> and when to use the word <u>bring</u>.

14.3 Adds emphasis to a word or phrase.

<u>He</u> did it, not Bill

Gazetteer

Akron, AL, OH
Alameda, CA
Albany, GA, NY
Albuquerque, NM
Alexandria, LA, VA
Alliance, OH
Aliquippa, PA
Amarillo, TX
Anaheim, CA
Anniston, AL
Ann Arbor, MI
Appleton, WI
Asheville, NC
Ashville, AL
Atlanta, GA
Attleboro, MA
Aurora, CO, IL
Auburn, NY

Baltimore, MD
Bartlesville, OK
Baton Rouge, LA
Bayonne, NJ
Beaumont, TX
Belvedere, CA
Belvidere, IL, PA
Berkeley, CA, PA
Berkley, MI
Bethlehem, PA
Biloxi, MS
Birmingham, AL
Booneville, AR, MD

Boonville, IN, MO
Boston, MA
Bridgeport, CT
Brockton, MA
Buffalo, NY

Cedar Rapids, IA
Charleston, IL, MS,
    MO, SC, WV
Charlestown, IN
Champaign, IL
Chattanooga, TN
Chicago, IL
Chula Vista, CA
Cicero, IL
Cincinnati, OH
Cleveland, OH
Columbus, OH
Concord, CA, MA, NH
Corpus Christi, TX
Costa Mesa, CA
Cucamonga, CA

Dallas, TX
Daly City, CA
Danville, VA
Davenport, IA, ND
Dayton, OH
Daytona Beach, FL
Dearborn, MI
Decatur, AL, IL
Denton, TX

Denver, CO
Des Moines, IA
Des Plaines, IL
Detroit, MI
Dobbs Ferry, NY
Dodge City, KS
Douglas, AK
Dover, DE
Dubuque, IA
Duluth, MN
Dumont, NJ
Dundee, OR
Durham, NC

East Providence, RI
Easton, PA
Eatonton, GA
Eatontown, NJ
East St. Louis, IL
Eau Claire, WI
El Dorado, AR
El Paso, TX
Elyria, OH
Englewood, NJ
Erie, PA
Eureka, CA
Everett, WA

Fall River, MA
Fond du Lac, WI
Fredericksburg, PA,
    VA

Fort Collins, CO
Fort Lauderdale, FL
Fort Wayne, IN
Fort Worth, TX
Fremont, CA
Fresno, CA

Gadsden, AL
Gainesville, FL
Galesburg, IL
Galveston, TX
Gloucester, MA
Grand Rapids, MI
Greensboro, NC

Hammond, IN
Hampton, VA
Hartford, CT
Hialeah, FL
Honolulu, HI
Houston, TX
Huntington, WV

Idaho Falls, ID
Independence, MO
Indianapolis, IN
Inglewood, CA
Iowa City, IA
Iron City, GA
Irvine, CA, KY
Irving, TX
Irvington, NJ, NY
Ithaca, NY

Jackson, MI, MS

Jacksonville, FL
Jamestown, NY
Janesville, WI
Jefferson City, MO
Jersey City, NJ
Johnson City, TN, TX
Johnstown, PA
Joliet, IL
Joplin, MO

Kalamazoo, MI
Kankakee, IL
Kansas City, KS, MO
Kearny, NJ
Kennebunk, ME
Kenosha, WI
Kettering, OH
Key West, FL
Kingsport, TN
Kingston, NY
Kingsville, TX
Kirkland, WA
Kirkwood, MO
Knoxville, TN
Kokomo, IN

Lafayette, IN
Lakeland, FL
Lakewood, CA, OH
La Mesa, CA
Lancaster, PA
Lansing, MI
Laredo, TX
Las Vegas, NV
Lawrence, KS

Litchfield, CT
Little Rock, AR
Livonia, MI
Long Beach, CA
Lorain, OH
Los Angeles, CA
Louisville, KY
Lubbock, TX
Lynchburg, VA

Marietta, GA
Marseilles, IL
Maywood, IL
Memphis, TN
Meridian, MS
Meriden, CT
Mesa, AZ
Miami, FL
Middletown, CT, NY
Milford, CT
Milwaukee, WI
Minneapolis, MN
Modesto, CA
Moline, IL
Monroe, LA, NY
Montebello, CA
Montgomery, AL
Muncie, IN
Muskegon, MI

Nashua, NH
Nashville, TN
Newark, DE, NJ
Newport, KY, RI
Newport Beach, CA

Santa Rosa, CA
Savannah, GA
Schenectady, NY
Scranton, PA
Seattle, WA
Selma, AL
Sheboygan, WI
Shreveport, LA
Sioux City, IA
Skokie, IL
South Bend, IN
Spartansburg, SC
Springfield. IL,
   MO, OH
Spokane, WA
Stamford, CT
Steubenville, OH
Superior, WI
Syracuse, NY

Tacoma, WA
Tallahassee, FL
Tampa, FL
Taunton, MA
Temple, TX
Terre Haute, IN
Texarkana, AR, TX
Toledo, OH
Topeka, KS
Torrance, CA
Trenton, NJ
Tucson, AZ
Tulsa, OK
Tuscaloosa, AL

Tyler, TX

Union City, NJ
University City, MO
Uxbridge, MA

Vallejo, CA
Valdosta, GA
Valparaiso, IN
Vicksburg, MS
Victoria, TX
Vineland, NJ
Vincennes, IN

Waco, TX
Waltham, MA
Warren, OH
Warwick, RI
Washington, DC
Waterbury, CT
Waterloo, IA
Watertown, NY
Waukegan, IL
Waukesha, WI
Wausau, WI
Wauwatosa, WI
West New York, NJ
Wheeling, WV
White Plains, NY
Whittier, CA
Wichita, KS
Wichita Falls, TX
Wilkes-Barre, PA
Williamsport, PA

Wilmington, DE, NC
Winston-Salem, NC
Woburn, MA
Woonsocket, RI
Wooster, OH
Worcester, MA
Wyandotte, MI
Wyoming, MI

Xenia, OH

Yakima, WA
Yazoo City, MS
Yoakum, TX
Yonkers, NY
York, PA
Yorktown, TX, VA
Yorktown Heights, N
Youngstown, OH
Yuma, AZ

Zanesville, OH
Zapata, TX
Zuni, AZ, NM

Abbreviations

A.A.U. Amateur Athletic Union

A.A.U.P. American Association of University Professors

A.A.U.W. American Association of University Women

A.B.A. American Bar Association

A.B.M. antiballistic missile

abr. abridged

abs. absolute

acad. academic

acct. account

A.C.L.U. American Civil Liberties Union

A.D.A. Americans for Democratic Action

A.D.C. Air Defense Command

adm. administration

A.D.P. automatic data processing

adv. adverb

advt. advertisement

A.E.C. Atomic Energy Commission

A.F.C. American Football Conference

AFL-CIO American Federation of Labor and Congress of Industrial Organizations

agcy. agency

agr. agricultural

AID Agency for International Development

a.m. ante meridiem

A.M.A. American Medical Association

Amer. America

amp. ampere

amt. amount

anon. anonymous

approx. approximate

apptd. appointed

apt. apartment

A.R.C. American Red Cross

arr. arrival

ASCAP American Society of Composers, Authors, and Publishers

asgmt. assignment

assn. association

asst. assistant

atm. atmosphere

atty. attorney

ave. avenue

avg. average

BASIC Beginner's All-purpose Symbolic Instruction Code

B.B.C. British Broadcasting Corporation

bbl. barrel
bd. board
bf. boldface
biog. biographical
bldg. building
blvd. boulevard
bot. botanical
br. branch
bur. bureau
bus. business

ca around
C.A.B. Civil Aeronautics Board
cap. capacity
Capt. Captain
CARE Cooperative for American Relief to Everywhere
cc cubic centimeter
CC carbon copy
cf. compare
chap. chapter
CIA Central Intelligence Agency
C.L.U. chartered life underwriter
cm. centimeter
co. company
c/o care of
COBOL common business oriented language
COD cash on delivery
comdr. commander
conf. conference
conj. conjunction

contd. continued
C.O.R.E. Congress of Racial Equality
corp. corporal
CPA certified public accountant
C.P.S. certified professional secretary
CST central standard time
ctn. carton
ctr. center
cu. cubic
cwt. hundredweight

DAR Daughters of the American Revolution
dbl. double
deg. degree
Dem. Democrat; Democratic
depr. depreciation
dept. department
DEW distant early warning
dg. decigram
dia. diameter
diag. diagonal
dict. dictionary
dm. decimeter
D.M.Z. demilitarized zone
do. ditto
doc. document
dom. domestic
doz. dozen
D.P. data processing

DST daylight saving time
dwt. deadweight ton
dz. dozen

econ. economics
ed. edition
EDP electronic data processing
EDT eastern daylight time
E.E.G. electroencephalogram;
electroencephalograph
e.g. for example
E.K.G. electrocardiogram;
electrocardiograph
elem. elementary
equip. equipment
E.S.P. extrasensory perception
EST eastern standard time
est. established
et al. and others
et seq. and the following one
etc. and so forth

FAA Federal Aviation Agency
FBI Federal Bureau of
Investigation
FCC Federal Communications
Commission
FDA Food and Drug
Administration
fem. feminine
F.E.P.C. Fair Employment
Practices Commission

ff. and the following pages;
fortissimo
FHA Federal Housing
Administration
FICA Federal Insurance
Contributions Act
FORTRAN formula translation
FPC Federal Power Commission
ft. feet
FTC Federal Trade Commission
fwd. forward

gal. gallon
G.A.T.T. General Agreement on
Tariffs and Trade
gen. general
gm. gram
GNP gross national product
GOP Grand Old Party
(Republican)
govt. government

hdqrs. headquarters
HEW Department of Health,
Education, and Welfare
hgt. height
hm. hectometer
hr. hour
ht. height
HUD Department of Housing
and Urban Development
hwy. highway

ibid in the same place

ICBM intercontinental ballistic missile

ICC Interstate Commerce Commission

idem. that same work

IDP integrated data processing

i.e. that is

I.F.O. identified flying object

IRS Internal Revenue Service

ital. italic

jct. junction

jr. junior

jt. joint

kl. kiloliter

km. kilometer

kt. karat

kw. kilowatt

lat. latitude

lb. pound

lc lowercase

L.E.M. lunar excursion module

ll lines

L.S.D. lysergic acid diethylamide

Lt. Lieutenant

lv. leave

masc. masculine

MATS Military Air Transport Service

max. maximum

mdse. merchandise

mfg. manufacturing

mfr. manufacture

mgr. manager

mgt. management

M.I.C.R. magnetic ink character recognition

misc. miscellaneous

ml. milliliter

mm. millimeter

mo. month

mos. months

M.P. member of parliament

mpg miles per gallon

mph miles per hour

ms. manuscript

msgr. monseigneur

MST mountain standard time

mtge. mortgage

N.A.A.C.P. National Association for the Advancement of Colored People

N.A.M. National Association of Manufacturers

N.A.S. National Academy of Sciences

N.A.S.A. National Aeronautics and Space Administration

natl. national

N.A.T.O. North Atlantic Treaty Organization
n.b. note well
N.B.A. National Basketball Association
N.C.A.A. National Collegiate Athletic Association
n.d. no date
NEA National Education Association
N.F.C. National Football Conference
NLRB National Labor Relations Board
N.T. New Testament
N.Y.S.E. New York Stock Exchange

O.A.S. Organization of American States
obj. object
O.C.R. optical character recognition
op. opus
op. cit. in the work cited
org. organic
orig. original
o/s out of stock
O.T. Old Testament
oz. ounce

PBX private branch exchange (telephone switchboard system)
pcs. pieces
pct. percent
pd. paid
PERT Program Evaluation and Review Techniques
P.G.A. Professional Golfers' Association
PHS Public Health Service
pkg. package
P.K.U. phenylketonuria
pkwy. parkway
pl. place
p.m. post meridiem
P.O.W. prisoner of war
pp. pages
pres. present
prod. production
prs. pairs
psf pounds per square foot
psi pounds per square inch
PST Pacific standard time
pt. part
PTA Parent-Teacher Association

qt. quart
qty. quantity
q.v. which see, whom see

ref. referee
rep. representative

Rep. Republican
rev. revised
R.F.D. rural free delivery
rpt. repeat
rte. route

S.A.C. Strategic Air Command
S.A.M. surface-to-air missile
SBA Small Business Administration
SEC Securities and Exchange Commission
secy. secretary
sgt. sergeant
sic thus
S.O.P. standard operating procedure
S.P.C.A. Society for the Prevention of Cruelty to Animals
S.P.C.C. Society for the Prevention of Cruelty to Children
sp. gr. specific gravity
sr. senior
std. standard
stk. stock
supt. superintendent
supvr. supervisor

T.A.C. Tactical Air Command
tchr. teacher

tpk. turnpike
trans. transactions
transp. transportation
treas. treasurer
TVA Tennessee Valley Authority
TWX teletypewriter exchange

uc upper case
U.F.O. unidentified flying object
UHF ultrahigh frequency
UN United Nations
UNESCO United Nations Educational, Scientific, and Cultural Organization
UNICEF United Nations Children's Fund
USIA United States Information Agency
U.S.O. United Service Organizations
U.S.S.R. Union of Soviet Socialist Republics

v. see
VA Veterans Administration
VHF very high frequency
V.I.S.T.A. Volunteers in Service to America
viz. namely
V.O.A. Voice of America
vou. voucher
vv. verses

WATS Wide Area Telephone
Service

wf wrong font

W.H.O. World Health
Organization

whse. warehouse

whsle. wholesale

wk. week

w/o. without

wt. weight

yd. yard

YMCA Young Men's Christian
Association

YMHA Young Men's Hebrew
Association

yr. year

YWCA Young Women's
Christian Association

YWHA Young Women's Hebrew
Association

ZIP (code) Zone Improvement
Plan (U.S. Postal Service)

Two-letter State Abbreviations
(INCLUDING TERRITORIES AND POSSESSIONS)

Alabama	**AL**	Montana	**MT**
Alaska	**AK**	Nebraska	**NE**
Arizona	**AZ**	Nevada	**NV**
Arkansas	**AR**	New Hampshire	**NH**
California	**CA**	New Jersey	**NJ**
Colorado	**CO**	New Mexico	**NM**
Connecticut	**CT**	New York	**NY**
Delaware	**DE**	North Carolina	**NC**
District of Columbia	**DC**	North Dakota	**ND**
Florida	**FL**	Ohio	**OH**
Georgia	**GA**	Oklahoma	**OK**
Guam	**GU**	Oregon	**OR**
Hawaii	**HI**	Pennsylvania	**PA**
Idaho	**ID**	Puerto Rico	**PR**
Illinois	**IL**	Rhode Island	**RI**
Indiana	**IN**	South Carolina	**SC**
Iowa	**IA**	South Dakota	**SD**
Kansas	**KS**	Tennessee	**TN**
Kentucky	**KY**	Texas	**TX**
Louisiana	**LA**	Utah	**UT**
Maine	**ME**	Vermont	**VT**
Maryland	**MD**	Virginia	**VA**
Massachusetts	**MA**	Virgin Islands	**VI**
Michigan	**MI**	Washington	**WA**
Minnesota	**MN**	West Virginia	**WV**
Mississippi	**MS**	Wisconsin	**WI**
Missouri	**MO**	Wyoming	**WY**

Table of Metric Equivalents

Unit (Basic units are shown in bold type.)	Number of Basic Units	Approximate U.S. Equivalent	
LENGTH			
Millimeter	1/1,000	.04 inch	
Centimeter	1/100	.39 inch	
Decimeter	1/10	3.94 inches	
Meter	**1**	**39.37 inches**	
Dekameter	10	32.81 feet	
Hectometer	100	109.36 yards	
Kilometer	1,000	.62 miles	
Myriameter	10,000	6.20 miles	
AREA			
Square centimeter	1/10,000	.155 sq inch	
Centare	**1**	**10.76 sq feet**	
Are	100	119.60 sq yards	
Hectare	10,000	2.47 acres	
Square kilometer	1,000,000	.386 sq mile	
VOLUME			
Cubic centimeter	1/1,000,000	.061 cu inch	
Decistere	1/10	3.530 cu feet	
Stere	**1**	**1.310 cu yards**	
Dekastere	10	13.100 cu yards	

Unit (Basic units are shown in bold type.)	Number of Basic Units	Approximate U.S. Equivalent	
CAPACITY		*Dry*	*Liquid*
Milliliter	1/1,000	.0018 pint	.27 fluidram
Centiliter	1/100	.018 pint	.338 fluidounce
Deciliter	1/10	.18 pint	.21 pint
Liter	**1**	**.908 quart**	**1.057 quarts**
Dekaliter	10	1.14 pecks	2.64 gallons
Hectoliter	100	2.84 bushels	26.4 gallons
Kiloliter	1,000	28.4 bushels	264. gallons